Early Voices

EDITED BY MARY ALICE DOWNIE
AND BARBARA ROBERTSON
WITH ELIZABETH JANE ERRINGTON

Early Voices

Portraits of Canada by Women Writers, 1639–1914

NATURAL HERITAGE BOOKS
A MEMBER OF THE DUNDURN GROUP
www.dundurn.com

Project Editor: Jane Gibson
Copy Editor: Matt Baker
Design: Jennifer Scott
Printer: Transcontinental

Library and Archives Canada Cataloguing in Publication

Early voices : portraits of Canada by women writers, 1639-1914 / by Mary Alice Downie and Barbara Robertson ; with Elizabeth Jane Errington.

Includes bibliographical references.
Also available in electronic format.
ISBN 978-1-55488-769-9

1. Women pioneers--Canada--History. 2. Women--Canada--History. 3. Women pioneers--Canada--Biography. 4. Canadian prose literature--Women authors. I. Downie, Mary Alice, 1934- II. Robertson, Barbara, 1931- III. Errington, Elizabeth Jane, 1951-

HQ1453.E37 2010   971.0082   C2010-902451-6

1   2   3   4   5   14   13   12   11   10

We acknowledge the support of the **Canada Council for the Arts** and the **Ontario Arts Council** for our publishing program. We also acknowledge the financial support of the **Government of Canada** through the **Canada Book Fund** and **Livres Canada Books**, and the **Government of Ontario** through the **Ontario Book Publishers Tax Credit program**, and the **Ontario Media Development Corporation**.

Care has been taken to trace the ownership of copyright material used in this book. The author and the publisher welcome any information enabling them to rectify any references or credits in subsequent editions.

J. Kirk Howard, President

Front cover image: *Winter Scene* by Frances Anne Hopkins. Library and Archives Canada, C-013581.
Back cover image: W.D. Jordan Special Collections and Music Library, Queen's University.

Images on pages 11, 31, 67, 111, 155, 255.
Courtesy W.D. Jordan Special Collections and Music Library, Queen's University.

Printed and bound in Canada.
www.dundurn.com
Published by Natural Heritage Books
A Member of The Dundurn Group

Dundurn Press
3 Church Street, Suite 500
Toronto, Ontario, Canada
M5E 1M2

Gazelle Book Services Limited
White Cross Mills
High Town, Lancaster, England
LA1 4XS

Dundurn Press
2250 Military Road
Tonawanda, NY
U.S.A. 14150

For Mary: the tradition continues.

Contents

PART V: BRITISH COLUMBIA AND NORTHERN REGIONS

The hills all round, as seen from our celebrated platform, are of the most lovely autumn colours, and, covered as they are with red and orange trees, they really look like flames in the distance, or like gigantic flower-gardens; for our trees are quite as brilliant as your best flowers, and if you can imagine your conservatory magnified a million times, and spread over miles and miles of hill and dale, you will begin to understand how we do things in this Canada of ours.

THE MARCHIONESS OF DUFFERIN AND AVA,
My Canadian Journal 1872–78

Acknowledgements

Jane Errington contributed far more than she can have anticipated when initially agreeing to write an introduction. Sarah Robertson proved herself her mother's daughter with her amusing and judicious editorial comments. Merna Summers joined enthusiastically in the hunt for elusive sources. Lynette Nunn supplied unexpected details about the post-Canadian career of her great-great-grandmother, Mrs. Beavan in Australia. Lorne C. Paul provided lively memories about the adult life of his aunt, Maryanne Caswell. Anne Hart led us to the touching memories of Lydia Campbell. Marsha Skrypuch, Frances Swyripa, and Jars Balan were guides to the Ukrainian pioneers.

Thanks to Franklin Foster, Trudy Powlowski from the Saskatoon Public Library, Nadine Charabin, Saskatchewan Archives Board, and Roberta Staples of Lady Margaret Hall Library, Oxford. The Stauffer Library at Queen's University was, as ever, the mother ship for our searches. The staff of W.D. Jordan Special Collections and Music Library patiently descended many times into the gold mine of the stacks. Paul Banfield, Queen's University Archivist was as helpful as ever.

Thanks also to Kelly Bennett, Carol Martin, Diana Birchall and P.G. Rooney, J.S. Pritchard, and M-A Thompson for a brilliant suggestion. We are grateful to Jane Gibson and Barry Penhale of Natural Heritage

Books for seizing the publishing moment, and to Michael Peterman for his advice and gracious words.

John Downie lived uncomplainingly for months among mounds of books and papers, while sharing both his study and his computer skills. Merriment along the trail was added by five young Abernethys and Eklunds.

Our Assorted Ancestors

By Mary Alice Downie

Many of the writings of the women who came to Canada during the last four centuries have been published. There are the letters of Marie de l'Incarnation, the intrepid Ursuline who sailed from Dieppe for the New World in 1639, and the journal of Baroness von Riedesel, wife of the general of the Hessian mercenaries during the American Revolution. Letitia Hargrave's account of life in the remote fur-trading post of York Factory in northern Manitoba is available, as are Juliana Horatia Ewing's descriptions of the garrison town of Fredericton just after Confederation, and Lady Aberdeen's expressions of dismay of the violence of hockey in late nineteenth-century Ottawa. (She was later to change her mind and become a fan.)

The books of the expatriate branch of the redoubtable Strickland sisters, Catharine Parr Traill and Susanna Moodie, and *Winter Studies and Summer Rambles* of the Victorian scholar Anna Jameson are valued staples of Canadian literature. Unfortunately, it is specialists rather than the general reader who are familiar with these other illuminating materials. Although feminist scholars are devotedly tilling the field, with some exceptions, they tend to write *about* the early writers, using brief excerpts to support a thesis.

Some — too many — years ago, Barbara Robertson and I decided to make a collection, providing substantial examples of writing by 29 women, known and unknown, professional and amateur, who visited or lived in Canada between the seventeenth and early twentieth centuries, allowing *them* to portray their lives in the woods, in the Maritimes, Quebec, in "muddy York," on the desolate or flower-strewn prairies, in British Columbia, and the Far North. We hope to send people to the library or bookstore — or, increasingly, online — to share their reactions to a frequently difficult, sometimes terrifying, but ultimately satisfying New World. We have Mrs. Jameson, eminent scholar and friend of Browning, exhilarated by her trip with the voyageurs to Lake Superior: "the wildest and most extraordinary tour you can imagine." Susan Allison, living in a cabin near Kelowna, without potable water, rattlers dangling among the pots and pans, home schooling her 14 children, writes: "I lived a perfectly ideal life at that time."

What relevance do these letters home, journals, memoirs, and biographies have for the modern reader? Certain themes, significant and minor, recur and resonate still: the welcome breakup of ice, the sweet pleasures of trips to the sugar-camp, the risks of mushrooms, the finding of fiddleheads. We continue to suffer annually from the blight of black flies and "no see 'ems," to dread that ominous buzz described by "Janey Canuck" in her sprightly riff on mosquitoes. Winter was more dangerous then, but even with central heating we must endure the cold on venturing outside in January. Indeed, with the unpleasant prospect of a future of ever-increasing hurricanes, droughts, floods, and forest fires, we can profit by reading early settlers' accounts. They were better able to cope with extreme conditions than we are. Six days of the Ice Storm in Kingston, shared with indignant cats, convinced us of that.

Margaret Dickie Michener's aching loneliness at sudden widowhood and Letitia Hargrave's heartbreak at losing a child speak to all generations. Today's working mothers, juggling children and careers, will enjoy the vignette recorded elsewhere of Nellie McClung's son Horace, leading home his young brother, "much spattered with mud, and one stocking at half mast, hurrying him along the lane and in through the secret entrance in the back fence, saying: 'Quick, now! It's a good thing I got you before the *Telegram* got a picture of you — Nellie McClung's neglected child!' — this with bitter scorn." And any twenty-first-century writer will feel a pang of recognition reading Catharine Parr Traill's final letter, written two days before her death at 97, on the return of a manuscript about a history of Canadian birds: "I had many misgivings as to the merits of the composition, &c — In fact I never see any good in my writings till they are in print and even then I wonder how that event came to pass."

In the creation of this anthology there were problems, of course. Every reader is her own anthologist; reviewers always complain because a favourite has not been included. Just for sport, we decided to use Catharine Parr Traill's letter about visiting Government House in Ottawa rather than an example of her balanced advice to settlers or botanical works. We did not include Elizabeth Simcoe, who to the consternation of observers, happy as a lark, camped out in Captain Cook's "canvas house" in "bowers made from the limbs of trees." Many biographies and place names preserve her memory. Our decision to omit Moodie may seem perverse when, as distinguished critic Michael Peterman writes: "she has so much to say and in such interesting and compelling ways. " Indeed, her description of canoeing is as lyrical as any of Anna Jameson's or Juliana Horatia Ewing's accounts of Canadian nature:

> The pure beauty of the Canadian water, the somber but august grandeur of the vast forest that hemmed us in on every side and shut us out from the rest of the world, soon cast a magic spell upon our spirits, and we began to feel charmed with the freedom and solitude around us. Every object was new to us. We felt as if we were the first discoverers of every beautiful flower and stately tree that attracted our attention, and we gave names to fantastic rocks and fairy isles, and raised imaginary houses and bridges on every picturesque spot which we floated past in our aquatic excursions. I learned the use of the paddle, and became quite a proficient in the gentle craft." ("The Wilderness, and Our Indian Friends")

We would have had no difficulty in finding an entertaining selection. But she is so well-represented elsewhere, the one early woman writer everyone has heard of, that we decided to use our limited space to introduce our readers to lesser-known voices.

We wrestled with the fact that, so often, our writers were well-educated upper- and middle-class British women. With glad cries we fell upon *A Home-help in Canada* by Ella Sykes — "At last," we thought, "a sturdy working-class observer!" Alas, the frontispiece of the book portrayed a *grande dame* in a magnificent hat worthy of Freya Stark. Her other books, such as *Through Persia on a Side-Saddle*, compelling reading still, reflect her experiences as sister and frequent hostess of diplomat — and spy — Sir Percy Sykes during his postings in Central Asia.

We admit to gaps — we would like to have had more examples from other groups. We consulted scholars who confirmed our impression that either the women simply weren't here, weren't writing in English, or did not have the luxury of time to write at length. We regard the discovery of half-Chinese Sui Sin Far, also known as Edith Maude Eaton, as a triumph. (The novelist and journalist, Onoto Watanna, looked promising, until we discovered that she was Sui Sin Far's sister Winifred, masquerading as an exotic half-Japanese.) No doubt, the minute we send in final proofs, a splendid Mennonite or Tibetan diary will appear.

As always, there was the dreaded question of order. Should it be geographical, chronological, by subject? The book is shaped by the pattern of settlement moving across the country in time and space. We wrestled with which passage to choose and how to select — as there was such richness. Where possible, we have kept a particular passage complete, but demands of length did sometimes require selective editing noted with ellipses. Spelling and punctuation are presented as in the original publication.

Not all our discoveries were made in the library. There were serendipitous surprises while travelling. The Quails' Gate Winery in the Okanagan now operates the Allison House Market, refurbished from the days of Susan Allison as a centre for local artisans' works and books — as well as picnics. After visiting the landmark Cliff House in San Francisco, we enjoyed reading Lady Dufferin's account of it in 1876, although late on a winter afternoon, accompanied by two tired small girls, we didn't see "close to the hotel ... some great rocky islands, upon which sea-lions are basking in the sun, and pelicans stand combing out their feathers," nor could we dine on their celebrated fare of "oysters, 'Porter-hall steak,' and omelette." It's still possible to admire "the terrifying but majestic sight" of Montmorency Falls from the spot where Governor Haldimand built "a little hut which hung directly over the waterfall" as a surprise for Baroness von Riedesel.

There have been other agreeable connections. For a time, co-editor Barbara lived next door to descendants of Baroness von Riedesel. A friend who grew up in Peterborough has memories of being chased home from school, pelted with snowballs by modern Stricklands.

Even in the twenty-first century it is possible to have a strong feeling of relationship with our assorted ancestors. Much of the work was done at an old wooden cottage on an island in the Rideau Canal, with no heat except for a big brick fireplace. (We don't go there in winter.) As we shiver on chilly fall mornings — it's often colder inside than out — it's easy to identify with the past. Hepaticas peep from the leaves in spring, trilliums carpet the land, just as Mrs. Traill described them. We have shared a sunset with a racoon family, admired the Egyptian profile of the Blue Heron standing splendidly on the end of the dock, heard the crash of a golden maple leaf when it lands in the silence of October. As I listen to the wolves — really coyotes — howling in the distance at night, it brings memories of a cherished sylvan legend in my own family. My great-grandmother was chased through the woods by wolves, barefoot, with my infant grandfather in her arms.

One great sadness is attached to the completion of this anthology. Barbara Robertson and I collaborated three times: on *The Wind Has Wings, The Well-filled Cupboard,* and *Chatzkel the Hunter.* We laughed and argued, brandishing the latest treasure from the library, commiserated with each other on difficulties with books we wrote separately. For many years, during weekly lunches at Queen's University Faculty Club, we shared the problems and joys of family life. (Like Mother Lears, we had three daughters each.) Just after the bulk of the reading was done, the manuscript accepted, Barbara suffered a devastating stroke. She lingered and died in 2006. My literary journeys were then solitary, at least until Jane arrived. As a passionate Canadian historian, how Barabara would have enjoyed and significantly contributed to the final stages. Nellie McClung wrote of *her* friend and collaborator, Emily Murphy — although on a grander stage: "It was fitting that the last thing recorded of her was that she had gone to the library seeking information."

The Diversity of Voices

By Elizabeth Jane Errington

In the last 20 years or so, women's voices have begun to make their way into our consciousness. It is no longer extraordinary to find biographies of or by women on our bookshelves, and some of our most celebrated novelists and poets are women. It is nonetheless surprising how unfamiliar we are with women authors of our past. We still tend to see New France, British North America, and nineteenth-century Canada as worlds inhabited by strong men and silent women. Although a number of scholars have been exploring the texture of these women's lives, their voices continue to be muffled, lost amid the panoply of accounts about politicians and priests, soldiers and farmers, canal workers and immigrant labourers who were, many continue to believe, the "real" makers of the nation. When women are discussed, they most often are placed in the private realm of hearth and home — living apart from and in a world that was fundamentally different than that of their male companions. Because many did not "work" for wages, or engage in politics or business, it is frequently assumed that most of our foremothers had little to say or, when they did, they spoke with one voice that reflected their shared domestic culture and view of the world.

This wonderfully eclectic collection challenges these assumptions. Ranging widely in time and space, we are presented with a collage of colours and a cacophony of sound. The authors here and the women they wrote about spoke with many voices and had varied reactions to the world around them. Their lives were invariably shaped and mediated by their class, their race, their age, their marital status, when they arrived or lived on the continent, and, of course, their personal expectations and beliefs. There is no question that many of the women who appear in these brief excerpts shared experiences that, in some ways, collapsed time and space. Although pioneering wives on the Canadian prairies had little in common with the wife of a visiting governor general, the delights and difficulties of being a wife and mother in one century were often echoed in another; and the aspirations of a woman adventurer in Newfoundland in many ways are reflected in stories of trekking across the Rocky Mountains. But each author had her own unique reaction to her world, and these both mirrored and helped to shape the rich record of Canadian experience.

Some of the authors, like Anna Jameson, Ella Sykes, and Ladies Dufferin and Aberdeen, were just visitors, and they wrote to inform their readers — either family members or a much broader general public — about what they saw and felt. Such often carefully crafted accounts contrast sharply, in tone as well as in content, with settler Margaret Michener's very private diary, in which she recorded her daily activities and which also seems to have provided her with a vehicle to begin to come to terms with her husband's death. Anne Langton's and Charlotte Bompas's personal journals, on the other hand, or Juliana Ewing's letters to her mother, although never intended for publication, were written for the benefit of anxious family members and friends. These three women, and many others, wanted both to convey something of the rhythm of their lives and to reassure those at home that all was well in this new world. Some authors here, like new arrivals Mary Ann Shadd and Emily Elizabeth Beavan, consciously wrote to inform and to persuade prospective emigrants about the advantage of moving to Canada; as Emily Carr, Laura Salverson, and others recounted stories of their childhood, they wanted to convey to an interested public something of a world gone by.

Whether by visitor or new settler or resident, almost all the accounts that appear here chronicle a personal journey. Some were clearly travellers coming to a new land. Like so many who dared to cross the Atlantic under sail, Mère Cécile confronted the ravages of storms and fears of shipwreck. Lady Dufferin and adventurers Anna Jameson, Mary Warren, and Mina Hubbard wrote about their travels within the continent itself, and were determined to capture — in words and sometimes with photographs — the texture and variety of the nation. In her letter to a daughter of an old friend, Catharine Parr Traill recounted her visit to the rarefied world of Canadian high society. Nellie McClung and Maria Adamowska told stories of their childhood and of family journeys to find and make new homes. Emily Carr travelled into her family's past; Margaret Michener, Letitia Hargrave, and Sui Sin Far found themselves on an often heart-wrenching emotional journey.

What is fascinating is that for so many of these women the Canadian landscape was an ever-present and often central character in their accounts. European travellers, including Anna Jameson and Lady Dufferin, and adventurers like Mina Hubbard and Mary Warren, were intrigued and delighted by the majesty and expanse of the land. Marie de l'Incarnation drew fantastic images as she tried to describe to her son the physical and emotional devastation that accompanied an earthquake in New France. What to some was a land of beauty and awe was to others a menacing barrier. Pioneering settlers, whether newly arrived to the continent or moving from one province to another, had to confront and try to vanquish the endless stands of trees or miles of grasslands just to eke out a living. As Loyalist Mary Fisher knew all too well, building a home was backbreaking, never-ending work and the land could be unforgiving. Mary Warren's delight once she arrived at a mountain meadow contrasts sharply with Maria Adamowska's bitter "disenchantment" with the family's first home in Manitoba. And Emily Murphy's satirical and humorous depiction of the dreaded mosquito belies the very real concern that Anne Langton's mother had of being bitten by mosquitoes and blackflies.

To many who appear here — Emily Beavan, Nellie McClung, and Emily Carr, for example — Canada was the promised land. At the same time, the very vastness of the territory was often daunting, particularly for women. Anna Jameson revelled in "the feeling of remoteness, of the profound solitude, that added to the sentiment of beauty" of the

Upper Canadian bush. For Laura Salverson's Great-Aunt Steinun, that same remoteness meant that medical help for her husband was miles and many hours away. The loneliness of the land was often compounded by the difficulties many settlers had maintaining contact with those at home. Juliana Ewing "longed for letters" from her mother; and Charlotte Bompas, living "an immense distance from civilization," could hardly wait for the "great annual mail." One has the sense that a number of the women who inhabit these pages felt a little like intruders on the landscape, and the experience was disquieting.

For many, their response to the land was intimately linked to their reactions to the often harsh climate. Juliana Ewing told her mother that "the summer heat at times" oppressed her head; Charlotte Bompas noted that "the very sharp experience" of the extreme cold of a northern winter, and the very short days that accompanied it, was one of her "greatest trials." And there is no question that the Fisher and Adamowska families suffered unimaginable hardship during their first winter in Canada. A number of writers went to some length, however, to reassure their readers that, as long as one was prepared, neither the cold nor the heat was as bad as one imagined. Moreover, without snow, the Beavan family would not have been able to move their house on a sled; it was a heavy snowfall that permitted Laura Salverson's great aunt to even think of pulling her husband to get medical help; and it was the freezing cold that afforded Lady Aberdeen the opportunity to learn to enjoy sledding in Ottawa. In her letter to prospective immigrants from the United States, Mary Ann Shadd, echoing sentiments of other travellers and advice writers of the time, was determined to set the record straight — the weather in the Canada's was healthy, she stated emphatically.

Another integral and often more daunting part of the landscape was the local inhabitants. Anna Jameson and Mina Hubbard were intrigued when, in their travels, they came across evidence of local native populations, and Maryanne Caswell happily played among abandoned Aboriginal camps and gravesites. And it must be remembered that many women came to Canada because of its aboriginal population. Although Sister Marie Morin often feared it was "our dying day" when Iroquois raiding parties attacked the settlement in New France, she and other

French *religieuses* "knew" that the "Savages" could, with God's grace, be saved and civilized. Bishop's wife and helpmeet, Charlotte Bompas, took considerable satisfaction in working with her mission children and was delighted when they began to instruct local Aboriginal women in the scriptures. A number of pioneering women obviously lived in dread of meeting a Canadian Aboriginal, however. They knew, from stories heard at home, that the "savages" were variously fierce, depraved, inscrutable, dirty, and dangerous — an unknowable other. To some, this land was "only fit for Indians and squaws." A young Maria Adamowska "froze on the spot" and tried to hide when she encountered a small party of "elderly Indians." Laura Salverson told of an old charwoman who had a terrifying night when "the menace of redskins" invaded her little house. That they saved her from an intruder was cause for considerable relief and she (and undoubtedly others) wondered if she had "misjudged the wanderers." It was not just First Nations peoples who were seen as foreign. Baroness von Riedesel was quite fascinated by the French Canadian population that she encountered as she made her way to Quebec City and then to her husband's posting at Sorel. Lady Dufferin described in considerable detail a Mennonite community that she visited in Manitoba. Residents there, she judged, were a wonderful asset to the nation, despite their "peculiar tenets." To some, Americans (or as Emily Beavan called them, "the Yankees") were even seen as a different kind of people — either as Mary Fisher remembered, hard drinking "bad characters," or, as a young Emily Carr discovered, "uncomfortable rushers."

That Canada was a new and different land few of the authors here would have disputed. A number were also conscious that encounters with the land could and often did create a new people. Ella Sykes very soon recognized that her "English ways" were quite different than those of her employer, Mrs. Brown. Life on a western dairy farm also made her aware that Canadians did not share English distinctions of class; in this land "full of splendid opportunities," she noted, it was the self-made man or woman who was valued. A young Maryanne Caswell told her grandmother about the visit of a contingent of the North West Mounted Police. They were "nice, polite Englishmen," she wrote, and by implication quite different than others in the neighbourhood. Emily

Carr was perhaps the most explicit about how the new world could transform settlers. She recounted how her father, after returning home to England, having lived for a time in California, had "chaffed at the limitations of the Old" world. British Columbia offered him and his new wife a congenial alternative and, there, he quickly became British. Although the gardens around his home were decidedly English, the family also maintained what they called a "Canadian" field, complete with a snake fence and natural grasses. For her part, Emily was decidedly Canadian, even if this meant that she was "slower" than her American neighbours. Emily Murphy, too, proudly declared her heritage, writing under her pen name Janey Canuck. Not all welcomed this transformation. Maria Adamowska clung tenaciously to her identity as a Ukrainian, even though she had left the old home at the age of nine. Others longed to become Canadian. As a Chinese-English child in Montreal, Sui Sin Far was aware that she was a "stranger." She was an oddity to her school mates and neighbours, and neither the English and the Chinese communities nor her parents really knew quite what to make of her. "I cheer myself ... that I am but a pioneer," she concluded, even if this meant that she had to "glory in suffering."

Most did not share Sui Sin Far's intense sense of alienation. Despite the scattered nature of settlement and Canada's relatively sparse population that often resulted in terrible loneliness and isolation, new arrivals and settlers could turn to family and their local community for solace and support. And it is here that one is conscious that, despite their differences of experiences and expectations, these women sometimes did share a common understanding of the world and their place within it.

From the seventeenth to the early twentieth century, there is no question that women's lives were fundamentally shaped by the very nature of the land, with its seasonal and climatic variations. Moreover, many of these authors and the women they wrote about were wives and mothers, and family was the fulcrum of their lives. They were also housekeepers and helpmates and neighbours, and they faced similar situations and dilemmas. Monica Hopkins, with her misadventures with the washing, would have recognized Anne Langton's difficulties with making bonnets and refashioning her dresses. Maria Adamowska's memories of being "without a piece of bread" echo Mary Fisher's concerns about having sufficient provisions to see the family through their first winter. Both Anne Langton, in the backwoods of Upper Canada, and Ella Sykes, working on the dairy farm in Alberta, ruefully commented that being a rural housekeeper was a "life of slavery." And yet, both these women and many others took satisfaction and some pride in their skills and their ability to make do with the limited resources that they had. For those like Juliana Ewing in New Brunswick and Monica Hopkins in Alberta, who seemed to have had to learn how to cook and clean after they arrived in Canada, the novelty of the situation was cause for laughter. For many others, keeping house, looking after children, and attending to a myriad of chores was not even cause for comment. Colonial and Canadian housekeepers knew that many hands made light work — and indeed, they needed the assistance of their children, their husbands (even when, as Monica Hopkins discovered, their husband's help created more work!) and their neighbours. In their accounts of their own childhood, Maryanne Caswell and seven- or eight-year-old Nellie McClung described helping out in the kitchen and the garden as a natural part of the daily routine. A few women could afford to hire "help." But even then, as Ella Sykes commented, the most "quick and capable" Canadian housekeeper usually found herself in the clutches of the "Demon of Work." When family was not enough, households turned to neighbours for help. The Beavan's house could not have been moved or the Langton's land cleared without the "frolic," or neighbourhood working bee.

Not all women (or men for that matter) were suited to life in Canada. As Mrs. McClung commented about the young couple that the family met on the trail, the land needed women, not "a painted doll." Mothers and wives and housekeepers had to have skills, tenacity, and be willing to turn their hand to a multitude of tasks. Many had to cope without the amenities of shops, or what Monica Hopkins called the "modern" gadgets of the city. They had to assume the responsibility of teacher and farm worker. Women in Canada had to be resilient, like Mary Fisher, who had left everything when she and the family had fled north after the American Revolution, or Susan Allison, who watched her home of many years be taken by the floods and had, without complaint, begun anew. Lydia Campbell, born on a Labrador outpost, remembered that although the family's closest white neighbours were some 30 miles away, they were never in want. Everyone in the family worked hard; at the same time, "we would enjoy ourselves pretty well." Being a wife and mother sometimes meant having to endure the heart-wrenching loss that came with the death of a child or a husband. But a young Margaret Michener and Letitia Hargrave had to carry on — to help neighbours cope with their own catastrophe or to look after other members of their families.

Not all the women who appear in *Voices* had chosen to come to or settle in Canada. Marie de l'Incarnation, Mère Cécile, Monica Hopkins, and others had consciously decided to make their homes in this new world. Others had followed their husbands. Children arrived with their families. Some, including Ella Sykes's mistress, were sometimes desperately unhappy. But as wives and mothers, they had a duty to fulfill, and a large part of that was to support their husbands. For many of these women, their faith in God gave them strength and solace. For most of them, their ties to their families — and the support of neighbours and friends — made what could have been an intolerable situation tolerable and, at times, enjoyable.

Single women travellers and visiting wives did not share such anguish. For Baroness von Riedesel, Lady Aberdeen, and Lady Dufferin, their time in the new world was an adventure that they knew would be relatively short lived and they could go home. As women of some considerable means and attached to men of power and influence, these upper-class women also had other women and men to do much of the housework, to look after the children, and to mediate the difficulties that could occur "in the colonies." In many ways, they stood apart from the world that most Canadian and pioneering women experienced. While someone else cooked or managed the household, they attended hockey games or learned to sled, or could read and write letters home, or keep a journal. Self-styled adventurers like Anna Jameson, Mary Warren, and Mina Hubbard, too, were in some ways privileged. As single women, without families to attend to and with the freedom that came with having an income and time, they could explore the world around them and delight in looking at it without having to live in it.

The stories told here — of hardships and laughter, of work and play, and of family and community — are not particularly unique. Most women who came to the colonies or Canada — as visitors or travellers, as pioneer settlers, as adventurers, and as wives and mothers — would have recognized themselves in at least some of these vignettes. They also would have appreciated that there was not an overarching experience that all of these women shared. It made a difference if one was the wife of the governor general or that of a recently arrived, struggling emigrant; being a mother and wife brought responsibilities that children or single women did not share, or even appreciate. Living in the backwoods of New Brunswick or the flat grasslands of Manitoba or along the banks of a mighty river fundamentally shaped the rhythms of one's life. Someone who was visiting the land saw different things and came away with a different understanding of the place than those who actually lived there. And yet, in the end, the worlds that these women were writing about were definitely new — and often foreign. And how they responded to it, in part at least, was a reflection of being women and all the concerns that accompanied this.

PART I

Maritimes

1

Mary Barbara Fisher

(1749–1841)

Mary Barbara Fisher, née Till, was "the mother of a very large family and a woman of resolute spirit, which she transmitted to her descendants." She was married to Lewis Fisher, who fought for the Crown with the New Jersey Volunteers during the American Revolution. Her four oldest children were born on Staten Island. In 1783 about 34,000 American Loyalists fled to Nova Scotia, including the Fisher family, and more than 14,000 settled in what is now New Brunswick. In October of that year, some 2,000 went up the St. John River Valley to Ste. Anne's Point.

Mrs. Fisher's son Peter is regarded as that province's first English-language historian; much of the material in his *Sketches of New Brunswick* (1852) comes from her memories. This excerpt is based on a manuscript by her granddaughter Georgianna, written in the 1880s or 90s, in which she recalls conversations with her grandmother. It shows the appalling difficulties of that first cruel winter faced by the original settlers of what is now the mellow town of Fredericton.

Weary Loyalists arriving in Nova Scotia after fleeing persecution and a difficult sea voyage would have rejoiced at this tranquil view. The Lower End of Halifax Harbour *is a page from the ship logbook, kept and illustrated by James S. Meres (active 1786–1835) a crew member of the* H.M.S. Pegasus.

THE GLOOMY PROSPECT

We sailed from New York in the ship "Esther" with the fleet for Nova Scotia. Some of our ships were bound for Halifax, some for Shelburne and some for St. John's river. Our ship going the wrong track was nearly lost. When we got to St. John we found the place all in confusion; some were living in log houses, some building huts, and many of the soldiers living in their tents at the Lower Cove. Soon after we landed we joined a party bound up the river in a schooner to St. Ann's. It was eight days before we got to Oromocto. There the Captain put us ashore, being unwilling on account of the lateness of the season, or for some other reason, to go further. He charged us each four dollars for the passage. We spent the night on shore and the next day the women and children proceeded in Aboriginal canoes to St. Ann's with some of the party, the rest came on foot.

We reached our destination on the 8th day of October, tired out with our long journey, and pitched our tents at the place now called Salamanca, near the shore. The next day we explored for a place to encamp, for the winter was near and we had no time to lose.

The season was wet and cold, and we were much discouraged at the gloomy prospect before us. Those who had arrived a little earlier had made better preparations for the winter; some had built small log huts. This we could not do because of the lateness of our arrival. Snow fell on the 2nd day of November to the depth of six inches. We pitched our tents in the shelter of the woods and tried to cover them with spruce boughs. We used stones for fireplaces. Our tent had no floor but the ground. The winter was very cold, with deep snow, which we tried to keep from drifting in by putting a large rug at the door. The snow, which lay six feet around us, helped greatly in keeping out the cold. How we lived through that awful winter I hardly know. There were mothers, that had been reared in a pleasant country enjoying all the comforts of life, with helpless children in their arms. They clasped their infants to their bosoms and tried by the warmth of their own bodies to protect them from the bitter cold. Sometimes a part of the family had to remain up during the night to keep the fires burning, so as to keep the rest from freezing. Some destitute people made use of boards, which the older ones kept heating before the fire and applied by turns to the smaller children to keep them warm.

Many women and children, and some of the men, died from cold and exposure. Graves were dug with axes and shovels near the spot where our party had landed, and there in stormy winter weather our loved ones were buried. We had no minister, so we had to bury them without any religious service, besides our own prayers. The first burial ground continued to be used for some years until it was nearly filled. We called it "The Loyalist Provincials Burial Ground."

...

When the Loyalists arrived there were only three houses standing on the old St. Ann's plain. Two of them were old frame houses, the other a log house (which stood near the old Fisher place). There were said to have been two bodies of people murdered here. It could not have been long before the arrival of the Loyalists that this happened.

Many of the Loyalists who came in the spring had gone further up the river, but they were little better off for provisions than we were at

St. Ann's. Supplies expected before the close of navigation did not come, and at one time starvation stared us in the face. It was a dreary contrast to our former conditions. Some of our men had to go down the river with hand-sleds or toboggans to get food for their famishing families. A full supply of provisions was looked for in the spring, but the people were betrayed by those they depended upon to supply them. All the settlers were reduced to great straits and had to live after the Indian fashion. A party of Loyalists who came before us late in the spring, had gone up the river further, but they were no better off than those at St. Ann's. The men caught fish and hunted moose when they could. In the spring we made maple sugar. We ate fiddleheads, grapes and even the leaves of trees to allay the pangs of hunger. On one occasion some poisonous weeds were eaten along with the fiddleheads; one or two died, and Dr. Earle had all he could do to save my life.

As soon as the snow was off the ground we began to build log houses, but were obliged to desist for want of food. Your grandfather went up the river to Captain McKay's for provisions, and found no one at home but an old colored slave woman, who said her master and his man had gone out to see if they could obtain some potatoes or meal, having in the

Explorers and settlers have long appreciated the virtues of the shrubby plant found from Labrador to the Yukon. Sir John Franklin, while navigating the Polar Sea found that it produced a refreshing beverage "in smell much resembling rhubarb." A strong infusion, boiling hot, "very much relieved" David Thompson of "a violent dysentery." The artist is William George Richardson Hind (1833–89).

house only half a box of biscuits. Some of the people at St. Ann's, who had planted a few potatoes, were obliged to dig them up and eat them.…

In our distress we were gladdened by the discovery of some large patches of pure white beans, marked with a black cross. They had probably been originally planted by the French, but were now growing wild. In our joy at the discovery we called them at first the "Royal Provincials' bread," but afterwards "The staff of life and hope of the starving." I planted some of these beans with my own hands, and the seed was preserved in our family for many years. There was great rejoicing when the first schooner arrived with corn-meal and rye. In those days the best passages up and down the river took from three to five days. Sometimes the schooners were a week or ten days on the way. It was not during the first year alone that we suffered from want of food; other years were nearly as bad.

The first summer after our arrival, all hands united in building their log houses. Dr. Earle's was the first that was finished. Our people had but few tools and those of the rudest sort. They had neither bricks nor lime, and chimneys and fireplaces were built of stone laid in yellow clay. They covered the roofs of the houses with bark bound over with small poles. The windows had only four small panes of glass.

The first store was kept by a man named Cairnes, who lived in an old house on the bank of the river near the gate of the first Church built in Fredericton [in front of the present Cathedral]. He used to sell fish at one penny each and butternuts at two for a penny. He also sold tea at $2.00 per lb. which was to us a great boon. We greatly missed our tea. Sometimes we used an article called Labrador, and sometimes steeped spruce or hemlock bark for drinking, but I despised it.

There were no domestic animals in our settlement at first except one black and white cat, which was a great pet. Some wicked fellows, who came from the States, killed, roasted and ate the cat, to our great indignation. A man named Conley owned the first cow. Poor Conley afterwards hanged himself, the reason for which was never known.

For years there were no teams, and our people had to work hard to get their provisions. Potatoes were planted among the black stumps and turned out well. Pigeons used to come in great numbers and were shot or caught by the score in nets. We found in their crops some small round beans, which we planted; they grew very well and made excellent green beans, which we ate during the summer. In the winter time our people had sometimes to haul their provisions by hand fifty or a hundred miles over the ice or through the woods. In summer they came in slow sailing vessels. On one occasion Dr. Earle and others went up the river to Canada on snowshoes with hand sleds, returning with bags of flour and biscuits. It was a hard and dangerous journey, and they were gone a long time.

For several years we lived in dread of the Indians, who were sometimes very bold. I have heard that the Indians from Canada once tried to murder the people on the St. John River. Coming down the river they captured an Indian woman of the St. John tribe, and the chief said they would spare her if she would be their guide. They had eleven canoes in all, and they were tied together and the canoe of the guide attached to the hindermost. As they drew near the Grand Falls, most of the party were asleep; and the rest were deceived by the woman, who told them that the roaring they heard was caused by a fall at the mouth of the stream which here joined the main river. At the critical moment the Indian woman cut the cord which fastened her canoe to the others and escaped to the shore, while the Canada Indians went over the fall and were lost.

In the early days of the settlement at St. Ann's, some fellows that had come from the States used to disturb the other settlers. They procured liquor at Vanhorne's tavern and drank heavily. They lived in a log cabin which soon became a resort for bad characters. They formed a plot to go up the river and plunder the settlers — provisions being their chief object. They agreed that if any of their party were killed in the expedition they should prevent discovery of their identity by putting him into a hole cut in the ice. While they were endeavouring to effect an entrance into a settler's house, a shot, fired out of a window, wounded a young man in the leg. The others then desisted from their attempt, but cut a hole in the ice and thrust the poor fellow in, who had been shot, although he begged to be allowed to die in the woods, and promised, if found alive not to betray them, but they would not trust him.

"The Grandmother's Tale" in *The First History of New Brunswick*, Peter Fisher.

2

Mrs. F. Beavan

(1818–1897)

Emily Elizabeth Beavan, née Shaw, also known as Mrs. F. Beavan, born in Belfast, Ireland, was the daughter of sea captain Samuel Shaw, who made frequent trips between Belfast, Dundalk, and Saint John, New Brunswick. Around 1836, she went to New Brunswick, where she attended school and was later employed as a teacher. In 1838 she married a surgeon, Frederick Williams Cadwalleder Beavan, and the couple settled in Queens County. Between 1841 and 1843, Mrs. Beavan published at least 10 tales and five poems in *Amaranth*, New Brunswick's first literary journal. In 1843 the family moved to England, but after the 1845 publication of her *Sketches and Tales*, intended as a handbook for settlers, she vanished, until recently, from our literary history. Thanks to the researches of her great-great-granddaughter, Lynette Nunn, it is now known that in 1852 they sailed for Australia, where Mrs. Beavan continued to write for newspapers and published at least four more books. The New Brunswick poet and critic Fred Cogswell considered the book, with its wide-ranging descriptions of settlement life and vivid settings, to be of greater value than Thomas Halliburton's and Susanna Moodie's better-known works, as well as "extremely useful to the student of history, education, agriculture, religion, and sociology." In this description of the Maritimes half a century later than Mrs. Fisher, it is clear that while there was still much backbreaking physical toil, life was altogether merrier. The account of trips to the sugar-bush and the annual joy of spring flowers will strike a chord with modern readers.

BEES AND MAPLE SYRUP

… No one attempts to live in the country districts without a farm. As the place where we lived had but a house and one acre of land, none being vacant in that immediate neighbourhood, and finding firing and pasturage expensive, and furthermore wishing to raise our own potatoes, and, if we liked, live in *peas*, a lot of two hundred acres was purchased in the settlement, styled, "*par excellence*," "the English," (from the first settlers being of that illustrious nation,) a distance of two miles from where we then lived. Our house was a good one. We did not like to leave it. Selling was out of the question: so we e'en resolved to take it with us, wishing, as the Highland robber did of the haystack, that it had legs to walk. A substitute for this was found in the universal resource of New Brunswickers for all their wants, from the cradle to the coffin, "the tree, the bonny greenwood tree," that gives the young life-blood of its sweet sap for sugar — and even when consumed by fire its white ashes yield them soap. I have even seen wooden fire-irons, although they do not go quite so far as their Yankee neighbours, who, letting alone wooden clocks, deal besides in *wooden hams*, nutmegs, and cucumber seeds. Two stout trees were then felled (the meanest would have graced a lordly park), and hewed with the axe into a pair of gigantic sled runners. The house was raised from its foundation and placed on these. Many hands make light work; but, had those hands been all hired labourers, the expense would have been more than the value of the house, but 'twas done by what is called a "frolic." When people have a particular kind of work requiring to be done quickly, and strength to accomplish it, they invite their neighbours to come, and, if necessary, bring with them their horses or oxen. Frolics are used for building log huts, chopping, piling, ploughing, planting, and hoeing. The ladies also have their particular frolics, such as wool-picking, or cutting out and making the home-spun woollen clothes for winter. The entertainment given on such occasions is such as the house people can afford; for the men, roast mutton, pot pie, pumpkin pie, and rum dough-nuts; for the ladies, tea, some scandal, and plenty of "*sweet cake*," with stewed apple and custards. There are, at certain seasons, a great many of these frolics, and the people never grow tired of attending them, knowing that the logs on their own fallows will disappear all the quicker for it. The house being now on the runners, thirty yoke of oxen, four abreast, were fastened to an enormous tongue, or pole, made of an entire tree of ash. No one can form any idea, until they have heard it, of the noise made in driving oxen; and, in such an instance as this, of the skill and tact required in starting them, so that they are all made to pull at once. I have often seen the drivers, who are constantly shouting, completely hoarse; and after a day's work so exhausted that they have been unable to raise the voice. Although the cattle are very docile, and understand well what is said to them, yet from the number of turnings and twistings, they require to be continually reminded of their duty. Amid, then, all the noise and bustle made by intimating to such a number whether they were to "haw" or "gee," the shoutings of the younger parties assembled, the straining of chains and the creaking of boards, the ponderous pile was set in motion along the smooth white and marble-like snow road, whose breadth it entirely filled up. It was a sight one cannot well forget — to see it move slowly up the hill, as if unwilling to leave the spot it had been raised on, notwith-standing the merry shouts around, and the flag they had decked it with, streaming so gaily through the green trees as they bent over it till it reached the site destined for it, where it looked as much at home as if it were too grave and steady a thing to take the step it had done. This was in March — we had been waiting some time for snow, as to move without it would have been a difficult task; for, plentifully as New Brunswick is supplied with that commodity, at some seasons much delay and loss is experienced for want of it — the sleighing cannot be done, and wheel carriages cannot run, the roads are so rough and broken with the frost — the cold is then more intense, and the cellars, (the sole store-houses and receptacles of the chief comforts) without their deep covering of snow, become penetrated by the frost, and their contents much injured, if not totally destroyed — this is a calamity that to be known must be experienced — the potatoes stored here are the chief produce of the farm, at least the part that is most available for selling, for hay should never go off the land, and grain is as yet so little raised that 'tis but the old farmers can do what is called "*bread themselves*": thus the innovation of the cellars by the *frost fiend* is a sad and serious occurrence — of course a deep bank of earth is thrown up round the house, beneath which, and generally its whole length and breadth, is the cellar; but the snow over this is an additional and even necessary defence, and its want is much felt in many other ways — in quantity, however, it generally makes up for its temporary absence by being five and six feet deep in April. About this season the warm sun begins to beam out, and causes the sap to flow in the slumbering trees — this is the season for sugar-making, which, although an excellent thing if it can be managed, is not much attended to, especially in new settlements, and those are generally the best off for a "*sugar-bush*;" but it occurs at that season when the last of the winter work must be done — the snow begins to melt on the roads, and the "saw whet," a small bird of the owl species, makes its appearance, and tells us, as the natives say, that "*the heart of the winter is broken*." All that can be done now must be done to lessen the toils of that season now approaching, from which the settler must not shrink if he hope to prosper. Sugar-making, then, unless the farmer is strong handed, is not profitable. A visit to a sugar-camp is an interesting sight to a stranger — it may, perhaps, be two or three miles through the woods to where a sufficient number of maple trees may be found close enough together to render it eligible for sugar-making. All the different kinds of maple yield a sweet sap, but the "rock maple" is the species particularly used for sugar, and perhaps a thousand of these trees near together constitute what is called a *sugar-bush*. Here, then, a rude hut, but withal picturesque in its appearance, is erected — it is formed of logs, and covered with broad sheets of birch bark. For the universal use of this bark I think the Indians must have given the example. Many beautiful articles are made by them of it, and to the back settlers it is invaluable. As an inside roofing, it effectually resists the rain — baskets for gathering the innumerable tribe of summer berries, and boxes for packing butter are made of it — calabashes for drinking are formed of it in an instant by the bright forest stream. Many a New Brunswick belle has worn it for a head-dress as the dames of more polished lands do frames of French willow; and it is said the title deeds of many a broad acre in America have been written on no other parchment than its smooth and vellum-like folds. The sugar-maker's bark-covered hut contains his bedding and provisions, consisting of little save the huge round loaf of bread, known as the "shanty loaf" — his beverage, or substitute for tea, is made of the leaves of the winter green, or the hemlock boughs which grow beside him, and his sweetening being handy bye, he wants nothing more. A notch is cut in the tree, from which the sap flows, and beneath it a piece of shingle is inserted for a spout to conduct it into troughs, or bark dishes, placed at the foot of the tree. The cold frosty nights, followed by warm sunny days, making it run freely, clear as water, and slightly sweet — from these troughs, or bark dishes, it is collected in pails, by walking upon the now soft snow, by the aid of snow shoes, and poured into barrels which stand near the boilers, ready to supply them as the syrup boils down. When it reaches the consistence required for sugar, it is poured into moulds of different forms. Visits to these sugar camps are a great amusement of the young people of the neighbourhood in which they are, who make parties for that purpose — the great treat is the candy, made by dashing the boiling syrup on the snow, where it instantly congeals, transparent and crisp, into sheets. At first the blazing fire and

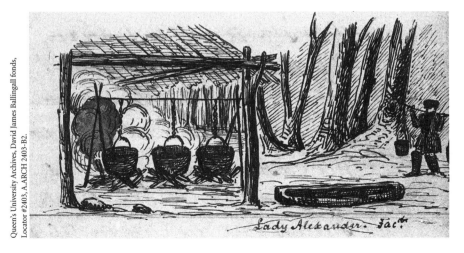

Queen's University Archives, David James Ballingall fonds, Locator #2403, A.ARCH 2403-B2.

This lively vignette of life in the sugar bush was sketched by Lady Eveline Marie Alexander (1818–1906), artist wife of a British officer stationed in Canada.

boiling cauldron look strange, amid the solemn loneliness of the forest, along whose stately aisles of cathedral-like grandeur the eye may gaze for days, and see no living thing — the ear hear no sound, save it may be the tapping of the woodpecker, or the whispering of the wind as it sighs through the boughs, seeming to mourn with them for the time when the white man knew them not. But these thoughts pass away when the proprietor, with his pale intelligent face, shaded by a flapping sun hat from the glaring snow, presses us hospitably to "take along a junk of candy, a lump of sugar," or a cup of the syrup. He sees nothing picturesque or romantic in the whole affair, and only calculates if it will pay for the time it occupies; at the same time, with the produce of his labours he is extremely "*clever*," this being the term for generous or hospitable, and one is sometimes startled at its application, especially to women; the persons in England, to whom it is applied, are so unlike the clever women of New Brunswick, those dear old creatures, who know not the difference between Milton and Dilworth, and whose very woollen gowns are redolent of all-spice and apples.

Towards the latter part of March and April the breaking up of the ice goes on gradually — some seasons, however, a sudden storm causes the ice and snow to disappear rapidly, but generally a succession of soft warm winds, and days partly sunshine and rain, does it more effectually, and prevents the heavy freshets in the rivers, which are often destructive, overflowing the low banks and carrying away with resistless force whatever buildings may be on them. After the disappearance of the snow, some time must elapse ere the land be in a fit state for sowing, consequently fencing, and such like, is now the farmer's employment, either around the new clearings, or in repairing those which have fallen or been removed during the winter. This, with attending to the stock, which at this season require particular care, gives them sufficient occupation — the sheep, which have long since been wearied of the "durance vile" which bound them to the hay-rick, may now be seen in groups on the little isles of emerald green which appear in the white fields; and the cattle, that for six long weary months have been ruminating in their stalls, or "chewing the cud of sweet and bitter fancy" in the barn yards, now begin to extend their perigrinations towards the woods, browsing with delight on the sweet young buds

An elegant young Mi'kmaq woman demonstrates the art of weaving baskets in a charming, if romanticized, watercolour by Nova Scotian artist Mary McKie (active 1840–62).

of the birch tree. At this season it is, for obvious reasons, desirable that the "milky mothers" should not stray far from home — many "a staid brow'd matron" has disappeared in the spring, and, after her summer rambles in the woods, returned in the "fall" with her full-grown calf by her side, but many a good cow has gone and been seen no more, but as a white skeleton gleaming among the green leaves. To prevent these mischances, a bell is fastened on the leader of the herd, the intention of which is to guide where they may be found. This bell is worn all summer, as their pasture is the rich herbage of the forest. It is taken off during the winter, and its first sounds now tell us, although the days are cold, and the snow not yet gone, that brighter times are coming. The clear concerts of the frogs ring loudly out from marsh and lake, and at this season alone is heard the lay of the wood-robin, and the blackbird. The green glossy leaves of the winter green, whose bright scarlet berries look like clusters of coral on the snow, now seem even brighter than they were — the blue violet rises among the sheltered moss by the old tree roots, and the broad-leaved adder tongue gives out its orange and purple blossoms to gladden the brown earth, while the trees are yet all black and barren, save the various species of pine and spruce, which now wear a fringe of softer green. The May flowers of New Brunswick seldom blossom till June, which is rather an Irish thing of them to do, and although the weather has been fine, and recalls to the memory the balmy breath of May, yet I have often seen a pearly wreath of new fallen snow, deck the threshold on that "merrie morn."

Mrs. F. Beavan, *Sketches and Tales Illustrative of Life in the Backwoods of New Brunswick.*

3

Juliana Horatia Ewing

(1841–1885)

Juliana Horatia Ewing, née Gatty, was the author of more than 30 popular books for children, including *Jackanapes, Lob Lie-by-the-Fire* and *The Story of a Short Life*. Several of her stories — such as *The Trinity Flower* (1871), a legend about the trillium — have Canadian settings. The English novelist and critic Arnold Bennett wrote of her work: "I conceive that Rudyard Kipling must have read Mrs. Ewing when he was young, and I wish I had." Juliana, born in Yorkshire, was the daughter of the redoubtable Victorian children's editor/author and seaweed expert Mrs. Margaret Gatty, and granddaughter of Canon Scott, Lord Nelson's chaplain. Juliana was at the start of her career when she married Major Alexander Ewing, composer of "Jerusalem the Golden." One week after their wedding they sailed for Fredericton, where his regiment had been posted, arriving in the midst of Confederation celebrations. Juliana was enchanted with her new life in this civilized military cathedral town, which she described in many letters home. She botanized, wrote, sketched, and, despite chronic ill health, revelled in snowshoeing, sleigh riding, and canoeing. The Ewings were recalled to England in 1869.

During their time in Fredericton, both Ewings were much involved with the life of Christ Church Cathedral. Mrs. Ewing wrote of Bishop Medley, "he is very clever, & awfully amusing, & told me the funniest anecdotes." The artist for this circa 1850 painting was Lady Anne Maria Head.

Canoes

8 June 1868. Fredericton

My dearest Mother —

Does the above give you the faintest idea of what it is to paddle up & down these lovely rivers with their smaller tributaries & winding creeks — on a still, sunny afternoon? It really is the most fascinating amusement we have tried yet. Mr. Bliss took us out the other day — it being the 1st time either of us was in a canoe & Rex took one of the paddles, & got on so well [and was so charmed] with it that we are going to set up our own canoe. Peter is building it — & I hope soon to send you a sketch of him "paddling his own canoe." Of us — I may say — for I tried a paddle today

— & mean to have a little one of my own to give my valuable assistance in helping the canoe along. Next month when Rex can get away, we think of going up the river to "Grand Falls" (the next thing to Niagara — they say) by steamer, taking our canoe with us — & then paddling ourselves home with the stream. About 80 miles. Of course we should do it by bits — sleeping at stopping places. One art Rex has not yet acquired, & it *looks* awful! A sort of juggler's trick — that of *carrying* his canoe. Imagine taking hold of the side of a canoe that would hold six people, throwing it up, & overturning it neatly on your head — without injuring either your own skull or the canoe's bottom.…

Your snow shoes are ordered with our canoe! And also a "pipe of peace" to add to Maggie's collection — I hope to send them by the Bishop in July.

I am longing for letters. Of course I was prepared to get none by the intermediate mail but now that the Halifax mail has had to put back to Liverpool — it seems a very long wait! — We shall probably get the ones via New York quite as soon if not sooner than those written by the mail before. This canoeing is really a source of great pleasure to us, & will more than double the enjoyment of summer to me. You see, having no carriage — nor unlimited means to hire *conveyances* — we get about *very* little — & in a lovely country which one may leave any day never to return — it seems a pity. Now with a canoe, Rex can "pull" me to 100 places where a short walk from the shore will give me sketching, botanizing — & all I want! — Moreover the summer heat at times oppresses my head — & then to get on the water gives a cool breeze — & *freshens one up* in a way that made me think of what it must be to people in India to get to "the hills." I have never wished for some of you more than on this lovely river — gliding about close to the water (you sit on the very bottom of the canoe) — all the trees just bursting into green, & the water reflecting everything exquisitely — kingfishers — & all kinds of birds flitting about & singing unfamiliar songs. Boblinks going "twit twit" — little yellow birds — king birds — crows & the robin: thrushes everywhere — I landed today at one place — & went into a wood to try & get flowers. I only got one good one — but it was very lovely! Two crows were making wild cries for the loss of one of their young ones which some boys had taken — & as I went on I heard the queer chirrup (like a bird's note) of Ajidomo the Squirrel! & he ran across my path, & into a hollow tree. It is a much smaller squirrel than ours — about the size of a water rat — & beautifully striped. The flower was a little pinkish bell on a pretty stalk & leaves of an orchidaceous appearance

We have joined an archery club — Not that *I* shall become a toxopholite — I have irons enough in the fire! But it will be sociable & pleasant — & Rex will do the archery for me. I certainly *do* wish I were a better hand at drawing. One does see lovely bits!! —

The only drawback to the paddling is that the beloved Hector cannot go with us. He would endanger the safety of the canoe. One has to sit very still! —

My garden gets on very jollily. At a sale on Saturday I bought some plants rather cheap. One silver geranium I gave less than ˢ1/- for, & I have got a dozen cuttings from it already besides the mother plant. It was a great straggling thing & I got it to cut up. The season is still very backward — & we have a great deal of rain — & some really cold days. Before the sun comes out we breakfast with a fire — & I put on my warmest winter jacket to go out in. When the sun once shines it is so powerful that one can hardly walk about with comfort. But I have enjoyed the Spring thoroughly — I much prefer it to plunging into boiling heat at once. Mrs. Medley has been very ill, but is nearly all right again. The Bishop has gone to Halifax. We are greatly looking forward to hear of Maggie & Frank & how the wedding went off. We had a bottle of champagne in honour of our own wedding day — I hope you remembered us. Today is the day we sailed from Liverpool! I do thank GOD for all the happiness I have had in this "strange land." It is bedtime dearest Mum — Ever your loving daughter, J.H. Ewing.

[Aug 15, 1868]

… I meant to have written to the dear Mum but do not know if I shall have time. What I wanted to say was in reference to the climate. Rex said long ago he wld be sure to frighten you as the dear old man is very strong on the subject. But you have no idea how charming the winter is — all said & done. The figures on the thermometer are very alarming — but you never have beheld or felt — what it is to walk over a glittering plain — of pure, dry, exquisite snow — under a sun as hot & a sky as pure, deep, & unclouded a blue as if you were in Italy. There *are* bitter days when the wind takes your breath, & freezes your nose & fingers — but ladies can simply stay indoors — where the heat would make you stare!!! The Bishop has knocked about in these winters for 27 or 29 years — going long day's journeys of 50 miles in sleighs or ricketty stages — & yet with all the hard work of a Colonial Bishop's life — you see him as active & lively as a man of between 60 & 70 can well be. As to the overshoe story — I think he has confounded me with Bessy Roberts who has a knack of forgetting her goloshes & leaving them in Church, especially when she has got a "throat" — to his great disgust. I never wear winter overshoes — always moccasons. The warmest & most comfortable of footgear! — & Rex would turn Fredericton upside down with indignation if *I* ran any risks from forgotten overshoes &c.!!! As to the fatigue of walking on snow-shoes — I don't think it fatiguing — It is charming — Moreover you *needn't* walk

"I took my first walk upon snowshoes yesterday, and got along very well and didn't tumble once!!!!!!" Mrs. Ewing felt awkward on skates and preferred snowshoes. Captain Francis G. Coleridge (1838–1923) painted Two Women on Snowshoes *in 1866.*

on them! It is an amusement, like skating — & is quite optional. I much prefer them to skates — & think it the greatest fun possible. It is a swinging, rather dignified gait & you get over a wonderful lot of ground with little trouble. It is a little troublesome to remember all one's wraps when one goes out in winter, but what is it? — 3 minutes more time to spend in dressing & undressing perhaps! — I *wish* the Mum *could* realize what the climate really is. *For life* — it *is* trying to delicate women. Years of extreme changes seem to affect the feminine constitution as a rule, in the *long run*. But people live here to great ages, & the mortality among regiments stationed here is *exceptionally low*. And it is so magnificently dry & bracing — & there are so few days & nights when you can't be out in the year, that I cannot fancy its being otherwise than a boon to *anybody* for a time. Just now it is splendidly fine. *Such* a sun! — such a sky! — such breezes — & cool nights — it is lovely. With melons, & squash, & tomatoes ripening in your garden…. Finally, tell the Mum above all not to fidget about our £.S.D. matters. We are perfectly comfortable. Of course it was a little expensive starting — & the remains of some old matters at home not quite cleared off that came on poor old Rex — we have been anxious to clear off whilst in this cheap living place. I just allude to this to show you that when we have no extras — but only to *live on* our income — we should be *perfectly comfortable* if the Scheme hangs fire till Michaelmas 10 years. I made up my mind (knowing that we had furniture to buy &c. &c. &c. &c.) that we would live at the rate of £250 a year as set forth in Domestic Economy. We have full £300. Whilst Sarah was with me — I did not always manage it. *Now* we live if anything on less. Moreover on that scale £31 is allowed for "rent & taxes." We pay only £25. Our *living, washing,* & *wages* only cost between £2 & £3 a week — & we have meat 3 times a day — a small bill of *good* wine (paid monthly) from the "Mess" (22d) — beer in barrel as at home — & everything we want. I have my dripping "clarified" to help out with cakes & pastry, & we get 2 lbs of delicious butter per week — which I *make do*. Just now the "feed" is beginning to be very good, as birds of all kinds are coming into season — We have vegetable marrows — tomatoes — & lots of all kinds of vegetables, besides supplying many of our neighbours. Tell the Mum we have *abundance* & live in the utmost comfort, & have champagne whenever there is an excuse for it! Rex ordered a bottle on my birthday — & if the Mum will get quite well — we will have 2.... Mrs. Parry & I have great fun over our domestic concerns. She thinks me a great hand I believe!!!!!! & has now got Domestic Economy — & started her accounts on my principle!!!!!!!!!!! — Tell the Mum housekeeping is only *amusement* to me. Our income is *more than ample* here. It is a splendid place for that. We *could not* live in London on 1/2 as much again with *comfort* & the feeling of being like other people. Here we are rather wealthy & swell than otherwise. Rexie never complains of anything — & lets me do it all my own way, & says he & I live on less than he could manage to live on alone!!!!

I must stop darling —

Your everloving old
Judy

Margaret Howard Blom and Thomas E. Blom, eds., *Canada Home: Fredericton Letters, 1867–1869.*

4

Margaret Dickie Michener

(1827–1908)

Margaret Michener, née Dickie, turned her hand to many occupations — shoemaking, teaching, farming, operating a telegraph — during her long life. She was born of Planter Baptist stock in the shipbuilding centre of Hantsport, Nova Scotia. In 1849 she married Simeon Michener, a mariner. After his untimely death, she taught school and furthered her studies. In 1856 she married Robert McCulloch, a ship's caulker. The couple settled on a farm in Delaware in 1867, but soon returned to Nova Scotia. In 1881 they moved to a farm near Tuscola, Michigan, where Margaret was active in the Baptist Church and served for two terms as a school inspector. Even in old age she earned a tidy sum, knitting double mittens for a woollen factory. The journal she kept for much of her adult life provides a vivid picture of her family and community. Several of her poems and excerpts from her diaries were published in the *Wolfville Acadian*.

WIDOWHOOD

April 13th, 1850

I am so busy most of the time I neglect to keep my journal, though I might find much to write. Simeon went to Cheverie on Monday and came back this evening; it has been a lonesome week without him. I wish he might obtain work on shore so he could always be at home. I like my occupation quite well. Sometimes when I talk to my scholars they pay great attention and make free to ask questions. They appear to know what is right, and willing to do the right, but forget sometimes. Every day some little differences come up between them, but they are soon all friends again.

19th

My brothers and Ann came down last evening to study as usual. Our attention is turned to Wisconsin and Michigan where Simeon, Capt. Curry and some others talk of emigrating to as it is good farming country. We women will be glad to have our husbands give up the seafaring life; we are willing to go — brothers, sisters and all, but what the outcome will be I know not....

...

25th

We visited Abigail last evening. This afternoon Simeon told us he was to leave tomorrow. I was quite surprised that he is to go so soon, so I sent for my brother and Ann to come down....

28th

Well, I am now alone as Simeon has gone away. I had no school yesterday as we were busy getting ready for his departure for Michigan, or some place that way. We arose early yesterday morning and took a walk; I suppose it will be our last one for some time. I was busy all the morning and got an early dinner; Capt. Curry and Simeon were running back and forth. After dinner Capt. Curry came in and asked me to take a walk

The three-masted Forest King, *built in 1877 was typical of the many wooden ships built in Hantsport. Painting by John Lowes (1889).*

with them to the shore. Maria would go if I would. So I got ready and we went. I suppose some thought if they were in our place they would not have gone, but they wished us to and we wished to see them as long as we could. They were taking some things to the vessel; we sat down on the bank watching them. John sung out to us — he being up in the "Hantsport" rigging. Mr. J. Frost came along and sat with us a long time, talking about the States and the people there; but the time soon came when we must be parted. They bade us Adieu with many good wishes to both parties, hoping to meet again ere many months shall pass. They stood waving their hats as we watched them sail away. We stopped at Olivia's and she came home with me, so I had my attention engaged. Joe came up in the evening and then they all went home. Maria came over and we talked on the departed ones with many hopes and fears. We slept soundly, but I was dreaming all night about vessels. When I arose this morning I took a walk down the new road to the shore and back on the old one before breakfast. Sister Ann was here when I returned. I am glad Maria is so near by as we can be together often. I have been reading in

Mason's Self Knowledge; it is a nice book and teaches one many things it is well to know.

May 1st

Mother was here to see me today and visited Mary also. It seems she and father are very much stirred up over our plans for going to the States. They do not like the idea at all and are feeling badly.

…

7th

My scholars number 32 now. I find it a trial sometimes to be patient, they are so noisy. I am kept busy. I would like to know where Simeon is. I hope he may make the journey in safety. I received my American Messenger yesterday; there is some very nice reading in them.

…

June 1st

The month has come in cold and rainy. I went up to Father's after school last night, and called into Charlotte Barber's and Sarah Whitman's on my way. I found the men busy with the farm work and Mother was spinning. I went upstairs and heard rain on the roof; it reminded me of bygone days, and many pleasing recollections were presented to mind as I looked around. After the men came in Robert read aloud about the trial of Dr. Webster. I arose early this morning and returned home. I read some in Comb's Constitution of Man, and find it a very good book. Jane Fielding is here and will stop the night with me. It is five weeks today since Capt. Curry and Simeon went away. I suppose they are in Michigan now.

6th

The "Orbit" came in from Halifax last night and brought some supplies to Mrs. Dorman for her store. There is great rejoicing among the old ladies as they all have been out of tea. I lent all I had as I do not drink it.

12th

John came down last night and went over to the Post Office. When he returned he had letters for father, Maria and me. Simeon wrote that they were fresh water sailors going to Ohio. They had a great time going from Albany to Buffalo in a canal boat. Simeon slept on the table and the cabin was crowded. They are going to cruise around for awhile before going to Michigan. They will write again soon. Maria and I had a great laugh at their description of their voyage.

21st

Friday morning. I had looked forward all week to Thursday, hoping it would be a fine day so we might attend the exercises at the College. I arose early and went up home. We started a little before seven o'clock — John, Robert, Ann and I. Robert called at Mr. Elder's for them. They soon came along … in another carriage…. we went in to the College where people were gathering. We stood a while gazing at the beautiful scenery around and then went in and found the room all decorated with festoons and garlands of flowers, vines of evergreens and wreathes. There were many ministers there, among the number we saw Rev's Rand, Dickie and Burpee. Mr. Rand is the missionary among the Micmac Indians; R.B. Dickie is a relation, and one of our favourite ministers and Mr. Burpee is our foreign missionary just returned from India. The program began with singing followed by prayer by our Venerable Father Harding.

Mr. Henry Johnston delivered his essay on the Ice World…. Mr. Thomas Crawley received the B.A. degree and then spoke on the tendencies of the age to brotherhood, showing how society was advancing, new discoveries being made — the inventions, all calculated to bring the people of the world closer together. Mr. David Freeman spoke on Instinct, Reason and Faith, showing how we all are fitted to our station; the animals having instinct to guide them, and we, being so much above them have reason, reflection and faith united with reason, productive of happiness. The exercises were varied by singing, the last piece being the national anthem…. It was nearly six o'clock before we started for home.

Mrs. Michener must have found some solace from her grief at early widowhood while living amidst such pastoral Nova Scotian scenery. This view from retreat farm, Windsor, Nova Scotia, was painted by William Eager in 1840.

July 3rd

… After school yesterday I took a walk across the fields back of the meeting house and beyond; the scene from the hill is delightful, looking down upon our pretty village to the adjacent river, with a glimpse of woods and houses in the distance. I was thinking of the last time I was there — about a year ago with Simeon.… I came to father's and stopped all night, and would like to have spent the day also, but had to return to my school.…

…

18th

We arose early this morning hoping it would be a fine day for our picnic, so we were all much pleased to see such a beautiful morning. The scholars assembled as usual, except they had on their Sunday dress. We went through with the morning lessons. Marianne Davidson and Ann came down and I set them to making wreaths of flowers. Susannah Davidson was chosen as the prettiest girl and we decorated her to represent "Flora." Between eleven and twelve o'clock we started to march down near the shore. We marched by couples, "Flora" and I leading the way. We soon arrived at the spot I had chosen under some trees in Mr. Davidson's pasture. We took our dinner seated on the ground after which the children played around for awhile, then recited some hymns they had learned. They sang some pieces beautifully, then Ann played some for them on the accordion. We also gave each of them a present with which they seemed much pleased. We took a walk along the beach and up to the top of the bank, where we sat for a while to rest. Louise joined us there and then we marched back home quite well pleased with the day's enjoyment, and they asked when we could have another picnic.

. . .

[Aug.] 20th
… I met Mr. Harris as I was coming home and he said there was a letter for me. I found it was one from Simeon, written long ago from Cork, and there was some money enclosed. I wonder where it has been all this time.

25th
I had company yesterday afternoon; Ann Eliza West, Mary and Ann were here. We had a very pleasant time talking over days that are past and gone. Ann Eliza likes to talk on phrenology and physiology, and we agree there. They are good subjects for conversation. She stopped all night and we did not go to sleep till after midnight. This morning after breakfast Ann Eliza and her son returned to her father's and I went to S. School as usual.

Sept. 9th
It rained and blew hard all night. After supper I went over to Maria's. I read a while in the "Life of John Bunyan", then sat and thought on by-gone days. Every scene with which Simeon was associated came to my mind. I could not refrain from tears, thinking, "What if I never should see him again." At last such a desolate feeling came over me, I had to start for home in the rain. Maria came with me.

10th

Maria went to Capt. Holmes yesterday afternoon, and after school I went too. She, Elmira and I took a walk down to the brook. We had to make a bridge to cross over as the rains have raised the water quite high. We went over to a beautiful grove, the same place Rebecca Elder, Elnira and I sat and sang three years ago. There is a lovely view from there and we saw Capt. Toye's brig come sailing up. We looked forward to the evening hoping to get letters from our loved ones. I went to Maria's and watched, as the bridge by Bishop's is up, and the coach came this way and left the mail at Harris's. We went over, but there were no letters for us. We felt sad and fear they are sick. We think maybe they are coming home, or perhaps their letters have gone astray. Time will tell and we must wait patiently.

...

24th

I have been shopping over at Aunt Sally's. She sells a great deal; there is someone in there the most of the time. Grandfather got in last night. I have just received my share of plums, a peck or more. After school I went down to Olivia's. Maria went in the afternoon. ... The boys came in and said there was a letter in the office for Olivia. Oh, how we wished there were some for us. We soon heard that Joe was in New York and was coming to Halifax. He said that on Sunday the 25th, Chipman fell from the top sail yard to the sea. It was a dark and stormy night but he was rescued. It made us tremble when we heard of it, and very thankful to know he was saved.

27th

Maria came in this evening and we have been taking turns reading aloud from a book called The Young Emigrant; it is about two families who move to Ohio. It shows how many difficulties the first settlers have to encounter in a new country.

Oct. 2nd

How changed are all my prospects. What shall I write? I know not what to say or think. My beloved Simeon is no more! Can it be possible I will not see him again, or hear his sweet voice? I went to Mary's last night to wait till the mail would come in. Ezra went over and returned with three letters. I got a light and saw that two letters were for Maria. It was with fear and trembling I read my letter from Simeon; he was in quite good spirits when he wrote but not too well. I found Curry had received Maria's letter but Simeon did not get mine. I read my letter to Mary and Ann, and then in haste went up to Marcia's where Maria was. The road never seemed so long before; I could not go fast enough. At last I gave her the letters, wishing yet dreading to know the contents. I told her to read the latest one first. I arose ready to start at the news she looked; I saw her drop the letter and I went into the bedroom as I wished to hear no more. I knew Simeon was dead yet dared not ask.

Oct. 3rd

Simeon wrote to me on Sept. 10th and died on the 13th at 5 o'clock in the morning. Capt. Curry attended him until his last moments; he died easily as if going to sleep. If only I could have been with him it would have been a mournful pleasure. I walked the floor nearly all night. I cannot realize he is gone never to return. This forenoon I felt as if I wished to see my parents and glad I was to see my father coming in. Emily Ann and Mrs. James were in a while this morning and mother came in this afternoon. I am glad to have their sympathy. Aunt Sally came to see me. She well knows the bitterness of losing a friend in a foreign port, but all the sympathy in the world cannot heal the wound. How many pleasant scenes I have to look back upon. How kind and good Simeon was! I was unworthy of such a good and loving companion. Oh, could I but see him once more, but the cruel grave has torn him from me. How can I bear it!

4th

I went up home with mother Wednesday evening; how lonely all things seemed, as all things remind me of the happy hours spent here with Simeon. I walked about from room to room and cannot put my mind on anything.... Oh, how rebellious my heart; how keen the smart when I see my sisters enjoying the society of their husbands. I feel I cannot submit to lose mine. Ann came down with me tonight. She will stay at

Olivia's a while, when she and Joe go to Halifax. How keen was our grief upon entering my lonely home. Capts. Michael and Hibbart have been in. They seem to feel deeply the loss we have sustained. Maria is here to stop with me. May God help us to seek thee.

. . .

7th

I have come tonight to my lonely habitation. It is not the same as it has been all summer, for hope has departed. I was looking forward to winter when Simeon would be home. I took a walk down to Halfway River bridge and sat on the fence by the marsh to watch the flowing tide. I sat there till it came all around me as the tides are high — and ebbed again. I read a while there Pope's "Messiah," which Simeon had learned and wrote it off for me before we were married. It sounds so like him, I almost think I hear him repeat it. I seem to envy Maria the hope she has of Curry coming home, but why should I? Let me give up, and wish others all good success. Maria is here now; my friends are all very kind. I wrote to Rebecca Elder today. I feel some consolation in scribbling. I pray God may direct me.

9th

... I was looking over Simeon's letters this forenoon; it seemed my heart would burst. I had to leave off and could not get my mind settled for a long time. I try to pray but I fear I am too much attached to the creature rather than the Creator....

13th

... I feel comforted whilst reading the many promises in scripture. I trust in the promises and hope although this affliction is for the present grievous it will work for my good. I feel to cling more closely to Him who has promised to be the widow's God.

. . .

21st

Monday evening finds me alone at my table scribbling. Yesterday was a drizzly day and a melancholy one. Rev. Vaughan preached a funeral sermon from the text, "Be ye also ready, etc." It seemed as if it was a call to all of us. I felt as though I wished to have the body before me while the services were being held but alas! that was denied.... Oh, I felt if I could only see his body there to be interred, it would be some consolation, but perhaps I would feel no better....

...

28th

Monday morning. Well, my house looks as lonesome as ever when I enter it. I came home early this morning after having been away nearly a week.... While at father's I took a walk daily down the glen below the house and to the bridge to gaze at the flowing waters. It reminds me of the stream of time thinking our lives are going as fast. Saturday afternoon I had a great ramble around the most rugged and steep bank I could find, and up to the spot where Simeon and I sat so happily a little over a year ago. The melancholy winds and wild rambles suit my spirit better than anything I find....

As I was going to Hibbart's this forenoon he said, "There has more trouble come to our family." I asked, "What?" He said, "James Holmes has been brought home dead." I felt my grief afresh then, as I thought of poor dear Abigail. I came home and then Hibbart came for me to go to tell Abigail; he said he could not do it. She had gone to Ann Barker's with her boys to spend the day. I went over, but could not go in the room where she was. "Oh," I thought, "if she only knew it, I could see her." After awhile I went in and talked of what had happened, saying we knew not who would be affected next; then I spoke of James and said Hibbart had heard from him, and I went out of the room. Abigail followed me and demanded to know what I meant. I told her to be prepared for the worst. She began to scream. "You tell me he is dead!" and she shook me. After she knew, we thought she would lose her mind. Emily Ann came in and we talked to her about her children and tried to calm her. Capt. Michener and Mrs. Kendal came in and after awhile she prepared to go home; her father, Mrs. Kendal and

I went with her, Emily Ann and some others following after. A short time afterward the body was brought home.... There he was in his sailor clothes looking so natural. I feel great sympathy for Abigail. She has her three little boys to be with her in her widowhood; they look like their father, only gone a week last Saturday from his home, and now returned a corpse....

Dec. 4th

Here I am at my lonely dwelling for a few minutes writing. Father and I went to Windsor Tuesday afternoon. I called at Dr. Harding's to pass an examination to get a license for teaching school. Mr. Murdock gave me the license. In the evening we attended a lecture at the Temperance Hall. We stopped at Mr. McHeffey's all night, then, after doing some shopping we returned home....

13th

Ann went down to Mrs. E. Holmes to watch, as her child is very ill.

14th

Saturday night I went to stay the night [at Mrs. Holmes]; about half past eleven the child died in my arms. It was the first time I had ever seen one die; it sank away so gently I hardly knew it was gone. I thought how sweet to die and be at rest from the tumult of this world. Dear little babe, it looked more beautiful in death than when living, for it was a great sufferer. Mrs. Hicks and Jane Lynch sat with me. Mrs. Hicks is a widow for three years. She has six children. I feel a nearness to widows.

Jan. 4th 1851

Two years ago tonight, I sat as a bride beside my husband. I knew not then what time we would spend together, but now I know, for it has fled. Dear Simeon, how happy we were.... I have taught school for a week now and like it.

"Margaret Dickie Michener Diary" in Margaret Conrad, Toni Laidlaw and Donna Smyth, eds. *No Place Like Home.*

PART II

Quebec

5

Mère Cécile de Sainte-Croix

(CIRCA 1609/10–1687)

Mère Cécile de Sainte-Croix, an Ursuline from Dieppe, was the third nun to join Marie de l'Incarnation on her mission to found a seminary for the education of young Aboriginal and French girls in the new colony of Quebec. The three sisters disembarked on May 4, 1639, with three Augustine nuns from Dieppe who were to found a hospital. Both establishments survive today, continuing their work of educating girls and healing the sick. Although Mère Cécile served in many capacities as teacher, apothecary, and cook in the convent — and learned to make sagamite (cornmeal boiled with plums), a favourite Native food — she was "so quiet and unassuming that no one troubles to mention her during the 48 years which she spent serving the Canadian Mission. In all the documents of the period she is mentioned only once" (Mother Denis Mahony). But a stalwart during the seminary's difficult early years, she was greatly valued by Marie de l'Incarnation. An early Ursuline document provides a touching account of her funeral. In 1686 the convent had burned down (for the second time) "to a glowing heap of ruins"; the nuns were ensconced in a "miserable hovel" for a year, waiting to rebuild. For three weeks that September, Mère Cécile suffered fever, died, and then "there was no more convenient spot for her grave than the ruins of their former lovely Choir! To add to the sadness of the burial ceremony, a heavy autumnal rain came pouring its waters over the funeral cortege as they bore the dear remains across the open court to the last resting place of the dead."

The Voyage Out

[2nd December 1639]

My very dear Mother,

Peace and love of Our Lord!

I wrote you on the sea, about a hundred and fifty leagues from Dieppe, by way of some fishermen. I do not know if you have received the letter. Thank God, we have been preserved from the danger to the ships that I reported to you, but we have incurred a great many others that I will tell you about.

With regard to the food, in which one commonly endures much at sea and of which I have heard many to complain, we have been spared and much better treated than if we had been in our convent, especially while we were in M. Bontemps' ship, who gave an order that we were not to be refused anything we asked. It is, thank God, the least mortification that one has food. I have tested it: we have felt more content with *la molue* without butter than if we are left without enough meat. It has often crossed my mind that it is another thing to experience the inconveniences of the sea than only to have heard of them. When one sees oneself within an ace of death one finds oneself very astounded. The first lesson that I have learned from the reverend Father Le Jeune, and that I have found very true, is that there is no Cross in Canada except those one brings from France. I have tested it every day.

We had a furious storm that lasted fifteen days, with very little interval, with the result that all the week of Rogations, including Ascension day, we were prevented from hearing holy Mass and holy Communion. We had the same mortification on Pentecost; the ship was so shaken during all this time that it was impossible to stand, nor to take the least step without being supported, or one found oneself straightway rolling to the other side of the room. We were forced to take meals on the flat ground and to hold a plate with three or four, and yes, we had much trouble preventing it from spilling. Most of us were so sick that the most troubled, among others Madame de la Peltrie, no longer dreamed of Canada, that she usually called her dear country, but of having a little calm; and as a matter of fact, as soon as that happened, we were cured. After this evil, the worst discomfort of the ship is the foul smell and filthiness of the tar and tobacco.

The day of the Holy Trinity, around ten o'clock in the morning as we were saying None of the great Service, we heard the woeful cries of a sailor. Nevertheless, we did not stop to investigate, not knowing what it was, when the reverend Father Vimont came down to our room and said to us: "We are dead if Our Lord does not have mercy on us: there is an iceberg that is going to collide with the ship, and it is no more than ten paces from us, and large as a town." And when kneeling down, and we also, he said those words Saint Francis Xavier had said in the past in a similar danger: "Jesus, my Saviour, be merciful to us!" That done, he said to us: "I am going to the sailors, and then I will return here to give you absolution. We still have half an hour."

When I heard from the Father: "We are dead!" I had no fear previously. I had no time to break up, for immediately M. Bontemps came into the room and told us: "We are saved! But it is a miracle." And at once he showed us the iceberg behind the ship, the top of which we could not see, because of the mist which was extremely thick and lasted a long time, so that we saw ourselves once again in danger, close to lands we could not see. We have attributed our deliverance to the prayers you have offered for us. A single man who was at the helm, then turned the ship so skilfully, which was going with great speed to sink into the iceberg that one would have thought it impossible for a man to do that.

The next day we left the flagship to embark on the Saint-Jacques, which is the only one of the three that goes up to Quebec, and is in the command of M. Ancot. There our quarters were cramped; we all sat around a chest which was used to say four masses every day. We remained

Peter Rindisbacher's painting of a ship sailing perilously near danger conveys the magnificent menace of icebergs.

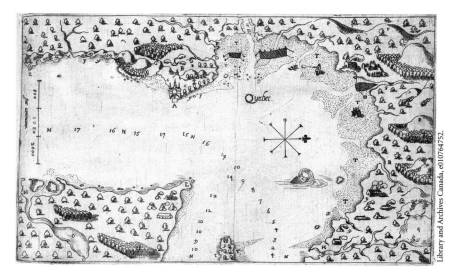

The Ursulines would have known the maps from Samuel de Champlain's Voyages, *published in 1613. Among his many gifts, he was a superb cartographer.*

in the Saint-Jacques until Friday July 9, which we left because the winds were against us, and we set off in a boat which went up to Quebec. There was no place to shelter ourselves, only a little room which was full of *molue* almost to the top, so we could stick there only by lying against one another like loaves of bread in the oven. And, as it was impossible, because of the stench and the heat of the hot *molue*, to stay for long; all our group was obliged to remain on the deck in the rain, which was very tiresome, night as well as day.

The afternoon of the day of Saint Ignace, when we were expecting to arrive at Quebec — but they could not because of the bad weather — the rain began and lasted five or six hours without slackening, and as I was one of those who could not endure the room, I was compelled to receive all the rain that wanted to fall on me. I remained so soaked, like many others, that for many days after our arrival in Quebec, our petticoats remained without drying, which was a little mortification for me, to be seen so dirty by so many well-bred people. The holy father Vimont, seeing us so soaked, and her Reverence also like the others, and who had no way of making a fire on the boat to dry us, requested the master of the boat to put us on shore, which was quite close. They lit a good fire for us and we dried ourselves in part. They made us a hut, Indian-style, and even though our bed was a simple cover on the ground, it did not prevent me from sleeping well. The next morning we returned to the boat, and arrived at Quebec at eight o'clock in the morning, the day of Saint Peter-ès-liens.

As soon as they saw the boat in which we were coming, the Governor sent two men in a canoe to see who it was and as soon as he had made certain, he sent us a covered boat to put us ashore. He came ahead with M. de Lisle, his lieutenant. As soon as we landed, we knelt down and the holy father Vimont made a prayer for us. We went straight to church and we sang the Te Deum, heard mass and took communion, then afterwards the Governor came to welcome us to his house, where we dined. Then they took us to that one which Madame de la Peltrie has praised the Gentlemen of the Company for, which consists of two quite large rooms, a cellar and an attic, situated on the bank of the great river. We have the most beautiful view in the world. Without leaving our room we can see ships arriving, which remain always in front of our house, all the time they are here. They have made for us a fence of stakes which are about the height of a little wall. They are not so close together that we are unable to see through, if we want to take care of the nearby property.

The next day they had us go to Sillery, which is the place where many Savages live, as many Christians as catachumens. There is a residence for the Fathers. The church is like a little parish for the Savages. This place is about one and a half leagues from Quebec.

We went out again Friday and Saturday to holy mass, and we have not gone out since. I have still so many things to tell you, if there were time, but I must stop. Farewell, my very dear Mother.

Sr Cécile de Ste-Croix

La Mère Cécile de Ste-Croix a la Supérieure des Ursulines de Dieppe. *De Tours à Québec 1639.*

(Translated by Barbara Robertson.)

6

Marie de l'Incarnation

(1599–1672)

Marie de l'Incarnation, née Marie Guyart, founder of both the Ursuline Order in Quebec City and the first school for girls in North America, has been described as "a mystic imbued with a sense of action." She longed for the cloister from an early age, but had a brief, unsatisfactory marriage. Widowed at 20, with a six-month-old baby, she eventually took her vows in 1633 with the Ursulines in Tours, despite a wrenching separation from her young son, Claude. Inspired by a dream of God taking her "to a vast country full of mountains, valleys and heavy fogs" (and by the Jesuits writing home from the mission to New France), she landed in Quebec City on August 1, 1639, never to return to France. Marie took an active part in the life of the colony, managed the farm and gardens, was consulted and confided in by governors, Jesuits, and officials, and learned several Aboriginal languages in which she wrote dictionaries and catechisms. Frequently superior of the convent, she contended with fire, earthquakes, financial problems, and the threat of Iroquois raids. In the midst of this busy life, she wrote two spiritual autobiographies, many devotional works, and between 13,000 and 20,000 letters. The geologist Dr. Nick Eyles notes that her description of the tides shifting in the St. Lawrence in this excerpt is the first document of a tsunami in Canada.

A faithful copy of the original of a portrait Marie, that was lost in the fire of 1686. After an elaborate funeral in 1672, her body was taken out of the vault and it is thought that Abbé Hughes Pommier (circa 1637–86) was the artist who made "a perfect likeness of this gentle face which was stamped with the marks of beatitude."

EARTHQUAKE

Quebec, 20 AUGUST 1663

My very dear son:

I have waited to give you an account separately of the earthquake this year in our New France, which was so prodigious, so violent, and so terrifying that I have no words strong enough to describe it and even fear lest what I shall say be deemed incredible and fabulous.

On the 3rd day of February of this year 1663 a woman Savage, but a very good and very excellent Christian, wakening in her cabin while all the others slept, heard a distinct and articulated voice that said to her, "In two days, very astonishing and marvellous things will come to pass." And the next day, while she was in the forest with her sister, cutting her daily provision of wood, she distinctly heard the same voice, which said, "Tomorrow, between five and six o'clock in the evening, the earth will be shaken and will tremble in an astonishing way."

She reported what she had heard to the others in her cabin, who received it with indifference as being a dream or the work of her imagination. The weather was meanwhile quite calm that day, and even more so the day following.

On the fifth day, the feast of St Agatha, Virgin and Martyr, at about half past five in the evening, a person of proven virtue [Mother Marie-Catherine de Saint-Augustin], who has frequent communication with God, saw that he was extremely provoked against the sins committed in this country and felt at the same time disposed to ask him to deal with these sinners as they deserved. While she was offering prayers for this to divine Majesty, and also for souls in mortal sin that his justice be not without mercy, also beseeching the martyrs of Japan, whose feast was being held that day, to consent to make application for this as would be most suitable to God's glory, she had a presentiment — or rather an infallible conviction — that God was ready to punish the country for the sins committed here, especially the contempt for the ordinances of the Church.

She could not refrain from desiring this chastisement, whatever it might be, since it was fixed in God's decree, though she had no indication of what it would be. Forthwith, and a little before the earthquake came to pass, she saw four furious and enraged demons at the four corners of Quebec, shaking the earth with such violence it was evident they wished to turn it right over. And indeed they would have succeeded in this if a personage of wondrous beauty and delightful majesty, whom she saw in the midst of them, giving vein to their fury from time to time, had not restrained them just when they were on the point of destroying everything.

She heard the voices of these demons saying, "Now many people are frightened. There will be many conversions, we know, but that will last but a little time. We will find ways to get the world back for ourselves. Meanwhile let us continue to shake it and do our best to turn everything over."

The weather was very calm and serene and the vision still had not passed when a sound of terrifying rumbling was heard in the distance, as if a great many carriages were speeding wildly over the cobblestones.

This noise had scarcely caught the attention than there was heard under the earth and on the earth and from all sides what seemed a horrifying confusion of waves and billows. There was a sound like hail on the roofs, in the granaries, and in the rooms. It seemed as if the marble of which the foundation of this country is almost entirely composed and our houses are built were about to open and break into pieces to gulp us down.

Thick dust flew from all sides. Doors opened of themselves. Others, which were open, closed. The bells of all our churches and the chimes of our clocks pealed quite alone, and steeples and houses shook like trees in the wind — all this in a horrible confusion of overturning furniture, falling stones, parting floors, and splitting walls. Amidst all this the domestic animals were heard howling. Some ran out of their houses; others ran in. In a word, we were all so frightened we believed it was the eve of Judgement, since all the portents were to be seen.

So unexpected a calamity, when the young people were preparing to spend the carnival season in excesses, was a clap of thunder on everyone's head, they expecting nothing less. It was rather a clap of God's mercy upon the whole country, as was seen by its results, of which I shall speak elsewhere. From the first tremor consternation was universal. And as no-one knew what it was, some cried "Fire!", thinking it was a conflagration; others ran for water to extinguish it; others snatched up their arms, believing it was an army of Iroquois. But as it was none of these things, everyone strove to be first out of the houses, which seemed on the point of falling down.

No greater safety was to be found without than within, for we at once realized by the movement of the earth, which trembled under our feet like agitated waves under a shallop, that it was an earthquake. Some hugged the trees, which clashed together, causing them no less horror than the houses they had left; others clung to stumps, the movements of which struck them roughly in the chest.

The Savages, who were extremely frightened, said the trees had beaten them. Several among them said they were demons God was using to chastise them because of the excesses they had committed while drinking the brandy that the wicked French had given them. Some other less-instructed Savages, who had come to hunt in these regions, said it was the souls of their ancestors, who wished to return to their former dwelling. Possessed by this error, they took their guns and shot into the air at what they said was a band of passing spirits. But finally our habitants and our Savages, finding no more refuge on the ground than in the houses, grew weak with fear and, taking better counsel, went into the churches to have the consolation of perishing there after they had made their confession.

When this first tremor, which lasted more than half an hour, had passed, we began to breathe once more; but this was for only a little while, for at about eight o'clock in the evening the shaking began again and in the space of an hour was twice repeated. We said matins in the choir, reciting it partly on our knees in a humbled spirit, surrendering ourselves to the sovereign power of God. There were thirty-two new earthquakes that night, as I was told by a person that counted them. I, however, counted only six because certain of them were weak and almost imperceptible. But at about three o'clock there was one that was very violent and lasted for a long time.

These tremors continued for the space of seven months, though irregularly. Some were frequent but weak; others were rarer but strong and violent. So, since the evil only left us in order to pounce upon us with greater strength, we had scarcely time to reflect upon the misfortune that threatened us when it suddenly surprised us, sometimes during the day but more often during the night.

If the earth gave us reason for alarm, heaven did no less so — both by the howls and shrieking we heard resounding in the air and by distinct and frightening voices. Some said, "Alas!" Others said, "Let us go! Let us go!" and others, "Let us stop up the rivers!" The sounds were heard sometimes of bells, sometimes of cannon, sometimes of thunder. We saw fires, torches, and flaming globes, which sometimes fell to the earth and sometimes dissolved in the air. A man of fire was seen with flames pouring from his mouth. When our domestics went of necessity to bring in wood at night, they saw fires of this sort five or six times a night. Terrible spectres were also seen, and, as the demons sometimes join with the thunder, though it is but an effect of nature, it was easy to believe that on this occasion they had joined with the earthquakes, to increase the fear that agitated nature would cause us.

Apart from the dangers of earthquakes, epidemics, and Iroquois attacks, the monastery burnt down twice — in 1650, destroying "the fruit of ten years' solicitude and toil" and again in 1686.

Amidst all these terrors we did not know where the whole thing would end. When we found ourselves at the close of the day, we made ready to be swallowed up by some abyss during the night. When day came, we were in continual expectation of death, seeing no assured moment of our life. In a word we sickened in the expectation of some universal misfortune....

A month passed thus in fear and uncertainty of what was to come — but finally when the earth's movements began to diminish, being now rarer and less violent (except two or three times when they were very strong), we began to discover the usual results of violent earthquakes — namely, a great many crevices in the earth, new torrents, new springs, and new hills, where they had never been before; the earth levelled where there had formerly been mountains; in some places new chasms whence rose sulphurous vapours, and in others great empty plains that had formerly been laden with woods and brush; rocks overturned, farms moved, forests destroyed, some of the trees being uprooted and others buried in earth to the tips of their branches. Two rivers were seen to disappear and two new springs were found — one white as milk and the other red as blood. But nothing astonished us more than to see the great St Lawrence River which, because of its prodigious depth, is never changed, either by the melting of the snow that usually changes rivers or by the junction of more than five hundred rivers that flow into it, not to speak of the more than six hundred springs, very heavy for the most part — nothing astonished us more, I say, than to see this river change and assume the colour of sulphur and retain it for a week.

When several Savages that fear had driven from the woods wished to return to their cabin, they found it buried in a lake that had formed there. A granary near us was seen to lie first on one side, then on the other, and finally to settle upright again. At the Beaupré church, which is that of the parish of Château-Richer, the earth shook so roughly on Ash Wednesday that its walls trembled visibly, like cardboard. The Blessed Sacrament, which was exposed, likewise trembled. It did not fall, however, being retained by a little crown of artificial flowers. The lamp, which was extinguished, fell three times but, when the ecclesiastic who has the care of that church lit it and set it back in its place, it did not fall again.

We learned from some gentlemen that came from Tadoussac that the earthquake made a strange disorder there. For the space of six hours it rained ashes in such quantity that they lay an inch thick on the ground and in the barks. It is inferred from this that the fire enclosed in the earth touched off a mine and, through the opening thus made, flung up ashes, which were like burned sugar. These gentlemen say that the first tremors terrified them in the extreme because of the strange effects they caused; but what most alarmed them was that the tide, which has its regular hours to rise and fall and had been retreating then for some little time, reversed its direction suddenly with a frightful noise....

Halfway between here and Tadoussac there were two big capes that produced wind and were very inconvenient to vessels. They are now collapsed and sunk back level with the shore. And — what is marvellous — they used to jut farther into the water than the width of our Loire at its times greatest spate. They have kept their trees and verdure and now it is a level plain. However, I do not know who will dare to walk there first, although it has a fine, firm appearance. A young man, one of our neighbours, who was going to trade, wished to go down to the shore of a river that had never been seen before, curious to see what it was like; at his first step he sank so far that he would have perished if he had not been pulled out, which was accomplished with great difficulty.

Monsieur the Governor's [Davaugour] lieutenant [Jacques de Cailhault de la Tesserie] has just come from Tadoussac. He reports that earthquakes are still as frequent and as furious there as in their beginning. They take place several times each day and several times each night. Yet I write this on the 10th of June — that is to say that this scourge has now lasted for four and a half months.

The shallop that arrived a few days ago at our port, having left the large vessel at Gaspé to come on ahead, had great difficulty near Tadoussac. We learned from Monsieur the Governor's secretary [Louis Peronne de Mazé] and a young neighbour of ours, who has just returned from France, that the shallop leaped and trembled in a strange manner, rising at intervals to the height of a house, which terrified them the more since they had never experienced its like in navigation. In their fear they turned their eyes to the land, where there was a great high mountain; they saw it suddenly move and turn, as if in a pirouette, and all at once sink and be swallowed up until its summit was level with the ground and firm as glass. This made them quickly swing wide in the river lest fragments reach them.

The big ship took the same route some time afterwards and was also surprised by a tremor. A worthy man that was aboard told me that all those in the vessel believed they were dead and, being unable to keep their feet because of the agitation, they all got down on their knees and prostrated themselves on the deck to prepare themselves for death. They could not understand the cause of so unusual a mishap, for the whole great river, which is as deep there as an ocean, was shaking like the land. As an indication of the violence of the tremors, the heavy cable of the ship broke and they lost one of their anchors, which was a considerable loss to them.

I learned from people that arrived in these vessels that in more than twelve places between here and Tadoussac — a distance of thirty leagues — the great commotion caused by the earth's tremors has in several places, especially near the two capes of which I spoke, made the mountains of rock open. They saw several little hills or eminences that have detached themselves from their foundations and disappeared, forming little coves where the barques and shallops will be able to shelter during tempests. This is so surprising a thing we can scarcely conceive of it, and every day we learn similar prodigies. It was very much feared that these upheavals along the shores of the great river might hinder navigation, but we now believe they will not be able to harm it, providing ships do not sail during the night, for then it would be perilous....

The earth has not yet firmed and we are now at the 6th of July, for I write only by snatches and as I learn things. The burning exhalations that came continually from the earth have caused such drought that all the crops have yellowed, but several days ago there were whirlwinds and furious storms near Cape Tourmente; these took everyone by surprise, for they occurred during the night. There was a terrible noise caused by a huge deluge of water pouring wildly from the mountains. The mills were destroyed and the trees in the forests uprooted and carried away.

These new waters made the river change its course, leaving its former bed sandy and dry. A very fine granary, which was quite new, was carried intact for a distance of two leagues, where it broke up on the rocks. All the beasts of the region, which were very numerous because of the fine wide prairies in that neighbourhood, were carried away by the rapidity of the flood. Several of them were saved, nevertheless, thanks to the trees; they were found caught among them and were withdrawn after the full force of the torrent had passed. The unripened wheat was entirely ruined; and not only the wheat but all the soil was lifted from an area of twelve arpents, leaving only the naked rock. A worthy man, one of our neighbours, who was there at the time, assured us that for the six days he remained he did not sleep for two hours because of his fear of the earthquakes and storms.

At the same moment that the earthquake commenced at Quebec, it commenced everywhere and produced the same results. It made itself felt from the Notre-Dame Mountains to Montréal, and everyone was equally afraid.

New Holland was not exempt, and the Iroquois that are their neighbours were caught up in the same consternation as were the Savages of these regions. As the tremors of the earth were new to them and they could not divine the cause of so great a commotion, they went to the Hollanders to ask them about it. The Hollanders replied that it meant the world would not last more than three years. I do not know whence they obtained this prophecy.

On the 29th of July a bark arrived in our port of Quebec from New England. The persons that disembarked from this vessel said that on Shrove Monday at half past five, while they were at Boston, a beautiful city built by the English, they had an earthquake just as we had here and that it was repeated several times. They tell the same of Acadia and of Port Royal, a place that formerly belonged to Monsieur le Commandeur de Razilly and has since been taken by the English. The other side of Acadia, which belongs to Messieurs de Canger and [Nicolas] Denys of our city of Tours, felt the earthquake as everywhere else.

This bark brought back five of our French prisoners that were captives of the Agneronon [Mohawk] Iroquois and escaped through the good offices of the Hollanders, who treated them very humanely as they do all those that flee to them.

Some Savages of a very distant nation were pressed to retire to these regions, but to be instructed and assure their consciences rather than to avoid the earthquakes, which followed them everywhere. They have discovered something that has been sought for a long time — namely, the entrance into the great Sea of the North [Hudson Bay], in the vicinity of which there are immense peoples that have not yet heard of God. This will be a great field where the workers for the Gospel may satisfy their zeal and fervour. It is held that this sea leads to China and Japan; if this is so, the way there will be very much shortened.

I return to our regions, where we are still in fear, though we are beginning to become accustomed to it. A worthy man, one of our friends, had built himself a house with a very fine mill on the summit of a marble rock; the rock opened during a tremor of the earth, and house and mill were swallowed up in the abyss thus formed. We are now at the 13th of August: last night the earth shook very violently. Our dormitory and our seminary received a bad shaking, which woke us from sleep and renewed our fear.

I close this account on the 20th of the same month, not knowing where all this commotion will end, for the earthquakes still continue. But the wondrous thing is that amidst so great and universal a wreckage, no one has perished or even been injured. This is a quite visible sign of God's protection of his people, which gives us just cause to believe that he is angry with us only to save us. And we hope he will take his glory from our fears, by the conversion of so many Souls that had slept in their sins and could not waken from their sleep by the movements of interior grace alone.

Joyce Marshall, editor and translator, *Word From New France: The Selected Letters of Marie de l'Incarnation.*

7

Marie Morin

(1649–1730)

Marie Morin began her *Annales* (1659–1725) in 1697, leaving vivid descriptions of domestic life and portraits of such towering figures as Jeanne Mance, Marguerite Bourgeoys, and Paul Chomedey de Maisonneuve. She was the first nun born in New France. Her brother Germain was the first Canadian priest. In 1659 she was a boarder at the Ursuline Convent where Jeanne Mance and three Religious Hospitallers stayed en route to founding Hotel-Dieu of Ville-Marie. At 11, despite family opposition, she determined to enter that order, and became a novice at 13. Possessed of excellent business sense, she was appointed depository several times, and elected as the first Canadian superior in 1693 and 1708. Her invaluable "domestic chronicle" of the foundation of the convent, its destruction by fire (twice), grave financial concerns, siege, extreme cold — "their house having holes in more than 200 places" — with its engaging flashes of humour, was rescued from the fires, but has yet to be translated into English.

Such a handsome apothecary jar (circa 1710) might well have adorned the Hospitallers' shelves.

TOCSIN

Every time the tocsin rang to warn people to help those whom the enemy had attacked and those who were working in dangerous places to leave, which they did as soon as the bell sounded, my sister Maillet would faint from extreme fear and my sister Macé remained speechless and in a pitiable state all the time the alarm lasted, both going to hide themselves in a corner of the rood-loft before the Holy Sacrament, to prepare themselves for death, or in their cells. Since I knew where they were, I would go to comfort them as soon as I knew the Iroquois had gone. This restored them to life. My sister de Bresoles was stronger and steadfast despite her fear, which did not prevent her from looking after the sick and helping with those who were wounded or dead after these events. She even climbed with me to the bell-tower, when we had the time, to ring the tocsin so a man did not need to perform this task, but could pursue the enemy. From this elevated place, we sometimes saw the combat which, when it was very close, frightened us very much and made us go down, very soon, trembling, fearing we were at our dying day. Other times, when the enemy was farther away and our men the strongest, it was a pleasure to be above, to see everyone run to the aid of the brothers and risk their lives to save another's. Even the women, like Amazons, ran armed like the men. I have seen this many times. One or two of the priests ran there also, to hear the confessions of the dying, who very often only lived long enough for that and died after making it, on the field. Exposing their lives as often as necessary without taking any arms to defend themselves must count as an excellent zealousness and a sublime charity. But the others did not fail them, keeping them very well protected, each delivering many blows very handily. The first inhabitants of Montreal must be praised for their valour and considered unanimously as good soldiers for the noble defence they made against the enemy, who, for their part, wanted these lands more than any other in Canada, because they said they belonged to them, and their ancestors had always lived there as their habitation of choice and preference.

Do not believe, my sisters, that the terror we felt at being captured or killed by the Iroquois was baseless, for humanly speaking that could happen. Montreal was not like it is today, for in the first place we were in a miserable wooden house, very easy to set on fire, without men to defend us, except for the hospital servants who sometimes could not do it, and when they could, did not have arms, nor us for them. Mademoiselle Mance, who was our nearest neighbour, was little more able to defend her house than we ours, having only serving girls and a male cook, who in my time was an old man who would not have frightened the Iroquois if they had attacked us. I do not know even if he could have shot straight. Moreover, many people testified that the Iroquois lay in the yard, close to the windows of Mademoiselle Mance's house, which touched ours at one end. As a matter of fact, it was stone, but would have burnt with ours if they had set fire to it. They also lay in our yard and in that of the Congregation among the big mustard plants where they hid so no one could see them. They have since said that their aim was to capture those who had to go out in the night for some reason. Our Lord was conscious of the evil they would have been able to do. In looking after our patients, we went out in the night quite often and it would have been very easy for them to capture us if God had permitted it, but assuredly providence guarded us and his power saved us from our enemies.

Monsieur de Chomeday, who was Governor of Montreal, although our friend, out of a sense of duty put the Iroquois prisoners who were wounded in our hospital so they could be healed. Some were not so sick that they could not have killed or cut the throats of the Hospitallers which no one would have known about until the evil was without remedy. Sometimes he put a soldier as sentinel to guard them as much during the night as the day, but most often there was no one. Besides, one man could not resist three or four of these dogs who were as big and strong as Turks. I was there one day when one of them tried to suffocate my Sister Bresoles between a door and an armoire, where she was so pressed that she couldn't breathe, and this was during the day, which showed great boldness. I came to know his plan by chance while passing through, for it

This domestic tableau of women and children by an unknown artist appears in the Historiae Canadensis *by the Jesuit Françoise Du Creux, published in France in 1664. It provides a more peaceful view of Iroquois life.*

was quite a private place, and ran quickly to call the patients to help her. Many of them flung themselves from their beds and ran with all their hearts to rescue their dear mother for whom they would have given their lives. They beat Monsieur l'Iroquois and cheerfully gave as much as he could bear. For his part, he said skilfully and deceitfully by way of excuse, that he did not mean to injure her for she had done him a thousand kindnesses, attended to his wounds, given him medicines to cure him, made his bed comfortable so he could sleep, and everyday gave him sagamite of Indian corn with lard to eat. Taking cheerfully the blows they gave him, he said that he wishes only to make her fear the Iroquois, but he knew he'd been wrong. He was left after that and remained as before. It is true that they and generally all the Indians had a very remarkable esteem and reverence for her. They named her in their language "the sun which shines," because, they said, she restored the sick to life through care and medicines, as the sun gave life to the plants of the earth. And when they wished to flatter me, they would say, "One day you will be like your mother," believing me to be her daughter because I was almost always her companion in nursing and providing medicines. They said as much to me in relation to my sister Maillet, seeing them old and me young, and not knowing at that time, as they do now, that the *Religieuses* have no children, all of which provided us with amusement.

Marie Morin, *Histoire simple et veritable.*

(Translated by Barbara Robertson.)

8

Baroness von Riedesel

(1746–1808)

Friederike Charlotte Louise von Massow, Baroness von Riedesel, was the daughter of a Prussian general and the wife of the general in command of the Brunswick (Hessian) troops who served with the British during the American Revolution. With three small daughters, she followed her husband from Germany to Canada in 1776. The family took refuge in a cellar during the battle of Saratoga, with cannonballs rolling about overhead, and was held in captivity in Boston, then Charlottesville, Virginia, where they became friends with Thomas Jefferson. (Friederike sang duets with his wife.) The general was transferred to Quebec in 1781, in command of all German troops in Canada, headquartered at Sorel. The family returned to Germany in 1783. Baroness von Riedesel's journal and letters, intended as a manuscript for the family and published in a limited edition in 1800, aroused great interest and were translated into Dutch and English, with many subsequent editions. Written very much from the viewpoint of a German noblewoman, her journal provides an extraordinarily detailed portrait of domestic life in the midst of war and many significant social and political figures, such as the Marquis de Lafayette, General Burgoyne, and the British Royal family.

Canadian Habitans.

Millicent Mary Chaplin (active 1838–42) accompanied her husband when he was posted to Canada with the Coldstream Guards. She painted many scenes of life in and around Quebec City, such as this lively triptych of habitants.

Library and Archives Canada, C-000867.

HABITANT CUSTOMS

… The region through which we passed was like a picture indeed. Every inhabitant has a good house, which he takes the pains to clean every year. This gives them a very immaculate look, and makes them glisten in the distance. When sons marry, they build their houses close to their parents, as do also sons-in-law, with the result that handsome settlements spring up, for which reason these people are called *habitans*, and not peasants. These dwellings, to each of which adjoins a stable, an orchard, and a pasture, are situated along the St. Lawrence, and make a very picturesque sight, especially to those who sail up and down the river. Each house has an ice cellar, which is made with little difficulty. A hole is dug in the ground and lined around with boards, and it is filled with ice. Then water is poured in, which in freezing fills the crevices and makes all smooth as glass. Over this the inhabitants place a very clean board on which to put the items to be preserved, observing the greatest cleanliness and taking special pains to keep out of the ice cellar any straw or hay, which, they say, causes the ice to melt more quickly. These ice cellars are all the more indispensable, since everyone slaughters his own cattle, which otherwise would not keep in the heat of summer there. Ordinarily these ice cellars are dug under the barns.

These people keep a lot of livestock in the summer, which at the start of winter they slaughter and bring to the city for sale. The smaller stock — beefs, sheep, and swine — which they keep for themselves, they drive into the forest in the morning to graze, and only in the evening do they give them fodder in the stable. In this part of the country they also have a small fish, called small cod, which are caught under the ice. This is done by cutting large holes in the ice, three or four hundred paces apart. Into these are placed nets of stout cord fastened on strong beams. In this manner they sometimes catch five or six sledges full. They throw the fish onto the ice where they are frozen in a moment and where they remain until they are needed. Then they are gotten, thawed out, thrown directly into the kettle, and eaten. These fish taste particularly good when fried in butter.

The dwellings are very comfortable, and one finds the beds remarkably good and clean. All people of property have curtained beds, and as their living rooms are very large, they have their beds in them. They have large stoves, in which they also cook. Their soups are very substantial, and for the most part consist of bacon, fresh meat, and vegetables, which are cooked together in a pot and served as a side-dish. The Canadians make their sugar themselves from maple trees, which for this reason are called sugar-maples. Early in the year they go into the woods with kettles and pots, in which they catch the sap from cuts made in the trees. This they boil, and the part that comes to the top, which is the best, they particularly use. The only thing wrong with maple sugar is that it is brown; otherwise it is very good, especially for [troubles in] the chest. The natives are hospitable and jovial, singing and smoking all the time. Frequently the women have goiter. Otherwise the people are healthy and live to an old age. Not infrequently one sees people, old as the hills, living with their great-grandchildren, who take the best of care of them.

It was in the middle of September 1781 after an eight-week trip that we reached Quebec, where we were welcomed in the most friendly way. My husband soon gained the favour of the English Lieutenant General Haldimand, who was governor of the province and commanding general of the troops in Canada, although he had been represented as a man with whom it was difficult to get along and whom no one satisfied. I not only had the satisfaction of being warmly received by him, but of having won his friendship, which lasted as long as he lived. People tried to make us distrustful of him, but we did not listen to them. We were frank and sincere in our relations with him, for which he was all the more grateful to us, since he was little accustomed to such treatment there. Great changes had been made in the governor's mansion, since formerly it had appeared very much like a barrack. He had furnished and decorated it in the English style, and although he had only been there five years, his gardens already were full of excellent fruit and exotic plants, which one would not have believed could be grown in this climate. He had, however, taken advantage of a good southern exposure. The house was on high land, almost at the summit of a hill.

. . .

The winters there are very healthy, though severe, for since the weather is not changeable, one can take good precautions against the cold. Thus one takes cold there less than in our country. At the beginning of November people lay in their winter provisions. I was very surprised when people asked me how much fowl, and particularly how many fish, I wanted and where I should like to have the latter left, since I had no pond. In the attic, I was told, where they would keep better than in the cellars. Accordingly I took three to four hundred, which kept very well through the winter. All that had to be done when a person wanted meat, fish, eggs, apples, and lemons for the midday meal was to put them in cold water the day before. Thus the frost is thoroughly removed, and such meat or fish is just as juicy, even more tender than that we have at home. In addition to this, poultry is packed in snow, which forms such a crust of ice that one must chop away with a hatchet.

There is a fruit in Canada called ottocas. It grows in water, is red, and of the size of a small cherry, but without the stone. They are bought without stems, and are carefully gathered, especially by the Indians. It makes a very good preserve, especially after a hard frost. All other fruits are very rare there, and only in Montreal are there good, yes, even excellent, apples, but only *reinettes* and apples of a variety called *bourrassas* that is large, red, and good-tasting. They are packed in barrels, which have to be carefully sealed and covered with paper, for they remain good to the last apple. But they use small barrels, for once they are broken open they no longer preserve the apples. Fruit is very expensive, especially pears, which are far scarcer there than apples and which also do not keep as well. I ordered six barrels of apples and half a barrel of pears. One can imagine my horror when I had to pay twenty-one guineas for them. To be sure, I had asked the price beforehand, but they had not been able to tell me the exact price then. My husband had a large piece of land behind our house plowed up for a garden and had twelve hundred fruit trees planted there, which made a very pleasant and at the same time very useful garden, especially as few vegetables could be raised there. All grew excellently in our garden, and every evening we went into it and plucked one hundred and fifty to two hundred cucumbers, which I made into pickles, which were not known there and of which I made presents to all the people, especially our good General Haldimand, who found them excellent.

It was as though I were upon a magnificent farm. I had my cows, a great many fowl, and Virginia hogs, which are black and smaller than ours and are especially short-legged. I also made my own butter. For the soldiers this was truly a promised land, for they had nicely furnished barracks, near to each of which were gardens. My husband gave them seeds, and it was a pleasure to look in on their housekeeping, especially their cooking, an amusement we often had, especially when we were strolling. They exchanged half of the salted meat which they received for fresh meat, then put both together in a large kettle along with all kinds of vegetables and dumplings; [and then] there was rivalry among them then as to who was the best cook. All work was regularly divided among them. Some tended the gardens, others looked after the kitchen, still others cleaned the barracks, while still different ones went to cut wood, which they brought back themselves on little carts made especially for this purpose. My husband had fish nets made, and every company in its turn went fishing, and each time they were so considerate as to send us something of their catch. In this way they had fish to eat two or three times a week, and every six days they received a bottle of rum, rice, butter, and twelve pounds of flour for bread, and every day a pound of salt pork or a pound and a half of beef. In spite of all this, most of them longed for their native land.

My husband also had Indians under his command in Canada and became much beloved by them. His straight-forward ways won him their hearts. Even before I arrived in Canada one of his Indians, named Hansel, once heard that he was sick, that he had a wife, and that he was very uneasy that she had not yet arrived. Therefore, he came to my husband with his own wife and said to him: "Listen. I love my wife, but I love you too, and as an indication I give her to you." My husband answered, "I thank you, and I recognize your love, but I already have a wife whom I love, and therefore I beg you to keep yours." He seemed sad over this refusal and almost offended, and only with effort could be persuaded to take back his wife, who was quite pretty and whom I often saw later. To be sure, this Hansel was not born an Indian, but a German. However, he had been captured in his fifteenth year along with others in a battle with the Indians. All the others were killed, but his appearance and his brave resistance had so delighted the savages that they spared him his life, under the condition that he marry one of them and accept their customs and dress, which he then did. The life of the Indians must have something very attractive about it, since a nephew of General Carleton lived for a long time among them, even marrying an Indian, and became so accustomed to the restless but free and merry life, that not until after many years and repeated entreaties did he return to his uncle, whose sister-in-law, a pretty and pleasant person, he then married. But, I was told, he clung to his old ways and longed for his first wife, whom he had had when among the Indians, but whose marriage was later annulled. He served in the army, I believe as a major, and was a very pleasing person.

It was just at this time that I saw the famous Indian chief, Brant, of whose likeness an engraving had been made. Since he showed much intelligence and many talents while still very young, General Carleton sent him to England to the King, whom he pleased so very much that he had him educated and promised to take care of him. He took advantage of the instruction he received, but when he was between twenty and twenty-four years old he begged to be sent back again to his people. At that time, when we were there (in Canada), he was chief among the Indians. His language was good, his manners the best, and, moreover, he was held in high esteem by General Haldimand. I have dined with him at the General's table. He was dressed half as a soldier and half as an Indian, and his countenance was manly and clever. His character was very gentle. My husband also was once invited to a meeting of Indians, where they first made a speech to him and then bade him be seated among them. Then they offered him a pipe of tobacco, which is their highest token of honour and an indication of their high esteem and friendship. They also gave him a name, which in their language meant "The Sun." He, in turn, invited them to visit him and entertained them in accordance with the custom of the land with tobacco and rum.

One of them in particular was decorated with medals, which are the signs of bravery. We invited him to dinner and pressed him to have some drink, but he drank very little and said to us in broken French, "The savage is a good child as long as he is sober, but when he's had too much to drink — a ferocious animal!" My daughter, little Frederika, won his friendship. He begged her for a new ribbon on which to hang his medals, assuring her that he would then prize them the more highly for it. He really was a very good man, kind and courteous.

The Indians are great believers in dreams. Before our arrival a certain man named Johnson became rich because of this. The Indians often would come to him and say: "We have dreamed that we came to you and that you gave us rum and tobacco." He would then reply, "In that case I must make your dream come true," and give them as much as they wanted. This pleased them, and they often came back, repeating their dreams. But one day he went to them, saying, "My brothers, I dreamed that I came to you, and you were so satisfied with the friendship and frequent good hospitality that I have shown you, that you presented me with a large piece of land," at the same time describing just which tract of land this was. "How can it be," they exclaimed quite shocked, "that you dream this?" They immediately went out and held a council, the result of which they expressed on their return: "Brother Johnson, we give you the piece of land, *but dream no more.*"

The Indians customarily treat their bodies very cruelly, making cuts and marks on their faces, which they then paint with various colours to make themselves look more like warriors.

One day a youth was chosen chief of a tribe. This caused grumbling among the other tribes, and at a general council so many abusive things were said to him by another chief that after much exchange of words his anger was so aroused that he sprang up and split open the head of his antagonist with his tomahawk. But later after reflecting upon the consequences of his rash act, which among the Indians was cause for feud and bloody revenge between the tribes of the murdered and the murderer, he went to the house of the English commander, called for a black ribbon, pierced holes through both his arms, through which he drew the black ribbon, with which he had his arms tied at his back, and thus gave himself over to the tribe of the man he had killed, exclaiming that he acknowledged his guilt in killing one of their number in a rage. In order to prevent the bloodshed which could result between these two tribes, he had rendered himself defenceless and delivered himself to them in this condition. At this noble behavior and at his evident penitence and courage, the Indians of the aggrieved tribe were so moved and touched, that they not only forgave but adopted him into their tribe in the place of the man who was slain, and later even chose him for their chief.

The Indians behave bravely in battle as long as victory is on their side. But on retreats, for example before our capture at Saratoga, I saw them first running and then hiding themselves. But this conduct was, to be sure, probably prompted by fear of being captured and then killed.

In the summer of 1782 we spent several very pleasant weeks in Quebec. General Haldimand had a house built on a hill, which he named Montmorency, after the famous waterfall of that name hard by. There he took us. It was his pet, and certainly nothing could equal its location. The celebrated Montmorency Falls plunge from a height of one hundred and sixty-three feet with a dreadful deafening noise through a cleft between

Madam von Riedesel half a century earlier could have admired a similar view beneath Montmorency Falls, (named by Champlain), as painted by Mrs. Chaplin.

two mountains. While the General was showing us this magnificent spectacle, I accidentally made the remark that it would be wonderful to have a cottage right above the Falls. Three weeks later he took us there again, and had us climb by a steep path over rocks which were linked by little bridges, just as in descriptions of Chinese gardens. When at last we had reached the top he offered me his hand to lead me into a little hut which hung directly over the waterfall. He was amazed at my courage in entering it directly without any hesitation. But I assured him that I would never be afraid with a man so considerate as himself. Thereupon he showed us how the little house was fastened. He had had eight strong beams extended over the chasm through which the water cascaded. A third of their length rested upon the rocks, and on these beams stood the hut. It was a terrifying but majestic sight. One could not remain in there for long, since the din was dreadful. Above the Falls excellent trout are caught among the rocks, which, however, once cost an English officer his life. He was jumping from rock to rock in order to catch them, but his foot slipped out from under him, and he was swept away by the force of the water. Only a few of his shattered limbs were later found.

We were also there once in the winter, where the different and strange forms the ice had taken offered a magnificent spectacle, but the roar was missing then. It was so cold then that the General's Madeira wine froze in its bottles, from which, however, it does not suffer, keeping the same excellence when thawed out again. The General let us drink that day the quintessence of it, which had not been frozen, and we found it extraordinarily good.

"Assignment in Canada" in Marvin L Brown, Jr., editor and translator, *Baroness von Riedesel and the American Revolution.*

9

Sui Sin Far
(Edith Maude Eaton)

(1865–1914)

Sui Sin Far, also known as Edith Maude Eaton, was born in Macclesfield, England. Her father was an English artist and silk merchant, and her mother was Chinese. When she was seven, the family immigrated to New York. They eventually settled in Montreal, where, as in England, the 14 children experienced prejudice. As family finances deteriorated, Sui Sin Far left school at 11, although she was well-educated at home. She sold her father's artwork, then worked as a typesetter at the *Montreal Daily Star*, and as a stenographer, before becoming a journalist and short-story writer. At 32, she left Montreal to travel and work in Jamaica and the United States. She produced much significant journalism in magazines and newspapers, ranging from *The Los Angeles Express, The Chicago Evening Post, New England Magazine,* and *Good Housekeeping* to the *Youth Companion.* Plagued by ill health, she published one book, *Mrs. Spring Fragrance and Other Stories,* and was writing a novel before her premature death in Montreal. Forgotten for many years, she is now celebrated as the first Asian American to be published. Her work appears in anthologies and is the subject of considerable scholarly activity. A revered figure in Montreal's Chinese community, she is considered "the spiritual foremother of contemporary Eurasian authors."

Both photographer and date are unknown for this handsome study found among family papers. It is thought that it might have been taken to accompany a newspaper article or for publicity at the time of publication for Mrs Spring Fragrance.

Courtesy of Diana Birchall

Chinese in Montreal

The scene of my life shifts to Eastern Canada. The sleigh which has carried us from the station stops in front of a little French Canadian hotel. Immediately we are surrounded by a number of villagers, who stare curiously at my mother as my father assists her to alight from the sleigh. Their curiosity, however, is tempered with kindness, as they watch, one after another, the little black heads of my brothers and sisters and myself emerge out of the buffalo robe, which is part of the sleigh's outfit. There are six of us, four girls and two boys; the eldest, my brother, being only seven years of age. My father and mother are still in their twenties. "Les pauvres enfants," the inhabitants murmur, as they help to carry us into the hotel. Then in lower tones: "Chinoise, Chinoise."

For some time after our arrival, whenever we children are sent for a walk, our footsteps are dogged by a number of young French and English

Canadians, who amuse themselves with speculations as to whether, we being Chinese, are susceptible to pinches and hair pulling, while older persons pause and gaze upon us, very much in the same way that I have seen people gaze upon strange animals in a menagerie. Now and then we are stopt and plied with questions as to what we eat and drink, how we go to sleep, if my mother understands what my father says to her, if we sit on chairs or squat on floors, etc., etc., etc.

There are many pitched battles, of course, and we seldom leave the house without being armed for conflict. My mother takes a great interest in our battles, and usually cheers us on, tho I doubt whether she understands the depth of the troubled waters thru which her little children wade. As to my father, peace is his motto, and he deems it wisest to be blind and deaf to many things.

School days are short, but memorable. I am in the same class with my brother, my sister next to me in the class below. The little girl whose desk my sister shares shrinks close against the wall as my sister takes her place. In a little while she raises her hand.

"Please, teacher!"

"Yes, Annie."

"May I change my seat?"

"No, you may not!"

The little girl sobs. "Why should she have to sit beside a — "

Happily my sister does not seem to hear, and before long the two little girls become great friends. I have many such experiences.

My brother is remarkably bright; my sister next to me has a wonderful head for figures, and when only eight years of age helps my father with his night work accounts. My parents compare her with me. She is of sturdier build than I, and, as my father says, "always has her wits about her." He thinks her more like my mother, who is very bright and interested in every little detail of practical life. My father tells me that I will never make half the woman that my mother is or that my sister will be. I am not as strong as my sisters, which makes me feel somewhat ashamed, for I am the eldest little girl, and more is expected of me. I have no organic disease, but the strength of my feelings seems to take from me the strength of my body. I am prostrated at times with attacks of nervous sickness. The doctor says that my heart is unusually large; but in the light of the present I know that the cross of the Eurasian bore too heavily upon my childish shoulders. I usually hide my weakness from the family until I cannot stand. I do not understand myself, and I have an idea that the others will despise me for not being as strong as they. Therefore, I like to wander away alone, either by the river or in the bush. The green fields and flowing water have a charm for me. At the age of seven, as it is today, a bird on the wing is my emblem of happiness.

I have come from a race on my mother's side which is said to be the most stolid and insensible to feeling of all races, yet I look back over the years and see myself so keenly alive to every shade of sorrow and suffering that it is almost a pain to live.

If there is any trouble in the house in the way of a difference between my father and mother, or if any child is punished, how I suffer! And when harmony is restored, heaven seems to be around me. I can be sad, but I can also be glad. My mother's screams of agony when a baby is born almost drive me wild, and long after her pangs have subsided I feel them in my own body. Sometimes it is a week before I can get to sleep after such an experience.

A debt owing by my father fills me with shame. I feel like a criminal when I pass the creditor's door. I am only ten years old. And all the while the question of nationality perplexes my little brain. Why are we what we are? I and my brothers and sisters. Why did God make us to be hooted and stared at? Papa is English, mamma is Chinese. Why couldn't we have been either one thing or the other? Why is my mother's race despised? I look into the faces of my father and mother. Is she not every bit as dear and good as he? Why? Why? She sings us the songs she learned at her English school. She tells us tales of China. Tho a child when she left her native land she remembers it well, and I am never tired of listening to the story of how she was stolen from her home. She tells us over and over again of her meeting with my father in Shanghai and the romance of their marriage. Why? Why?

I do not confide in my father and mother. They would not understand. How could they? He is English, she is Chinese. I am different to both of them — a stranger, tho their own child. "What are we?" I ask my brother. "It doesn't matter, sissy," he responds. But it does. I love poetry, particularly heroic pieces. I also love fairy tales. Stories of everyday life do not appeal to me. I dream dreams of being great and noble; my sisters and brothers also. I glory in the idea of dying at the stake and a great genie arising from the flames and declaring to those who have scorned us: "Behold, how great and glorious and noble are the Chinese people!"

My sisters are apprenticed to a dressmaker; my brother is entered in an office. I tramp around and sell my father's pictures, also some lace which I make myself. My nationality, if I had only known it at that time, helps to make sales. The ladies who are my customers call me "The Little Chinese Lace Girl." But it is a dangerous life for a young girl. I come near to "mysteriously disappearing" many a time. The greatest temptation was in the thought of getting far away from where I was known, to where no mocking cries of "Chinese!" "Chinese!" could reach.

Whenever I have the opportunity I steal away to the library and read every book I can find on China and the Chinese. I learn that China is the oldest civilized nation on the face of the earth and a few other things. At eighteen years of age what troubles me is not that I am what I am, but that others are ignorant of my superiority. I am small, but my feelings are big — and great is my vanity.

My sisters attend dancing classes, for which they pay their own fees. In spite of covert smiles and sneers, they are glad to meet and mingle with other young folk. They are not sensitive in the sense that I am. And yet they understand. One of them tells me that she overheard a young man say to another that he would rather marry a pig than a girl with Chinese blood in her veins.

In course of time I too learn shorthand and take a position in an office. Like my sister, I teach myself, but, unlike my sister, I have neither the perseverance nor the ability to perfect myself. Besides, to a temperament like mine, it is torture to spend the hours in transcribing other people's thoughts. Therefore, altho I can always earn a moderately good salary, I do not distinguish myself in the business world as does she.

When I have been working for some years I open an office of my own. The local papers patronize me and give me a number of assignments, including most of the local Chinese reporting. I meet many Chinese

The Montreal Market would have been familiar to Sui Sin Far, the young reporter, as she tramped around the city. The photograph is by the Notman and Son Studio.

persons, and when they get into trouble am often called upon to fight their battles in the papers. This I enjoy. My heart leaps for joy when I read one day an article by a New York Chinese in which he declares, "The Chinese in America owe an everlasting debt of gratitude to Sui Sin Far for the bold stand she has taken in their defense."

The Chinaman who wrote the article seeks me out and calls upon me. He is a clever and witty man, a graduate of one of the American colleges and as well a Chinese scholar. I learn that he has an American wife and several children. I am very much interested in these children, and when I meet them my heart throbs in sympathetic tune with the tales they relate of their experiences as Eurasians. "Why did papa and mamma born us?" asks one. Why?

I also meet other Chinese men who compare favourably with the white men of my acquaintance in mind and heart qualities. Some of them are quite handsome. They have not as finely cut noses and as well developed chins as the white men, but they have smoother skins and their expression is more serene; their hands are better shaped and their voices softer.

Some little Chinese women whom I interview are very anxious to know whether I would marry a Chinaman. I do not answer No. They clap their hands delightedly, and assure me that the Chinese are much the finest and best of all men. They are, however, a little doubtful as to whether one could be persuaded to care for me, full-blooded Chinese people having a prejudice against the half white.

Fundamentally, I muse, all people are the same. My mother's race is as prejudiced as my father's. Only when the whole world becomes as one family will human beings be able to see clearly and hear distinctly. I believe that some day a great part of the world will be Eurasian. I cheer myself with the thought that I am but a pioneer. A pioneer should glory in suffering.

"You were walking with a Chinaman yesterday," accuses an acquaintance.

"Yes, what of it?"

"You ought not to. It isn't right."

"Not right to walk with one of my mother's people? Oh, indeed!"

I cannot reconcile his notion of righteousness with my own.

Sui Sin Far, *Mrs. Spring Fragrance and Other Writings.*

Part III

Ontario

10

Anna Brownell Jameson

(1794–1860)

Anna Brownell Jameson, née Murphy, the daughter of a talented min-
iaturist, was born in Dublin. In 1825 she married Robert Sympson
Jameson, a barrister, who was appointed Attorney General of Upper
Canada in 1833. The marriage was unsuccessful and the couple soon
separated, but she came to Canada at his request in 1836. By this time,
she was an established journalist and the author of *Diary of an Ennuyée*
(1826) and a study of Shakespeare's heroines, entitled *Characteristics of
Women* (1832). In 1837 she left her husband and returned to England
where she secured her reputation as a major literary and art critic, lecturer, and champion of women's rights. Her *Winter Studies and Summer
Rambles* (1838), enlivened with her own sketches and watercolours, is
treasured for its freshness and accurate, if occasionally biting, depiction
of life in Upper Canada on the eve of the 1837 Rebellion.

Summer Rambles

On the 6th of August I bade adieu to my good friends Mr. and Mrs.
MacMurray. I had owed too much to their kindness to part from them
without regret. They returned up the lake, with their beautiful child and

Indian retinue, to St. Mary's, while I prepared to embark in a canoe with the superintendent, to go down the lake to Penetanguishine, a voyage of four days at least, supposing wind and weather to continue favourable. Thence to Toronto, across Lake Simcoe, was a journey of three days more. Did I not say Providence took care of me? Always I have found efficient protection when I most needed and least expected it; and nothing could exceed the politeness of Mr. Jarvis and his people; — *it began* with politeness — but it ended with something more and better — real and zealous kindness.

...

There were two canoes, each five-and-twenty feet in length, and four feet in width, tapering to the two extremities, and light, elegant, and buoyant as the sea-mew when it skims the summer waves: in the first canoe were Mr. Jarvis and myself, the governor's son, a lively boy of four-teen or fifteen, old Solomon the interpreter, and seven voyageurs. My blankets and night-gear being rolled up in a bundle, served for a seat, and I had a pillow at my back; and thus I reclined in the bottom of the canoe, as in a litter, very much at my ease: my companions were almost equally comfortable. I had near me my cloak, umbrella, and parasol, my note-books and sketch-books, and a little compact basket always by my side, containing eau de Cologne, and all those necessary luxuries which might be wanted in a moment, for I was well resolved that I would occa-sion no trouble but what was inevitable. The voyageurs were disposed on low wooden seats, suspended to the ribs of the canoe, except our Indian steersman, Martin, who, in a cotton shirt, arms bared to the shoulder, loose trowsers, a scarlet sash round his waist, richly embroidered with beads, and his long black hair waving, took his place in the stern, with a paddle twice as long as the others.

The manner in which he stood, turning and twisting himself with the lithe agility of a snake, and striking first on one side, then on the other, was very graceful and picturesque. So much depends on the skill, and dexterity, and intelligence of these steersmen, that they have always double pay. The other men were all picked men, Canadian half-breeds, young, well-looking, full of glee and good-nature, with untiring arms and more untiring lungs and spirits; a handkerchief twisted round the head, a shirt and pair of trowsers, with a gay sash, formed the prevalent costume. We had on board a canteen, and other light baggage, two or three guns, and fishing tackle.

The other canoe carried part of Mr. Jarvis's retinue, the heavy baggage, provisions, marquees, guns, &c, and was equipped with eight paddles. The party consisted altogether of twenty-two persons, viz: twenty-one men, and myself, the only woman.

We started off in swift and gallant style, looking grand and official, with the British flag floating at our stern. Major Anderson and his people, and the schooner's crew, gave us three cheers. The Indians uttered their wild cries, and discharged their rifles all along the shore. As we left the bay, I counted seventy-two canoes before us, already on their homeward voyage — some to the upper waters of the lake — some to the northern shores; as we passed them, they saluted us by discharging their rifles: the day was without a cloud, and it was altogether a most animated and beautiful scene.

...

We bought some black-bass from an Indian who was spearing fish: and, *a-propos!* I never yet have mentioned what is one of the greatest pleasures in the navigation of these magnificent upper lakes — the purity, the coldness, the transparency of the water. I have been told that if in the deeper parts of the lake a white handkerchief be sunk with the lead, it is distinctly visible at a depth of thirty fathoms — we did not try the experiment, not being in deep water; but here, among shoals and islands, I could almost always see the rocky bottom, with glittering pebbles, and the fish gliding beneath us with their waving fins and staring eyes — and if I took a glass of water, it came up sparkling as from the well at Harrowgate, and the flavour was delicious. You can hardly imagine how much this added to the charm and animation of the voyage.

About sunset, we came to the hut of a fur trader, whose name, I think, was Lemorondière: it was on the shore of a beautiful channel running

Library and Archives Canada, e000835937.

Lake Huron is famous for its sunsets. Despite the unwelcome attentions of sand-flies and mosquitoes, Mrs. Jameson took time to sketch this scene.

between the main land and a large island. On a neighbouring point, Wai,sow,win,de,bay (the Yellow-head) and his people were building their wigwams for the night. The appearance was most picturesque, particularly when the camp fires were lighted and the night came on. I cannot forget the figure of a squaw, as she stood, dark and tall, against the red flames, bending over a great black kettle, her blanket trailing behind her, her hair streaming on the night breeze; — most like to one of the witches in Macbeth.

We supped here on excellent trout and white-fish, but sand-flies and mosquitoes were horridly tormenting; the former, which are so diminutive as to be scarcely visible, were by far the worst. We were off next morning by day light, the Yellow-head's people discharging their rifles by way of salute.

The voyageurs measure the distance by *pipes*. At the end of a certain time there is a pause, and they light their pipes and smoke for about five minutes, then the paddles go off merrily again, at the rate of about fifty strokes in a minute, and we absolutely seem to fly over the water. "*Trois* pipes" are about twelve miles. We breakfasted this morning on a little island of exceeding beauty, rising precipitately from the water. In front we had the open lake, lying blue, and bright, and serene, under the morning sky, and the eastern extremity of the Manitoolin Island; and islands all around as far as we could see. The feeling of remoteness, of the profound solitude, added to the sentiment of beauty: it was Nature in her first freshness and innocence, as she came from the hand of her Maker, and before she had been sighed upon by humanity — defiled at once, and sanctified by the contact. Our little island abounded with beautiful shrubs, flowers, green mosses, and scarlet lichens. I found a tiny recess, where I made my bath and toilette very comfortably. On returning, I found breakfast laid on a piece of rock; my seat, with my pillow and cloak all nicely arranged, and a bouquet of flowers lying on it. This was a never-failing *gallanterie*, sometimes from one, sometimes from another, of my numerous *cavaliers*.

...

My only discomposure arose from the destructive propensities of the gentlemen, all keen and eager sportsmen; the utmost I could gain from their mercy was, that the fish should gasp to death out of my sight, and the pigeons and the wild ducks be put out of pain instantly. I will, however, acknowledge, that when the bass-fish and pigeons were produced, broiled and fried, they looked so *appétissants*, smelt so savoury, and I was so hungry, that I soon forgot all my sentimental pity for the victims.

We found today, on a rock, the remains of an Indian lodge, over which we threw a sail-cloth, and dined luxuriously on our fish and pigeons, and a glass of good madeira. After dinner, the men dashed off with great animation, singing my favourite ditty:

> Si mon moine voulait danser,
> Un beau cheval lui donnerai!

— through groups of lovely islands, sometimes scattered wide, and sometimes clustered so close, that I often mistook twenty or thirty together for one large island; but on approaching nearer, they opened before us, and appeared intersected by winding labyrinthine channels, where, amid flags and water-lilies, beneath the shade of rich embowering foliage, we glided on our way; and then we came upon a wide open space, where we could feel the heave of the waters under us, and across which the men — still singing with untiring vivacity — paddled with all their might to reach the opposite islands before sunset....

We passed this day two Indian sepulchres, on a point of rock, overshadowed by birch and pine, with the sparkling waters murmuring round them; I landed to examine them. The Indians cannot here *bury* their dead, for there is not a sufficiency of earth to cover them from sight, but they lay the body, wrapped up carefully in bark, on the flat rock, and then cover it over with rocks and stones. This was the tomb of a woman and her child, and fragments of the ornaments and other things buried with them were still perceptible.

We landed at sunset on a flat ledge of rock, free from bushes, which we avoided as much as possible, from fear of mosquitoes and rattlesnakes; and while the men pitched the marquees and cooked supper, I walked and mused.

I wish I could give you the least idea of the beauty of this evening; but while I try to put in words what was before me, the sense of its ineffable loveliness overpowers me now, even as it did then. The sun had set in that cloudless splendour, and that peculiar blending of rose and amber light that belongs only to these climes and Italy; the lake lay weltering under the western sky like a bath of molten gold; the rocky islands which studded its surface were of a dense purple, except where their edges seemed fringed with fire. They assumed, to the visionary eye, strange forms; some were like great horned beetles, and some like turtles, and some like crocodiles, and some like sleeping whales, and winged fishes: the foliage upon them resembled dorsal fins, and sometimes tufts of feathers. Then, as the purple shadows came darkening from the east, the young crescent moon showed herself, flinging a paly splendour over the water....

...

They pitched my tent at a *respectful* distance from the rest, and Mr. Jarvis made me a delicious elastic bed of some boughs, over which was spread a bearskin, and over that, blankets: but the night was hot and feverish. The voyageurs, after rowing since daylight, were dancing and singing on the shore till near midnight.

Next morning we were off again at early dawn, paddled "*trois* pipes" before breakfast, over an open space which they call a "traverse," caught eleven bass fish, and shot two pigeons. The island on which we breakfasted was in great part white marble; and in the clefts and hollows grew quantities of gooseberries and raspberries, wild-roses, the crimson columbine, a large species of harebell, a sort of willow, juniper birch, and stunted pine, and such was the usual vegetation.

It is beautiful to see in these islands the whole process of preparatory vegetation unfolded and exemplified before one's eyes — each successive growth preparing a soil for that which is to follow.

There was first the naked rock washed by the spray, where the white gulls were sitting: then you saw the rock covered with some moss or lichens; then, in the clefts and seams, some long grass, a few wild flowers and strawberries; then a few juniper and rose bushes; then the dwarf pine, hardly rising two or three feet; and lastly, trees and shrubs of large growth: and the nearer to the main land, the richer of course the vegetation, for the seeds are wafted thence by the winds, or carried by the birds, and so dispersed from island to island.

We landed to-day on the "Island of Skulls," an ancient sepulchre of the Hurons: some skulls and bones were scattered about, with the rough stones which had once been heaped over them. The spot was most wild and desolate, rising from the water edge in successive ledges of rock to a considerable height, with a few blasted gray pines here and there, round which several pairs of hawks were wheeling and uttering their shrill cry. We all declared we would not dine on this ominous island, and proceeded. We doubled a remarkable cape mentioned by Henry as the *Pointe aux Grondines*. There is always a heavy swell here, and a perpetual sound of breakers on the rocks, whence its name. Only a few years ago, a trader in his canoe, with sixteen people, were wrecked and lost on this spot.

We also passed within some miles of the mouth of the *Rivière des Français*, the most important of all the rivers which flow into Lake Huron. It forms the line of communication for the north-west traders from Montreal; the common route is up the Ottawa River, across Lake Nippissing, and down the River Français into Lake Huron, and by the Saulte Ste. Marie into Lake Superior. Pray have a map before you during this voyage.

No one has captured the way of the voyageurs with more accuracy, beauty and vitality than Frances Anne Hopkins (1838–1919) who accompanied her husband, chief factor for the Hudson's Bay Company, on his journeys through the wilderness.

Leaving behind this cape and river, we came again upon lovely groups of Elysian islands, channels winding among rocks and foliage, and more fields of water-lilies. In passing through a beautiful channel, I had an opportunity of seeing the manner in which an Indian communicates with his friends when *en route*. A branch was so arranged as to project far across the water and catch the eye: in a cleft at the extremity a piece of birch-bark was stuck with some hieroglyphic marks scratched with red ochre, of which we could make nothing — one figure, I thought, represented a fish.

To-day we caught several bass, shot four pigeons, also a large water-snake — which last I thought a gratuitous piece of cruelty. We dined upon a large and picturesque island — large in comparison with those we usually selected, being perhaps two or three miles round; it was very woody and wild, intersected by deep ravines, and rising in bold, abrupt precipices. We dined luxuriously under a group of trees: the heat was overpowering, and the mosquitoes very troublesome.

...

I recollect that as we passed a lovely bit of an island, all bordered with flags and white lilies, we saw a beautiful wild duck emerge from a green covert, and lead into the lake a numerous brood of ducklings. It was a sight to touch the heart with a tender pleasure, and I pleaded hard, very hard, for mercy; but what thorough sportsman ever listened to such a word? The deadly guns were already levelled, and even while I spoke, the poor mother-bird was shot, and the little ones, which could not fly, went fluttering and scudding away into the open lake to perish miserably.

But what was really very touching was to see the poor gulls; sometimes we would startle a whole bevy of them as they were floating gracefully on the waves, and they would rise soaring away beyond our reach; but the voyageurs, suspending their paddles, imitated exactly their own soft low whistle; and then the wretched, foolish birds, just as if they had been so many women, actually wheeled round in the air, and came flying back to meet the "fiery death."

The voyageurs eat these gulls, in spite of their fishy taste, with great satisfaction.

I wonder how it is that some of those gentry whom I used to see in London, looking as though they would give an empire for a new pleasure or a new sensation, do not come here? If epicures, they should come to eat white-fish and beavers' tails; if sportsmen, here is a very paradise for bear-hunting, deer-hunting, otter-hunting; and wild-fowl in thousands, and fish in shoals; and if they be contemplative lovers of the picturesque, *blasés* with Italy and elbowed out of Switzerland, let them come here and find the true philosopher's stone — or rather the true elixir of life — *novelty!*

At sunset we encamped on a rocky island of most fantastic form, like a Z. They pitched my tent on a height, and close to the door was a precipitous descent into a hollow, where they lighted vast fires, and thus kept off the mosquitoes, which were in great force. I slept well, but towards morning some creature crept into my tent and over my bed — a snake, as I supposed; after this I slept no more.

We started at half-past four. Hitherto the weather had been glorious; but this morning the sun rose among red and black clouds, fearfully ominous. As we were turning a point under some lofty rocks, we heard the crack of a rifle, and saw an Indian leaping along the rocks, and down towards the shore. We rowed in, not knowing what it meant, and came upon a night-camp of Indians, part of the tribe of Aisence (the Clam). They had only hailed us to make some trifling inquiries; and I heard Louis, *sotto voce*, send them *au diable!* — for now the weather lowered darker and darker, and every moment was precious.

We breakfasted on an island almost covered with flowers, some gorgeous, and strange, and unknown, and others sweet and familiar; plenty of the wild-pea, for instance, and wild-roses, of which I had many offerings. I made my toilette in a recess among some rocks; but just as I was emerging from my primitive dressing-room, I felt a few drops of rain, and saw too clearly that our good fortune was at an end. We swallowed a hasty breakfast, and had just time to arrange ourselves in the canoe with all the available defences of cloaks and umbrellas, when the rain came down heavily and hopelessly. But notwithstanding the rain and the dark gray sky, the scenery was even more beautiful than ever. The islands were larger, and assumed a richer appearance; the trees were of more luxuriant growth, no longer the dwarfed pine, but lofty oak and maple. These are called the Bear Islands, from the number of those animals found upon them; old Solomon told me that an Indian whom he knew had shot nine bears in the course of a single day. We found three bears' heads stuck upon the boughs of a dead pine — probably as offerings to the souls of the slaughtered animals, or to the "Great Spirit," both being usual.

We dined on a wet rock, almost covered with that species of lichen which the Indians call wa,ac, and the Canadians *tripe de roche*, because, when boiled till soft, and then fried in grease, it makes a dish not unpalatable — when one has nothing else. The Clam and some of his people landed and dined at the same time. After dinner the rain came on worse and worse. Old Solomon asked me once or twice how I felt; and I thought his anxiety for my health was caused by the rain; but no — he told me that on the island where we had dined he had observed a great quantity of a certain plant, which, if only touched, causes a dreadful eruption and ulcer all over the body. I asked why he had not shown it to me, and warned me against it? and he assured me that such warning would only have increased the danger, for when there is any knowledge or apprehension of it existing in the mind, the very air blowing from it sometimes infects the frame. Here I appealed to Mr. Jarvis, who replied, "All I know is, that I once unconsciously touched a leaf of it, and became one ulcer from head to foot; I could not stir for a fortnight."

This was a dreadful night, for the rain came on more violently, accompanied by a storm of wind. It was necessary to land and make our fires for the night. The good-natured men were full of anxiety and compassion for me, poor, lonely, shivering woman that I was in the midst of them! The first thought with every one was to place me under shelter, and my tent was pitched instantly with much zeal, and such activity, that the sense of inconvenience and suffering was forgotten in the thankful sense of kindness, and all things became endurable.

The tent was pitched on a height, so that the water ran off on all sides; I contrived for myself a dry bed, and Mr. Jarvis brought me some hot madeira. I rolled myself up in my German blanket, and fell into a deep, sound sleep. The voyageurs, who apparently need nothing but their own good spirits to feed and clothe them, lighted a great fire, turned the canoes upside down, and, sheltered under them, were heard singing and laughing during great part of this tempestuous night.

Next morning we were off by five o'clock. My beautiful lake looked horribly sulky, and all the little islands were lost in a cold gray vapour: we were now in the Georgian Bay. Through the misty atmosphere loomed a distant shore of considerable height. Dupré told me that what I saw was the Isle des Chrétiens, and that formerly there was a large settlement of the Jesuits there, and that still there were to be seen the remains of "*une grande cathédrale.*" …

We spent the greater part of two days at Penetanguishine, which is truly a most lovely spot. The bay runs up into the land like some of the

Scottish lochs, and the shores are bolder and higher than usual, and as yet all clothed with the primeval forest. During the war there were dock-yards and a military and naval depot here, maintained at an immense expense to government; and it is likely, from its position, to rise into a station of great importance; at present, the only remains of all the warlike demonstrations of former times are a sloop sunk and rotting in the bay, and a large stone building at the entrance, called the "Fort," but merely serving as barracks for a few soldiers from the garrison at Toronto. There are several pretty houses on the beautiful declivity, rising on the north side of the bay, and the families settled here have contrived to assemble round them many of the comforts and elegancies of life....

There was an inn here, not the worst of Canadian inns; and the wee closet called a bed-room, and the little bed with its white cotton curtains, appeared to me the *ne plus ultra* of luxury. I recollect walking in and out of the room ten times a day for the mere pleasure of contemplating it, and anticipated with impatience the moment when I should throw myself down into it, and sleep once more on a Christian bed. But nine nights passed in the open air, or on rocks, and on boards, had spoiled me for the comforts of civilization, and to sleep *on a bed* was impossible: I was smothered, I was suffocated, and altogether wretched and fevered; I sighed for my rock on Lake Huron.

Anna Brownell Jameson, *Winter Studies and Summer Rambles in Canada.*

11

Anne Langton

(1804–1893)

Anne Langton was born in Yorkshire to a family "almost voracious in its pursuit of culture and learning." Her father was a merchant; her mother was connected to the Brontes. In 1815 Thomas Langton took his children on an extended six-year educational "Grand Tour" of Europe. After their return to Britain in 1821, in straitened circumstances, Anne kept house, visited friends, continued her art studies, and painted portraits on commission to supplement the family's now meagre income. Her brother John immigrated to Upper Canada in 1833 to Sturgeon Lake relatively near those other refined settlers, the Stricklands. In 1837, Anne, her mother, father, and aunt undertook "rather a wild scheme" and came to join him "to a waste wilderness of wood." Anne then turned her competent hand to making soap, glazing windows, even butchery, initially in a small log cabin, later in the more comfortable Blythe Farm. Her letters, journals, and sketches were sent home to relatives to "give some sort of a notion of what this world of ours is like."

Despite the constant chores of pioneer life, she ran the first school and circulating library in the area. (The Langtons had twelve hundred books on their shelves.) After her brother left the farm to enter politics — he was eventually to become Auditor-General of Canada — she paid several long visits to Britain, but decided to settle permanently with her

Interior of John's House: *"At last ... after all delays and disappointments, our long journey is accomplished. John looked very proud when he handed his mother into his little mansion. His arrangements for our accommodation are very snug.... My father has the hammock put up every night in the sitting-room, and John himself has a tiny apartment curtained off by a sail from the ante-room. Here we expect to make ourselves comfortable for perhaps a couple of months, or maybe more, if as many unexpected delays occur as have occurred in the preparations at 'the big house,' as our future habitation is elegantly denominated."* August 22, 1837.

brother's family where, as the nephew who edited her journals wrote, "she seemed a second mother, ever interested, helpful and devoted."

PURSUITS

Monday, July 1 [1839]. The season has only just commenced; a week ago we were still enjoying fires, and notwithstanding our early spring the country is in a very backward state, owing to the long continuance of high and cold winds.

I am rather in expectation of a stupid month, partly because the last was a stirring one. I do not mean that we have been stirring, for not one of us has once moved from the clearing, but our little world has been stirring around us. We had last week a large "Bee." At our little one last year to raise the root-house we had some ten or a dozen men, but this time there were near forty, and seven yoke of oxen. Six or seven acres were logged up during the day. We walked down to take a view of the black and busy scene. One ought to see at what cost of labour land is cleared to appreciate even our bustled prospect.... There are four fishing lights on the lake tonight, which look very pretty moving up and down, but this holds out no prospect of a dish of fish tomorrow. The Indians find it more convenient to take their produce at once to the Falls where they have a certain sale for it. We are pulling very wry faces tonight at the mosquitoes.

Tuesday, July 2. We have been getting all our mosquito blinds into order; they have not been required hitherto, as there has been so little to induce us to sit with open windows.... We have had a thunderstorm to-day. My mother amused herself during the storm with repeating poetry, a thing I have not done for a very long time. The old world is the world of romance and poetry. I daresay our lakes, waterfalls, rapids, canoes, forests, Indian encampments, sound very well to you dwellers in the sub-urbs of a manufacturing town; nevertheless I assure you there cannot well be a more unpoetical and anti-romantic existence than ours.

Thursday, July 4. We all joined in a little tirade against Canada this morning, my mother's ground of complaint being the slovenly nature of its inhabitants, instanced by the scattering of lime and water over her flower-beds. Poor country! It bears the blame of all the various sins of the motley herd that inhabit it, besides the sins inherent in itself that it has to answer for. I grumbled a little at the necessity of storing all your summer provisions in the winter, and at the annoyance of unpacking and repacking barrels of pork, boiling brine, etc., etc. Our caterer I find, instead of a box of candles, has brought us a cask of tallow, much to our disappointment, having already abundance of work on hand. I have sometimes thought, and I may as well say it, now that it is grumbling day — woman is a bit of a slave in this country.

...

Sunday, July 7. The mosquitoes are sailing about in all directions, and make a great commotion against us, producing some exclamations, jumps, clapping of hands, etc. It is no joke to anyone to be so worried, but to my mother it is a very serious annoyance. The bites inflame exceedingly with her, and sometimes even produce something in the nature of prickly heat, but this I think is due more to the black fly than the mosquito, and most happily that insect does not often come into the house, so that by keeping a close prisoner you can escape it. The mark, too, of the black fly is much more disfiguring, resembling much a little leech bite, the first prick being less painful. The blood is sometimes streaming from you in various directions before you are aware that you are much bitten. You would not readily imagine the amount of resolution it requires to sit still making a sketch when the flies are bad. The mosquitoes will bite through almost anything, and the black flies are most ingenious in finding their way through all defences, and once within the folds of a closely tied handkerchief they do more mischief than if you had left them free access. If John takes up my journal I expect he will quiz my long dissertation on flies. He is often inclined to laugh at us.

Tuesday, July 9. Yesterday we had a piping hot morning, which made the culinary operations of the day appear rather formidable. Fortunately a storm came on, or rather a succession of storms, which, as they did not deter the guests from coming, suited us very well.... The dinner served up to these illustrious personages was soup at the top, removed by (I am told) a very bad curry of my manufacture, boiled pork at the bottom, fried pork and ham at the two sides. Second course, pudding and tart. My biscuits, I presume, which appeared at dessert, were better than my curry: at any rate such ample justice was done to them that I am encouraged to give you the receipt — 4 oz. of white sugar with as much water as will dissolve it, 4 oz. of clarified butter. This mixture to be poured hot upon 4 eggs, beating it up until a little cool. Throw in a few carroway seeds, and stir in as much flour as will make it into a *stiff* paste. Roll it and fold it as often as your patience will allow you. Bake it in cakes about the thickness of two half-crowns, which must be pricked....

Thursday, July 11. Our breakfast table was graced this morning with eighteen newspapers, and, what was much better, with five English letters, yours of the 11th June amongst them. As that part of the day not occupied by the perusal of these interesting despatches was dull enough, I shall devote a page to comment and reply. In the first place, do not send me out any portable musical instrument. There has been time and money enough already spent on me. The day may come when the first of these at least may be of less consequence than at present, and then I can make the experiment of how much music there is left in my soul.

I am afraid I shall not be able to send an old shoe, I never have any. The article is in great request among the servants, and my remaining pair of well-fitting ones are too precious to part with. I am not, however, so badly off in that department as I feared. Some of the boots and shoes I thought unwearable when my foot had been expanding in moccasins I can wear now. They tire me in the long-run but do not hurt, so I can wear them very well occasionally. Some I have disposed of, others altered to fit, so that the actual loss is not very great, and in case of failure this time I will try a new store at Peterboro, where, I understand, they have nice shoes — rather dear, I daresay....

Saturday, July 13. I take credit to myself for getting through twelve days' journal without once writing the word regatta, a sound which must vibrate on the air of these lakes some hundred and fifty times a day. On Cameron's Lake it has been the topic for the last three months. We are only just getting drawn in. The Regatta, together with the steamboat at the Falls standing still, and the ship-carpenters being unemployed, has led to the building of several new boats, and very much increased our navy. The merits, expectations, and adventures of the *Calypso*, the *Waterwitch*, the *Wave*, the *Coquette*, etc., form interesting variations to the theme.

Sunday, July 14. We had an exceedingly small congregation to-day, and it assembled very late. There is a difficulty in getting any regularity to an hour where there are no watches, or village clocks, or church bells. This I feel exceedingly in my school, but I believe it is an irremediable inconvenience.

...

Tuesday, July 16. My chief occupation was rigging myself up a morning gown out of one of my mother's, and making a collar to it out of superfluous sleeves. My mother handled the hoe instead of the needle, and was engaged for some time in trimming up her front garden.

Wednesday, July 17. ... My mother was in her element today, tidying away the rubbish of the joiner's shop, the accumulation of ages. Miss Currer stuffed a pillow with feathers off the farm. The geese, however, were given up this year, they were so perpetually getting into the garden. I brought my gown to a conclusion, but am not at all satisfied with the performance. If, however, I have not succeeded in fashionizing the sleeves very gracefully, I have at least attained the object of the alteration, and got a neat little cape out of them.

Thursday, July 18. This morning, after sundry deliberations concerning the wind, and whether the southerly direction was likely to bring rain soon or not, it was determined that John and I should set out to carry our invitation to the Dunsfords. Accordingly I embarked for the first time on board the *Ninniwish*, and a very nice little boat it is, but I rather prefer a canoe for an expedition of moderate length. I don't know how I should bear the kneeling position for three or four hours in a canoe. I can take a paddle, and at least flatter myself that I do some little good, which is more agreeable than sitting in state at one end of the boat, and having nothing to do but observe my companion's exertions. But my canoeing days are over. John does not like the responsibility of taking me out in one, and thinks it altogether an unfit conveyance for so helpless a being as woman. I, having a due value for my precious life, should be sorry to urge the risk of it, but I am rather glad the idea did not spring up earlier. After we turned Sturgeon Point the wind was favourable. We put up a small sail, and proceeded more swiftly and easily on our voyage. It was the first time that I had been lower down than the Point since we came up — now almost two years ago. I think the lower part of the lake, upon the whole, superior to our end in point of beauty. Both shores are pretty, and the islands make an agreeable variety. Though at our end our own side is inferior to no part of the lake, the opposite coast is very monotonous. Mr. Dunsford's new house is a conspicuous object all the way down, and, I daresay itself commands a fine view, but it will be two or three months more, I fancy, before they will be able to get into it. We found the ladies luxuriating in the absence of all domestics, a variety of not unfrequent enjoyment in the backwoods. Their servant had taken her departure early one morning before the family were up, and since that the young ladies were taking it in turn to bake bread, make puddings, etc., and perform all the labours of the household. We can speak for the skill they have acquired in the first-named operation, for nicer bread was never laid on Canadian table than they placed before us, not even my own! After we had done justice to it, Mrs. Dunsford provided a further entertainment of harp and piano to enliven us during a thunderstorm. Our invitation was not accepted, which on some accounts I did not regret....

Monday, July 22. On Saturday we looked anxiously at the signs of the weather for the following day, and a fine one happily dawned upon us. About ten on Sunday morning two boats-full put off from the landing, and wended their way up the river to Fenelon Falls, and as soon as there was an appearance of the congregation assembling, we walked slowly up the hill to our little church. After morning service, at which from about eighty to a hundred people might be present, nine children were brought to be baptized, one or two of them about six or seven years of age, and afterwards one grown woman, who had officiated as sponsor to one of the children, came forward herself to be baptized. Being quite unable to answer the questions the clergyman put to her, he declined admitting her into the church at the time! Does not this show how much we stand in need of a regular minister amongst us? When this ceremony was over the time before evening service was so short that some of us preferred remaining in church to encountering another walk, and the gentlemen were so good as to bring up some sandwiches and a pail of water, which, with a little wine, was, I assure you, extremely refreshing, for we have now hot summer weather. Mr. Street, who was very quiet and unaffected both in and out of the pulpit, and, moreover, pronounced by some of us to be very like you, William, gave us an excellent short sermon in the afternoon, and about five we re-embarked on our homeward course. What an event in our lives! and once we went to church every Sunday.

Mrs. Hamilton is going down to Peterboro on Wednesday she says, to scold her daughter for going out to parties and coming home at one or two in the morning, when the doctor has ordered her never to be out after sunset. Aunt Alice, who has often talked of a journey to Peterboro, though it was not clear whether in joke or in earnest, at

Archives Ontario F1077-8-1-4-16

Peterborough from White's Tavern, 1837: *Anne's first impression of Peterborough in 1837, when there were only nine hundred inhabitants, was of "A waste wilderness of wood ... There were sticks and logs in every square yard of the little place before us, to say nothing of stumps...."*

length seriously determined to accompany Mrs. Hamilton, whose stay will be only a few days....

We must get you to send us the notes of some good simple old psalm tunes. There is a book of such amongst my old music. I believe I oftener think of my music books than of my piano. Some dim recollection of an old favourite passes through my mind's ear, and I fancy I should like to see the notes. The psalm tunes, I hope, will be wanted soon for the church. Yesterday our carpenter was the leader, and several voices were joined to his. These, I hope, will increase in number and in power as we get accustomed to hear ourselves....

Tuesday, July 23. Miss Currer's courage has been cooling gradually all day respecting this Peterboro journey, at which I am not surprised, for the weather has been growing hotter and hotter. In the afternoon I received the agreeable announcement that a young woman was come to take our place. She had brought her bundle as usual, ready to establish herself, without the smallest doubt of being engaged. I was going to put a few questions to her, but seeing her very much heated I said she had better get her tea before we talked to her. Going out a few minutes afterwards, I found her with her hands in the wash-tub hard at work already. This looks well, and put a stop to all enquiries concerning qualifications, leaving only the simple one about wages to be made. How differently our domestic arrangements are formed here and in England!

Sunday, July 28. ...We had a visit from Mr. and Mrs. Fraser on Friday. They arrived just in time to partake of our early dinner. Mrs. Fraser appeared very shy when they were with us for the Regatta last autumn, and no wonder, after a five years' seclusion. Her winter at Peterboro, and a further acquaintance here, have quite removed the shyness, or at least only left what with her foreign accent and nice appearance makes her a very interesting little person. We hope to see them again at the Regatta. Mr. Fraser is very gentlemanly, and after seeing nothing but young men for so long, it is quite a treat to converse with a middle-aged one. We want decidedly an admixture of ages, as well as of sexes, to render our society what it should be. The pursuits and occupations, too, of all its members are too similar to afford much variety in the general run of conversation, and this defect I expect to be on the increase, as the varieties of our several younger years belong more and more to a remote past.

I fancy after four days' trial I may be expected to mention my hopes and my fears respecting our new domestic. I am sorry to say the latter greatly predominate. The only source of the former is that she is young and willing, but the height of her ambition seems to extend to acting by dictation. I must keep out of the way entirely in order to put her upon thinking instead of asking, "Shall I set the potatoes on now?" "Do you think there is fire enough on the bake kettle?" So far she has been small relief, and I am somewhat downhearted on the subject. Possibly she may be less lost and bewildered in a little time. This is the peculiar and unavoidable trial of the backwoods, and it colours the stream and directs the current of all one's ideas, and makes us very dull and stupid journal writers.

Saturday, August 3. We are once more in the midst of dirt and confusion, and surrounded by work-people. Happily, however, they are outside the house this time. We came to the decision of plastering the whole house, on account of the absolute necessity of doing something of that kind to the gable-ends to keep the cold out. We shall be much the better for this operation when it is over, but meanwhile the state of affairs is not the most comfortable, and the disagreeables attending it are on the increase. John was obliged to go down to Peterboro to provide nails and some other things for our proceedings....

Mrs. Hamilton has had bad weather both going and coming — wet going down, cold coming up — so it was very well Aunt Alice had not joined her party. Moreover, Peterboro cannot at present supply the article she chiefly wanted, viz., crockery. Things will break here as elsewhere, and we want replenishing sadly. You have no idea of the extra value which glass, china, etc., acquire by removal to the wilderness. As for our candle lamp, it has become a perfect treasure, and we have as much care over it as if it were Aladin's own.

As this is not a letter, but a journal, I must give you something of the doings of the week. In the early part of it we were preserving ourselves a good supply of raspberries. It is a fruit we have in plenty, and much cheaper than in England. Pickling has also been the order of the day. We consume more in the way of ketchups, sauces, curry-powder, etc., than we used to do at home; on account of the many months we are without fresh meat....

The new girl will not do. I never, I think, saw one so thoroughly useless. She is inconceivable and indescribable. We continue, however, to like her, and therefore must consider ourselves comparatively well off. Mrs. Hamilton cannot hear of a servant. She has only a temporary one, whose child she has also to accommodate. Mrs. Fortye was without one, the Dunsfords are without — all very encouraging! ...

Aunt Alice said in a very melancholy tone the other day, "I did think and say when we were coming to Canada, 'Well, there is one good thing in it, however, there will be no bazaars!'" Poor Miss Currer! She finds us much further advanced in folly than she expected. We have not only bazaars, but regattas! By the bye, there was a bazaar in Canada the other day, at Kingston, which produced the large sum of forty pounds.

Sunday, August 4. ... Next to the biters our greatest insect pests are crickets. They are everywhere, and in such numbers that it is quite hopeless to attempt destroying them. Moreover they are very destructive. I find they have been feasting lately on my shoe leather. The noise of them at night is unceasing, but this we get quite accustomed to. There is a little beetle too, a great plague from its numbers, and a large kind of ant annoyed us a good deal last year in the sweetmeat cupboard. Beyond these we have nothing to complain of in the insect way. There are very few of the disgusting kinds which hot climates sometimes produce.

H.H. Langton, editor, *A Gentlewoman In Upper Canada: The Journals of Anne Langton.*

12

Mary Ann Shadd

(1823–1893)

Mary Ann Camberton Cary, née Shadd, perhaps one of the most signifi-cant women to grace our shores, has been neglected until recently. The daughter of an important free Black abolitionist — her family home was a "station" on the Underground Railway — she was born in Wilmington, Delaware. Educated at a Quaker school in Pennsylvania, after graduation, she returned to Wilmington to found a school for Black children, and also taught for several years in the area. After the passage of the Fugitive Slave Bill in 1850, she and her brother Isaac immigrated to Canada, where she founded what she hoped would be a racially integrated school in Windsor, with the help of the American Missionary Association. In 1852 — the same year as Susanna Moodie's *Roughing It in the Bush* was published — she wrote *A Plea for Emigration; Or, Notes of Canada West* in an attempt to persuade her compatriots to come to Canada. In 1853 she founded and edited a newspaper, *The Provincial Freeman*, although not under her own name. In the 1850s, she lectured widely throughout the U.S. and Canada, raising funds for the newspaper, which survived until 1859, and promot-ing her vision of "equality through education and self-reliance."

Mary Shadd married Thomas Cary in 1856 and the couple lived in Chatham. He died in 1860, a month before the birth of their second child. In 1863 she returned to the United States to become a recruiting

This youthful photograph of a pensive Mary Ann Shadd was taken circa 1845–55.

Library and Archives Canada, C-029977.

officer for the Union Army. After the Civil War, despite her admiration for Canada, she decided she could best serve her people by remaining in the U.S. to fight for equal rights. She founded a school for Black children, while attending evening courses at Howard University Law School. She was the first woman admitted and when she graduated in 1883, she was the first Black female lawyer in the U.S. In later life she worked for both civil and women's rights.

The Canadian Climate

The increasing desire on the part of the coloured people to become thoroughly informed respecting the Canadas, and particularly that part of the Province called Canada West — to learn of the climate, soil and productions, and of the inducements offered generally to emigrants, and to them particularly, since that the passage of the odious Fugitive Slave Law has made a residence in the United States to many of them dangerous in the extreme — this consideration, and the absence of condensed information accessible to all, is my excuse for offering this tract to the notice of the public.

The people are in a strait. On the one hand, a pro-slavery administration, with its entire controllable force, is bearing upon them with fatal effect. On the other, the Colonization Society, in the garb of *Christianity and Philanthropy*, is seconding the efforts of the first named power, by bringing into the lists a vast social and immoral influence, thus making more effective the agencies employed. Information is needed. Tropical Africa, the land of promise of the colonizationists, teeming as she is with the breath of pestilence, a burning sun and fearful maladies, bids them welcome; she feelingly invites to moral and physical death, under a voluntary escort of their most bitter enemies at home. Again, many look with dreadful forebodings to the probability of worse than inquisitorial inhumanity in the Southern States from the operation of the Fugitive Law. Certain that neither a home in Africa, nor in the Southern States, is desirable under present circumstances, inquiry is made respecting Canada.

I have endeavoured to furnish information to a certain extent, to that end, and believing that more reliance would be placed upon a statement of facts obtained in the country, from reliable sources and from observation, than upon a repetition of current statements made elsewhere, however honestly made, I determined to visit Canada, and to there collect such information as most persons desire. These pages contain the result of much inquiry: matter obtained both from individuals and from documents and papers of unquestionable character in the Province.

— *M.A.S.*

A PLEA FOR EMIGRATION
BRITISH AMERICA

British America, it is well known, is a country equal in extent, at least, to the United States, extending on the north to the Arctic Ocean, from the Atlantic on the east, to the Pacific on the west, and the southern boundary of which is subject to the inequalities in latitude of the several Northern States and Territories belonging to the United States government. This vast country includes within its limits some of the most beautiful lakes and rivers on the Western Continent. The climate, in the higher latitudes, is extremely severe, but for a considerable distance north of the settled districts, particularly in the western part, the climate is healthy and temperate: epidemics are not of such frequency as in the United States, owing to a more equable temperature, and local diseases are unknown. The Province claiming especial attention, as presenting features most desirable in a residence, is Canada, divided to East and West; and of these Canada West is to be preferred.

THE CANADAS AND THEIR CLIMATE

Canada East, from geographical position and natural characteristics, is not so well-suited to a variety of pursuits as the more western part of the Province. The surface is generally uneven, and in many parts mountainous; its more northern location subjects the inhabitants to extremely cold, cheerless winters, and short but warm summers. The land is of good quality, and vegetation is of rapid growth, but the general healthiness of the country is inferior to some of the other districts. The State of Maine presents a fair sample of Lower Canada in the general. Population (which is principally French) is confined chiefly to the valley of the St. Lawrence and the country contiguous.

In Canada West, the variation from a salubrious and eminently healthy climate is now here sufficient to cause the least solicitude; on the contrary, exempt from the steady and enfeebling warmth of southern latitudes, and the equally injurious characteristics of polar countries, it is highly conducive to mental and physical energy. Persons living in the vicinity of the Great Lakes and the neighbouring districts say that their winters are much less severe than when, in past years, vast forests covered that region — that very deep snows are less frequent than they were, and that owing to the great body of ice that accumulates in the Lakes, the people living in the States bordering suffer more severely from the cold than Canadians — the ice making more intense the north winds sweeping over it. If these statements admit of a doubt, we well know that many flourishing towns in Canada are farther south than a large portion of Maine, New Hampshire, Vermont, New York, Michigan and Oregon, and should, in considering this fact, have the full benefit of geographical position.

I have thought proper to allude to the cold, at first, for the reason that it is the feature in the climate most dwelt upon: the solicitude of friends, ignorant on this point, and of persons less disinterested, often appealing to fears having no foundation whatever, when the facts are fairly set forth.

The products of a country make an important item, in all cases in which this question is being considered; so in the present instance. In Canada we find the vegetation of as rank growth as in the middle and northern United States. In order to promote a luxuriance in the products of a country equally with another, the conditions necessary to that end must be equal. If by reference to facts, an approach to similarity can be made, that part of the subject will be settled for the present.

As early as March there are indications of permanent spring weather, and in June and July, the summer will compare with the same season south of the line. In January and February there are always cold spells and warm alternating, as in our experience; but when the warm season commences, the heat is intense, and the growth of vegetation is rapid, so that whatever deficiency may be attributed to a brief period, may be fully compensated for in the steady and equal temperature after the warm season has fairly set in. Though summer is late in beginning, it is prolonged into what is the autumn with us, and farmers harvest their crops of wheat and hay at a later period than in the Middle States, generally, August and September being the months in which hay, wheat, and some other crops are gathered in.

Taking this circumstance in connection with the regularity of the seasons, and uniform heat or cold when they have such weather, the superiority of many products, as wheat and fruit, may be accounted for. I say superiority because, in its place, I hope to give such evidence as will substantiate the assertion. Annexed is a table setting forth the greatest degree of cold and heat, in the years mentioned, as indicated by Fahrenheit's Thermometer, together with the highest and lowest range indicated in the months of September and December of 1851, which last has been said to be unusual (the lowest in twenty years) by the "oldest inhabitant."

A naturalization certificate was issued to Mary Ann Shadd in 1862, a year before she returned to the United States to recruit for the Union Army.

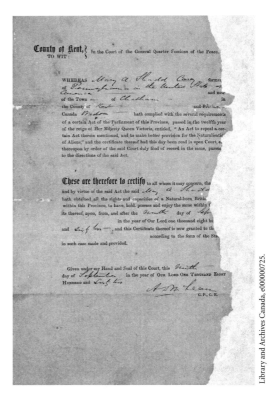

	GREATEST DEG. OF HEAT	LOWEST DEG. OF COLD
1840	82.4°	18.6°
1841	93.1°	6.7°
1842	91°	1.9°
1843	89°	9.4°
1844	96.8°	7.2°
1845	95°	4.2°
1846	94.6°	16.7°
1847	87°	2.9°

"These are the extreme ranges of cold and heat indicated at the Observatory, on one day during the seasons, but which do not last beyond a few hours; the mean temperature of the four months of summer and four of winter for the last eight years have been respectively: Summer 75.6°, Winter 26.7°, Fahrenheit." In addition to the usual state of the weather of the last year, as contrasted with former periods, the last summer and first autumn months were very warm, and in the month of September indicated 95° Fahrenheit in the shade, without eliciting remarks other than a similar state of weather, at that season, would have in the United States. In short, from much conversation with persons of many years' residence, I believe that climate poses no obstacle to emigration, but that it is the most desirable known in so high a latitude, for emigrants generally, and coloured people particularly.

In other parts of British America, as, for instance, Lower Canada, Nova Scotia, and New Brunswick, the cold is more intense; but when we think of the extent of Upper Canada, there would be no more reason for ascribing severe cold to the whole, than there would be to class the climate of the United States with that of the torrid zone, because of the great heat of the lower latitudes. In this Province the regularity of the seasons promotes health in a greater degree than in those countries subject to frequent changes, as in many of the United States, where cold and warm weather alternate in quick succession; and in the upper province especially, universal testimony to the healthiness of the climate obtains.

Mary A. Shadd, *A Plea for Emigration.*

13

Catharine Parr Traill

(1802–1899)

Catharine Parr Traill, née Strickland, was raised and educated in a highly literary family, chiefly in Reydon Hall, a seventeenth-century manor in rural Suffolk. She was the sister of Susanna Moodie, Samuel Strickland, and the biographer Agnes Strickland. In 1832 she married Orkneyman Thomas Traill, a half-pay officer, and they immigrated to the Rice Lake area near Peterborough in 1846. Blessed with a sunny disposition, a strong faith, and a keen interest in nature, she endured many hardships during her 70 years in Canada — the loss of two babies, a depressed husband, constant financial worries, and the destruction of their Rice Lake home in a fire. After the death of her husband in 1859, she lived at Westove, a cottage in Lakefield, enjoying respect if not monetary rewards from a long literary career. *The Backwoods of Canada* (1836) and *The Canadian Settler's Guide* (1855) are practical and judicious accounts of the difficulties and pleasures of the emigrant's life. *Canadian Wild Flowers* (1868), illustrated by her niece Agnes Fitzgibbon, later Agnes Chamberlin (Susanna's daughter), remains to this day a delightful guide for anyone with a cottage in the woods.

PARTY AT RIDEAU HALL

[LETTER TO ELLEN STEWART DUNLOP]

2nd March 1884

… Now my dear Ellen I must turn from business to pleasure and tell you some thing about my yesterdays visit by card to the Governors Saturday night grand fete — Well it was indeed the grandest sight that I ever witnessed and I shall never forget the delight it gave me. I must tell that the Marquis and Lady L — had especially expressed their wish that I should go with the Chamberlins if they did not fear my taking fresh cold and as I really felt much better I went in the cab with Mrs C — and Miss FitzGibbon and a lady friend — And though the glass was pretty low I was carefully wrapped up —

The drive through the avenue among the snow laden trees was delightful, the sky studded with stars and a splendid young moon just above the dark pine woods gave light-enough to make every old leafless oak and silvery birch stand out from the darker evergreens in bold relief — The grounds about Rideau have the picturesque charm of hill and dale and the dark background of sombre pines make grand depths of light and shade in the landscape that are very charming to such as love natural scenery and who could look abroad upon its beauties last night and be insensible to so varied and lovely a scene must be dull of heart

Lady Alexander's jolly sleigh scene reflects Mrs Traill's delight at the snowy drive to Rideau Hall.

indeed. As we drew nearer to the Hall I noticed a beautiful sight, a great vapoury cloud of smoke rising into the still air and spreading in fold after fold upwards above the trees, the lower part gilded till it appeared like a golden veil over the great solid banks of snow which were checked with the fantastic shadows of tree and bush and distant moving figures — The next turn revealed as by a sudden magical change of the picture a glorious sight — Long lines of radiant light — reaching down from the summit of the great snow slide to its far off terminus among the trees in the valley — The light dazzled one — for the grand bon-fire in the centre of the grounds blazed up and made visible masses of people moving or in stationary groups watching the swift toboggans as they flashed past on their downward descent with a speed that almost took away my breath to see their lightning like swiftness as they flew past us — for I was afraid of accidents happening — and one did occur to a young lady — a daughter of my old friend Professor Macoun, by which she was much hurt and her face wounded and bruised. The Governor shook hands very cordially with me and thanked me for a note that I wrote a few days before — he had previously expressed his acceptance of the dedication of my book in handsome terms.

The Marchioness was very friendly and kind chatting as we stood side by side on a platform above the slide, then we went through the wood path to see the skating on what Lord Dufferin called his own *pet rink* where too the Princess had had a log cabin built — It was a pretty lively sight, the girls skating on this wood-encircled sheet of ice lighted up by torches on a little islet in the far end of the rink — while all sorts of Chinese lanterns hung from the branches of the trees along the walk that led to this recess in the pine wood — and waved as the wind moved the boughs — We went into the log cottage and got warmed by the stove but a log-fire would have been more in keeping with the cottage — which by the bye was handsomely panelled with varnished wood inside — it was not a real log cabin — for it was not rough and chinked and plastered as the log houses used to be. This would have been a palace for a settler in the old settlement days of the Back woods. We should have been thought too luxurious altogether and the house out of keeping with the rude furniture, diet and dress of that time —

We turned home after some delay — it must have been nearly 12 o'clock, and I am none the worse for the frolic — but feel very well to day —

The only thing that I did not like was that when I was left in the tearoom everybody kept staring at me, and some edged nearly up to me, and I kept hearing — "That's her — That's Mrs. Traill — " and so on, and short people stood on tiptoe, and others peered over shoulders and pushed those before them aside peering at poor me as if I had been the show piece of the play. The poor old lioness squeezed herself into a corner (I believe some people expected her to roar or wag her tail) not being accustomed to be gazed at in that way — it was a little oppressive —

We had a lovely drive home through the park, and though I have not done justice to all I saw — I must leave the rest of the details of my second pleasant experience of Rideau Hall till we meet — There was first a refreshment table in the saloon of tea and delicious coffee and cakes of all sorts and fruit. I just drank a cup of coffee only — Lady L — had charged me to take refreshments herself — There was a grand supper at 11 — but we did not go into the room. There was such a crowd of hundreds of people — all seemed bent on making the *most* of the liberal hospitality of His Excellency.

Now my dearest Ellen, do not be afraid all the attention and flattery bestowed on me will turn my old head — it is pleasant from some, but seems almost too absurd from others — The only thing is — It is good for the book — as some will get copies out of curiosity now — Nor do I expect unadulterated praise — but some may like the pictures, and others the cover, and a few the letter press — and some will criticize — but that is the fate of those who "Write a book" — Now will you not be glad when I say — Good-bye — With much love to dear Charles and Mary, to my Kate if with you and to dear Anna, and all the dear friends. Ever yours,

C.P. Traill

Carl Ballstadt, Elizabeth Hopkins, and A. Michael Peterman, eds., *I Bless You in My Heart: Selected Correspondence of Catharine Parr Traill.*

14

Lady Aberdeen

(1857–1939)

Ishbel Maria Gordon, née Marjoribanks, was born into an affluent Liberal Scottish family and raised in London and the Highlands. In 1877 she married John Hamilton Gordon, 7th Earl and 1st Marquess of Aberdeen and Temair. They were to become an effective team, examples of those energetic and high-minded Victorians dedicated to good works. After Lord Aberdeen was appointed Governor General of Canada in 1893, the Aberdeens travelled throughout the country, meeting Canadians of all stripes and attempting to bring religious groups together. Lady Aberdeen provided a warm family life for her sensitive husband and "thought and fought for him in all his affairs" during a turbulent period that included four prime ministers, the Manitoba schools crisis, the completion of the Canadian Pacific Railway, and the Yukon gold rush. She became president of the National Council of Women in 1893 and founded the Victorian Order of Nurses four years later. Her journal — described by her editor, John Saywell, as "the most important single manuscript for the mid-1890s" — provides a vivid portrait of balls, theatrical per-formances, political figures, and sports. (Lord Aberdeen, it reveals, was "perhaps the best skater and curler ever to reside in Rideau Hall.")

Although this watercolour of a "Skating Party at Rideau Hall" by Robert W Rutherford (circa 1882) predates their vice-regal tenure, the debonair figures gliding about the ice do remind one of Lady Aberdeen's fond description of her husband: "Johnny does skate so beautifully and looks so graceful when doing it and goes at such a pace."

WINTER SPORTS

Jany 12th 1894
It is somewhat refreshing however in the midst of an entourage entirely possessed with a mania for winter sports all day & all night to find Sir John admitting that he has never seen a game of curling & Mr Blake saying he had never seen hockey.

…

Saturday Jany 20th 1894
… Went this evening with all our party to witness one of the championship hockey matches between Ottawa & Montreal. The latter expected to

win, but were beaten by 5 to 1. This game appears to be a most fascinating one & the men get wildly excited about it. But there can be no doubt as to its roughness, & if the players get over keen & lose their tempers as they are too apt to do, the possession of the stick & the close proximity to one another gives the occasion for many a nasty hit. Tonight one man was playing with his nose badly broken & the game had twice to be stopped, once because a man got hit in the mouth & the other time because one of the captains was knocked down unconscious & had to be carried out. When he recovered consciousness he came out & played again, but the amount of risk even in the ordinary way seems to be scarcely compensated for by the game — at least so it appears to some spectators at any rate. There are many men & boys here in Ottawa who practically live for hockey. It must be said that it is beautiful to see the perfection of skating that is involved in the playing of the game — the men simply run on the ice as if they were on the ground.

...

Thursday Jany 24th 1894
... Then today I ventured on to a toboggan with His Ex. — not from the top, needless to say. I am however confirmed in my belief that it leaves too much of one's inside behind one to be comfortable for such folk as me — still it wasn't bad.

...

Saturday Feby 3rd 1894
The day closed with a fiercely contested championship hockey match between Quebec & Montreal, won by Quebec by 4 to 2. I did not join the party till near the end. The more I see of hockey, the less I like it — it presents too fierce a temptation for roughness & unfairness for any average person. I am sure I should murder my opponents if I were to play at such close quarters & with a stick in one's hand. The referee is very strict in stopping the game the moment there is any unfairness, but the number of the hurt & the maimed & the disfigured

after from the effect of hockey is distressing. Mr Baldwin rather hurt this morning.

···

Saturday March 3rd [1894]
H.E. & staff went to a very exciting hockey match to-night, one of the championship matches. It was between Quebec & Ottawa — if the former won they would have the championship, if the latter, there would have to be three more matches between Quebec, Ottawa & Montreal before the matter was decided. Unfortunately Ottawa won.

···

Monday Jany 20th [1896]
Haddo's birthday — he is seventeen today & certainly looks pretty different to what one might have expected if one looks back to Jany 20th 1879.

I rashly asked him last night what we could do to give him a special treat — & he promptly had me by responding that I was to come down with him on the toboggan slide — So I, who have carefully avoided any such hare brained & undignified sports since my arrival in Canada except one furtive attempt with H.E. once, found myself an exhibition to my family & was taken down three times — the last one being from the top of the big slide — by Haddo. I must say he steers very well, but I own I am not sure whether I should not like a basin at the bottom — all one's insides goes from one, & one's brain too. However my fate is sealed now, for the other children announce their claim also to a pound of flesh. They all exalt in these adventures. Archie goes from the top of the steep slide on Norwegian skis, a performance none of the gentlemen can do, & they none of them mind anything — they standing or sitting or kneeling or any way so also do Babe and Lena.

···

Queen's University Archives, Queen's Picture Collection, Locator #V28 P-22.

"The ceremony was a decided ordeal & I simply quaked" Lady Aberdeen *wrote in her journal. On April 28, 1897, she was the first woman to be awarded an honorary degree at Queen's University, Kingston, or any other Canadian university — although women had been admitted to Queen's and granted degrees for thirty years. The students sang "For she's a jolly good fellow" & shouted "What's the matter with Lady Aberdeen. She's all right, you bet."*

Saturday March 21 [1896]

We had quite a successful last skating & tobogganing party today. It is quite an extraordinary event when the winter lasts long enough to allow of these skating-parties in March & the sun is so strong that the frost at nights does not avail to keep the skating rinks right. But the slides were in good condition & my conversion to the art of tobogganing is so complete that I no longer practice it only in seclusion with the children but steer past M.P.'s & others down myself. Today I took down Dr Weldon & Mr Herridge, Marjorie also took Dr Weldon & Mr Cockburn. Neither had ever been down before & the latter appeared to the onlookers in a fainting condition as he passed us. Marjorie said he leant more & more back & she thought would be pushed off altogether. "I first shut my eyes, & then I opened them & oh it was awful," he said. H.E. & I had a grand upset one day together & turned several somersaults.

...

Jany 31, 1897

Hockey has been played very regularly on our own rink this winter so far by the children, staff & household generally. Both Marjorie & Archie are very keen about it & are said to play well for their years. Monday & Thursday afternoons are regular hockey match days & often there are games on other days as well. John Keddie & Johnnie Cheyne distinguish themselves, & Frederick has been induced to resume his skates & even Aldridge joins in the fray with grave dignity. And A. too himself takes a hand not infrequently. They play just for an hour as a rule, as this is deemed long enough by the doctor.

Lady Aberdeen, *The Canadian Journal of Lady Aberdeen (1893–1898).*

PART IV

The West

15

Lady Dufferin

(1843–1936)

Hariot Georgina Blackwood, née Rowan-Hamilton, Marchioness of Dufferin and Ava, grew up in the Norman castle of Killyleigh near Belfast. In 1862 she married Lord Dufferin, great-grandson of Richard Brinsley Sheridan, and an accomplished orator and diplomat. In 1872 he was appointed Governor General of Canada. *My Canadian Journal*, based on weekly letters written to her mother, was published 20 years after their tenure. Although she claimed only distantly to allude to public events "in a somewhat light and irresponsible spirit," she often attended political debates and reported back to her husband. Her journal is a lively account of pleasures that included winter sports and stage plays for children at Rideau Hall. Lady Dufferin took obvious delight in their travels to every province, although there is a hint of tedium in her description of a visit to a boarding school: "... the girls played and sang and read to us. As they had decorated their bedrooms we had to go into each one."

The Dufferins loved Quebec, and it is to Lord Dufferin we owe the preservation of the fabled walls of Quebec. (Local officials wanted to tear them down in order to expand the city.) Lady Dufferin correctly prophesied that Dufferin Terrace, built from her husband's design, "promises to become one of the loveliest walks in the world." The Dufferins went on to serve in Russia, Turkey, India, Italy, and France, but Lady Dufferin later wrote that her happiest times had been spent in Canada.

MENNONITES

[August 1877]

MONDAY, 20TH — Another expedition! The first thing we heard this morning was the sound of rain, and the day looked most unpromising. However, we started about ten, the four gentlemen riding, Mrs. Littleton and her maid, Nellie and I in the ambulance drawn by four horses. We got on very well for the first three hours, when we came to some fearful swamps. Our horses plunged through water and mud, the wheels of our carriage sinking, first on one side and then on the other. Two or three times the horses in the carts sat down in despair, and once they sunk so deep in the mire that the whole caravan had to stop and help to pull them out. The rain came on in torrents, and there was thunder growling overhead. Altogether it was not a nice day for camping out.

Certain themes such as mosquitoes and the infamous Red River Gumbo recur in early writing. Lady Dufferin's account of sinking into the mire is echoed by William George Richardson Hind's drawing of an unhappy ox struggling across a river.

We expected to reach our destination at two, and to lunch there; but owing to our adventures in the bogs we did not get there till five, and were all wet and famished. The Lieutenant-Governor had arrived before, and he gave us shelter and tea, which revived us. Then the rain cleared off, we made up a nice fire, and things began to look better. Our cook had been in the most unfortunate cart, and had been over his knees in water most of the day; but the moment he arrived he lit his fire, and made us a dinner of good soup, mutton chops and potatoes.

It was next discovered that three tents had been left behind — three out of six; however, we managed very well without them. D., Nellie, and I had one tent. Mrs. Littleton and her maid another (our maids take the expeditions in turns — mine came last time), and the three gentlemen the third. We had stretcher-beds, with buffalo-robes and blankets on them, and dry hay on the floor; so we were really very comfortable. Our camping ground is near water, half river, half swamp, and as we can get wood, water, and milk, we shall return here for another night on our way back. I rather dread going through those bogs again!

TUESDAY, 21ST — We were awoke rather early by the noises of camp-life; wood being chopped up, conversations going on in every tent, etc., and I had some difficulty in keeping Nellie in bed till the orthodox hour of seven, but, as I am much afraid of her being over-tired on this expedition, I have to insist upon this.

The weather was much better — the sun shone, but the wind was very cold. It was nearly ten before everything was packed, and we were on our way to the Mennonite settlement. Four of those men met us on horseback, some way from their farms, and rode before us through their Reserve. You know the Mennonites have left Russia for conscientious reasons, in the same way they left their native land, Germany, and settled in Russia, because they will not fight, and these two countries require their subjects should serve in the army.

The Mennonites are most desirable emigrants; they retain their best German characteristics, are hard-working, honest, sober, simple, hardy people. They bring money into the country, and can settle in a woodless place, which no other people will do. Necessity (in Russia) has taught them to make a peculiar fuel-cake of manure, mixed with straw — which is kept a whole year to dry thoroughly, and which looks exactly like turf. With this they go through the long Canadian winter without wood or coal. They speak nothing but German, and are Lutheran, to which form of religion they add the Quakers' non-fighting doctrine.

They dress in the plainest and least decorative fashion; the women, from their birth to their graves, tie up their heads in coloured handkerchiefs fastened under their chins, and wear dark-coloured stiff gowns, the baby's being made after the same fashion as its mother's. The men shave, and wear black stocks round their throats. Partly in consequence of this unbecoming costume, all the people, men and women, are plain. One hundred and twenty families arrived in Canada three years ago and settled on this bare prairie one autumn day. For a week they had not a roof to cover them, and slept under their carts; then they dug up the sods, and with them made rude huts, in which they lived through one of our long and severe winters. This is, therefore, their third year here. Now I will tell you how we find them situated.

We drove about five miles through their Reserve, which is eighteen miles square, and in so doing passed through five or six villages of farm-houses. They are not in streets, each house being surrounded by land. The houses are cottages, very plainly built, roofed with thick hay thatch, the walls wooden, but covered with plaster. Next to, and opening into the living-house is a large building in which the cattle spend the winter.

Everything looks neat; home-made wooden furniture, flowers in the windows, nice gardens, etc. Each family is given 160 acres of land, and the way in which they work their farms enables them to do so very advantageously.

Supposing there are twenty families in a village, they put all the land together, and mark out the different spots which are best suited to particular crops. Thus, all the pasture is in one part, all the potatoes in another, and so on. Each man, however, works his own share of each crop, and has his profit to himself. Their church is most simple — plain deal forms without backs, and no ornament anywhere.

After driving through these prosperous-looking villages, and passing through great corn-fields, we saw before us on the open prairie an arbour erected, and in front of it at least 700 people. The men stood on one side, with specimens of their farm produce before them, corn grown from Russian seed, from Canadian seed, flax, etc. The women on the other side showed their garden produce. The babies and children were out too. In the arbour were three girls, with lace handkerchiefs on their heads, and trays with glasses in their hands, ready to offer us some Russian tea, which was most refreshing after our cold drive.

The arbour was prettily hung with garlands of flowers and bunches of corn mixed with poppies, and there were tables all round it, and little Christmas-trees on which hung bouquets with some German lines of welcome wrapped round each, the whole most charmingly done. Mr. Hespeler, the Mennonite agent who arranged the whole of this immigration, was with us, and acted as interpreter. The Mennonites' most learned man [Mr. Jakob Peters] read, and Mr. Hespeler translated, a very nice address, and D. replied in a speech which delighted them greatly. They never cheered, but when anything pleased them they lifted their caps. In allusion to their peculiar tenets he said:

> You have come to a land where you will find the people with whom you are to associate engaged indeed in a great struggle, and contending with foes whom it requires their best energies to encounter. But those foes are not your fellow-men, nor will you be called upon in the struggle to stain your hands with human blood — a task so abhorrent to your religious feelings. The war to which we invite you as recruits and comrades is a war waged against the brute forces of nature; but these forces will welcome our domination, and reward our attack by placing their treasures at our disposal. It is a war of ambition — for we intend to annex territory — but neither blazing villages nor devastated fields will mark our ruthless track. Our battalions will march across the illimitable plains which stretch before us as sunshine steals athwart the ocean; the rolling prairie will blossom in our wake, and corn and peace and

plenty will spring where we have trod.... In one word,
beneath the flag whose folds now wave above you, you
will find protection, peace, civil and religious liberty,
constitutional freedom and equal laws.

We walked around, muttered a few lame German sentences, and
were as speechlessly polite as we could be. This being over, after a song
from the school-children, Mr. Hespeler asked us over to his camp-fire,
where we had Rhine wine and German cake, and where he gave hot
coffee to the women from a distance. Nellie made love to all the babies,
and having nursed one for some time, its mother presented her with a
cucumber. It was very pleasant sitting by the fire and seeing the people
enjoying their coffee on the grass. After an hour and a half spent here
we walked to our camp, a quarter of a mile off. Some women showed us
their houses, and then we dined, and sat round our own fire. Presently
we saw fireworks rising from the other camp, so we got up an enormous
torch, which was seen and responded to by a distant cheer, and one line
of "He is a jolly good fellow."

The only other thing I have to say about the Mennonites is that the
great proportion of those here are young, and that everybody has at least
six children. Think what a gain they are to this country: in three years to
have eighteen square miles of country settled by such people.

WEDNESDAY, 22ND — We all slept very comfortably, and longer than
we did the first night. We were packed up about ten, and set off to drive
through some more villages. Mr. Hespeler showed us the domestic
arrangements. The only fault is that the stables open into the living-
rooms. The inhabitants will gradually leave off this nasty plan, but it
is their devotion to their cattle which makes them wish to have them
so near. The village herd and the village schoolmaster are the only two
paid labourers in the Mennonite vineyard; the clergyman receives no pay.
School is not kept during the three summer months.

We reached our new camping-ground early in the day, and the gentlemen went out shooting. They got a mixed, but not a good bag — prairie chicken, snipe, plover, duck and a bittern, the latter quite delicious

When not accompanying her husband on vice-regal journeys across the country, Lady Dufferin could have admired this view of Parliament from the dining-room of Government House. Sir Frances Clare Forde, aide-de-camp to Lord Dufferin was the artist.

to eat. In the evening we sat over our camp-fire, and Mr. McKay told us some interesting stories of his life. I must introduce him to you, for he is (to use a Yankee expression) the "boss" of our party. He arranges everything for us, provides the horses, carriages, tents, beds, etc.

The Hon. James McKay, M.P. (in the local Parliament), has been a mighty hunter in his day, but as he now weighs 320 lbs., he leads a quieter though still a very active life. He has a pleasant face, and is very cheery, and a thorough "good fellow," but so enormous! It is curious to see him filling up his buggy, and driving on before us, steering us through the bogs, and making signs to our driver to avoid dangers on the way. His boy of eleven rides on a pony with him, and promises to be as large. I never saw such a fat boy.

Mr. McKay is a half-breed. His parents had some French blood in them, and he speaks the three languages, but I believe he talks Indian at home. He has lost one thumb, and besides this gun-shot wound he has had several other narrow escapes of his life. One day he and an English gentleman killed seven grizzly bears; there was a bag! Mr. McKay shot four, and the Englishman three. But what seems to me the most wonderful feat is that he once killed a mother and two young cubs with a lasso. He had no gun with him, and the great bear came towards him on her hind paws; he quickly threw the lasso over her head, and, turning his horse quickly away, pulled her over on her back, and strangled her; then he killed the cubs too.

He said he had thought nothing of it, as he had killed a black bear with a lasso when he was fourteen years old. "Jemmie" (his fat boy) is always practising picking things off the ground when he is on horseback, with a view to future excellence with the lasso. Mr. McKay knows a great deal about the Indians, and it was interesting to hear him talk of them.

THURSDAY, 23RD — We had about twenty-five miles to drive home, and as we got a good deal shaken we were very tired at night and ready to go early to bed after reaching Silver Heights. The younger gentlemen, however, having gone to Mr. McKay's to see about some shooting, found dancing going on, and amused themselves by trying to learn the Red River Jig.

Lady Dufferin, *My Canadian Journal 1872–1878.*

16

Nellie L. McClung

(1873–1951)

Helen (Nellie) Letitia McClung, née Mooney, social activist, lecturer, journalist, and novelist, was born at Chatsworth near Owen Sound, Ontario. In 1880 the family moved to Manitoba, settling near Brandon. At 16, after only five years of formal education, Nellie went to Normal School in Winnipeg and then taught in rural Manitoba. In 1896 she married druggist Robert Wesley McClung who, she wrote, insisted "I would not have to lay aside my ambitions if I married him." Deeply influenced by her future mother-in-law, she had already campaigned for temperance and universal franchise. Her literary career began in 1902 when she entered a short story in a competition and an American publisher suggested that she expand it to a novel; *Sowing Seeds in Danny* sold an astounding 100,000 copies.

Nellie continued her lifelong battle for women's rights and temperance as a member of the Alberta legislature from 1921 to 1926. She was one of the "Famous Five" involved in the Persons Case, which led to a declaration by the British Privy Council that women were persons and thus eligible to become senators. A witty and dynamic speaker, she attracted large audiences across North America, as did her syndicated newspaper column "Nellie McClung Says." She was a delegate to the League of Nations in 1938 and a governor of the CBC from 1936 to 1942.

Her autobiography was originally published in two volumes, *Clearing in the West* (1935) and *The Stream Runs Fast* (1945).

Settling

When the first of September came, we began to watch the Portage road. Our men might come any day now. Mother had a pound cake made and set away in a crock, and the bread supply was not allowed to fall below three loaves and the stove got blackened every day.

One Saturday evening, as the sun was going down in a wine red mist, I saw two ox-wagons come over the rise in the Portage road, beyond the McMullen farm. I was sure it was our wagons, but I had been sure so many times before and utterly disappointed when the wagons went past, that I watched and said nothing. I was the only one on guard at the moment, and I hoped every one would stay where they were so I could have the "scoop." I wanted to run down to the road, but I had done that before and there was no luck in it. So I turned my head away and counted fifty before I looked. They were still coming! I counted another fifty and with masterly self control, refrained from sound or motion even though I could see a red ox, with a red and white ox, a red ox with a black and white ox. It must be them! I had to stuff my sun-bonnet into my mouth to keep from raising the glad shout. At last the first wagon turned in — and I lifted the alarm, which brought the other members of the family flying.…

Father and Will had come, leaving George behind to look after the place.

… There was so much talk, I sat up unobserved until ten, by making myself small, and quiet and I heard that we must be on our way in a week, and that father said he was glad we had not come with them in the spring, for between the smoke of the smudges and the mosquito bites there wasn't much to choose, and that we were going to get a pony and cart for it would save the oxen, and be a quicker way of getting around, when we got home.

…

The Sunday before we left we all went to church, walking the mile to the little English church of which Mr. Pinkham was the rector. We had attended there all summer and Mr. Pinkham had come to see us. We said goodbye to the friends we had made: Mr. and Mrs. Armstrong, Mr. and Mrs. Buckley and the Tait family — Mr. and Mrs. Robert Tait, Herbie, Ellen and Addie. Addie was a little older than I, a tall girl with reddish hair, who always had money and seemed to me like a princess in disguise. I think she bought candy every day at the store and in the mixture, when hard candies with a centre like flour paste appeared she threw them away. Ah me! I would have been glad of them, but of course, I couldn't take Addie's "leavings," so I heaped scorn on them too, but it was hard to forget them, in the candyless years that followed.

We left on Monday morning, early, with the poplar leaves stirring in the light of the rising sun. It was a glorious morning, with a smell all its own, dead leaves, ripening again, coffee and bacon, new boots and something else, maybe just adventure, the magic of the unknown.

...

We had two wagonloads of "Settler's Effects," — which was a broad term that included anything from a plow to a paper of pins. The little oxen, Jake and Brin, went first, for theirs was the lighter load of the two. In their wagon, wrapped in canvas and tarpaulins, were the things that would not be needed on the journey, flour, bacon, dried vegetables, extra bedding, chairs, tables, boxes of clothing. In the covered wagon, which the big oxen drew were the necessities for the days of travel, bedding, dry wood, frying pans, pots, clothing, ox harness, whiffletrees, a neck yoke, tools, spades for digging out mud holes, an axe, ropes and chains, and one bed made up and ready "in case of sickness."

Never had I experienced as great a moment as came to me, when the oxen's heads were turned west on Portage Avenue and the long trail received us unto itself. I felt that life was leading me by the hand and I followed on light feet. We would travel with the sun, until we came to that flower starred prairie where no stone would impede the plow; where strawberries would redden the oxen's fetlocks; where eight-hundred acres of rich black soil was waiting for us, and a running stream would stir the cat-tails in the current and I would have a little boat on it, with white sails and on hot days I could wade in its cool waters, and there would be shady pools and big trees, where I could build a seat and go there and read, when I learned to read, and it would be far enough away from the house, I could not hear any one calling me, and it would be almost the same as having a room of my own....

...

It was hot when the sun climbed higher in the sky, but there came heavy banks of clouds that gave us periods of shade and the faithful oxen plodded on, at their own unhurried pace. Wild geese passed into the south to remind us that winter was on our heels, but nothing could dim the radiance of that day of high adventure.

White-washed, Red-river frame houses, set in wide farm yards, well back from the road, stacks of hay and fields of ripe grain with men cutting it down with reapers, and in some fields with sickles and cradles — then long stretches of meadows, growing brown with autumn and then more houses. Over all the odor of wild sage, and golden rod, that grew beside the road, and in the air flights of crows and black-birds visiting the scattered grain fields, and sitting on wire fences, like strings of jet beads.

I wondered how these people could be content to stay on their little farms when there was better land ahead. Perhaps they did not know. Will had said their land was too heavy with gumbo and alkali to ever make easy farming, but they liked living close together with the river at their front door; and had their little circle of friends, and simple pleasures.

Part of the glow I felt in beginning this journey, came from the sense I had that we were well dressed for the occasion. We had dark print dresses and straw hats, lined with the same print as our dresses and banded with a fold of it, dark gray ribbed woolen stockings, hand knit, and good stout boots. Then we had olive green coats, made of homespun, mother's own weaving, with smoked pearl buttons. I remember these coats well, as well I may, for when I grew out of mine I stepped into Hannah's and when it proved inadequate, I got Lizzie's, so that olive green homespun with pearl buttons was my portion in coats until I was fifteen years old. My Aunt Ellen had made them and they were good-looking coats.

The bad roads began at Baie St. Paul, a great swampy place, dreaded by all prairie travellers. We met there, a tragic family who had turned back, discouraged and beaten. It was the wife who had broken down. She wore a black silk dress and lace shawl and a pair of fancy shoes, all caked with mud. She would have been a pretty woman if she would only stop crying. She hated the country, she sobbed, it was only fit for Indians and squaws and should never have been taken from them. Her two little girls were crying too. They had broken their garters and their legs were a mass of mosquito bites.

Mother was very sorry for their distress and tried to calm the weeping woman.

"You're not dressed right for a journey like this," she began. "No one can be happy going through mud in a fine silk dress and thin kid shoes."

"But these are the oldest things I have," she protested tearfully, "and I don't care if they do get spoiled."

"But your shoes are not comfortable," mother said, "and they are no protection to your feet, and you should have made yourself some print or gingham dresses."

"But I can't! I never made a dress in my life, mother always did my sewing," — and from her eyes came another freshet. "I want to go back to her; she never wanted me to come, but I thought it would be fun, and Willard was so crazy to get land of his own, but he can get his job back at the store."

Mother's zeal began to flag, "Take her back," she said to Willard, "she's not the type that makes a pioneer."

Willard nodded his head grimly, "I see that," — he said.

Mother invited them to stay and eat with us, for we were stopped for the noon meal and while she was making a bannock in the mouth of a flour sack, Will fried the bacon and made coffee; and Lizzie put Balm of Gilhead salve on the little girls' mosquito bitten legs and mended their garters.

"Poor Willard," mother said, as we saw them drifting down the backward trail. "He'll go on selling papers of pins and yards of tarleton,

A young Nellie McClung might well have watched a settler ambling along on his sulky plough. The artist is Edward Roper (1833–1909).

but all his life he'll dream of the yellow wheat fields that might have been his and his heart will wither with longing. But he made the mistake many good men have made — he married a painted doll, instead of a woman."

"She's a pretty little thing, too," my father said, looking after the wagon receding in the distance — "did you ever see a neater ankle?"

At High Bluff we bought a pony and cart, a Red-river cart that had not a nail in it, and whose wooden axle had never known the soothing touch of axle-grease. It rumbled and mourned, and creaked, and whined, as it turned protestingly. We bought the pony from a Methodist minister there, the Reverend Mr. Bray.

Ten miles was a good day's travelling. One day we made only one mile.

At Poplar Point we camped beside the home of Chatsworth people, who had left our neighbourhood years before. Mother had written to Mrs. Lance, but no reply had come, but Margaret Lance was the sort of woman who would not write and mother was not offended....

We knew they were now living at Poplar Point, so we would go to see them when we were so near.

They lived half a mile from the trail, in a long log house on the bank of a creek. We stopped our wagons on the other side of the creek which was running swiftly under the rough bridge and waited there on the bank opposite their house, while mother and father went across the bridge and up the bank to the house, attended by three barking dogs.

When Mrs. Lance came out of the kitchen door, there was a flurry of wings in the farm yard and hens and ducks raced toward her. Watching from the wagons we saw the meeting, though we could hear nothing above the uproar. A few black haired children came out of the house, the eldest boy vainly trying to quiet the dogs. There was a large duck pond on the side of the creek next to the house, where a flock of ducks were feeding, but they, hearing the commotion, climbed out of the water and waddled up in a body to find out what it was all about, making raucous comments as they went.

We were taken into the house and there we saw that although Mrs. Lance had not written she was expecting us. The kitchen table held a fresh baking of bread, and after the greetings were over, the eldest boy was sent out to catch and kill two chickens.

I remember the pattern of their farm buildings. The house was on one side of the creek; and the hen house and stables on the other. When we asked why they had built them this way, Mrs. Lance said she thought

A settler's home in Assiniboia near Carberry, painted by Edward Roper.

it best to keep the animals across the creek by themselves and while she
said it, a hen and chickens walked in the door of the kitchen. "We keep
her in the woodshed," Mrs. Lance said, "she's late with her chickens; this
is her second flock and I'm trying to build them up before winter. It's just
time for her boiled wheat and she knows it."

The hen cackled and stormed, sounding a hawk-alarm when she saw us.

Mrs. Lance apologized. "She doesn't like strangers," she said, "but
don't mind her, she is really a very friendly hen when she gets to know you."

On the top of the high oven a tin milk pan lined with hay contained
three young ducks that had been drenched with rain, Mrs. Lance said,
and had nearly died, but if she could just get them feathered out before
the cold weather, they would be all right.

"Don't you find it a long way over to the stables, down one hill and
up another, with the creek to cross?" mother asked, "how do you manage
in the spring when the water is high?"

"Oh! Johnny has a raft and it never lasts very long, maybe a week —
he likes it —" she said. "Johnny does like a bit of excitement, and the boys
are the same. He's so fond of animals — and he likes them around him.
He'd have the house full of them, if I would let him.... I don't believe
we'll be long here; there's people coming to settle near us and he doesn't
like to be crowded."

...

Johnny himself arrived home in the afternoon, with a bag of wild
fowl — he had been away shooting on the marsh, and gave us a riotous
welcome. Why couldn't we stay a week, and go shooting prairie chickens
on the plains? They were as thick as you ever saw black birds in the oat
fields in Ontario, and so tame, it was a crime to shoot them.

We could not stay. The weather might break any day and we were
only half way on our journey.

"Well, the North West is the place to live," Johnny said, as he drove the
hen and chickens out and shut the door. "The Garafraxa would choke
me now, if I went back. A man needs freedom! That's what drove me
out, and will drive me out again. It's different with women! They never

had freedom and so never miss it. I'll have to sell this place pretty soon and move on...."

"The trouble with me is, I won't take dictation from anyone," Johnny said. "Over here two miles away they're startin' a school. That will mean taxes and what do we need a school for?"

"What about your children; don't you want them to go to school?" mother asked indignantly.

Johnny was pressing tobacco into a black pipe, with his broad thumb.

"My boys can get all the education they need from me," he said. "And what good is it for girls? Makes them want to read books, when they should be patchin' quilts; Maggie here, would be a happier woman if she couldn't read at all."

Mother untied her apron before she replied to this.

"The only thing we live for is our children," she said in her Scotch voice, "and if we fail them, we have failed altogether. Every child has a right to an education and if you do not get that for them, you have cheated them."

"You're movin' the wrong way," he said, "if it's education you're after. There will be no schools out west where you're headin', for years. It will be like the bush in Grey County forty years ago when my folks went in. The schools came too late for me, and when they came, I was too big to go, but I don't know as I mind. I've done all right. One generation gets missed out in every new settlement, and you'll find that out too. The thing is not to get too much education in the next. It makes too wide a gap. I don't want my kids to get feeling they know more than I do; not that it would hurt me, but it wouldn't be good for the kids. You women are all the same — all for learnin', but I want my boys to stay with me, and this is one way to keep them. Ignorance holds families together."

"You don't mean it Johnny!" mother said at last. "No one could be so selfish as this, or as foolish" ...

"I do mean it! Look what education does for people! A man in the Portage forged a cheque and is in jail for it, a good fellow too, would he have done that if he had never learned to write? He had an idea he was smart — knew a little more than the rest of us. And if you do read a newspaper — what do you get? Murders, horse thieving, devilment of one kind or another. What good does her readin' do Maggie, here? Upsets her that's all. Gets her feeling too big for her boots."

That was too much for mother to stand. "Johnny Lance!" she said, "you married the prettiest girl and the best liked girl in Sullivan County. She jilted a good man to marry you — and she has roughed it with you, in this new country, and put up with you, done without things, and met all sorts of hardships and you would begrudge her the little bit of pleasure she gets from reading a book when her day's work is done, and you want to move on again, thinking always of your own wishes, your own pleasure, and not of your family. I wonder at you, Johnny!"

"You got me wrong, Mrs. Mooney," he defended, good-naturedly. "I don't begrudge it to her, if it did her any good, but I claim it don't. She reads in a paper that a man stole horses in Winnipeg and got away, and she's runnin' out all the time countin' ours. Or she reads a story about a man that left his wife and took up with a younger woman, one with yalla hair and I see her eyin' me, and I know she's afraid she might lose me. That's what I mean. My claim is it's a mistake to know more than you need to know; and that's why I like animals so well. They ask no questions, tell nothing, have no ambitions or regrets, or complaints, and take things as they come."

Mrs. Lance was making motions behind his head, and no more was said.

Before we left, Mrs. Lance defended her husband's wild talk.

"Johnny just talks to hear himself, but he doesn't mean it. He feels bitter about not ever being to school and covers it up by pretending he does not care. He's a good man to me, Lettie. I don't regret giving Billy Spicer the go-by. I'd have had an easier life, maybe, a good house and near town, but Johnny suits me, for all he's rough in his ways and he likes to talk big. He's a child in some ways, would rather be scolded than not noticed at all. He just loved having you pitch into him. I couldn't let you go thinking that Johnny is mean, for he isn't. He voted for the school and wants the boys to get an education as much as I do. I think most men take a little knowing, Lettie."

...

The weather broke the day we left the Lances and the real trouble of the journey began. Fortunately there were many travellers on the road and the mud-holes were the drag nets which brought them all together. Sometimes it took three yokes of oxen to draw a wagon out of a bad spot and even then the long grass beside the road had to be cut and thrown into the slippery, gummy mud to give the oxen a foot-hold.

The men wore long boots of leather and overalls of brown or blue duck, but I do not remember seeing any rubber boots. If the holes were not deep, Hannah and I were left in the wagon for our small weight would not make much difference. But it was like a nightmare to see the oxen go down, down into the mud, sprawling helplessly in its treacherous depths. But they did not get excited as horses would have and they did their best, without urging. In the worst part of the road we were fortunate to have Lord Elphinstone and his traders on the way to Fort Edmonton, and they gave assistance to all the wagons on the road....

I had a nightmare one night on the trail, when the whole world roared around me like a bursting sea. Only it was a sea of mud, black and greasy, licking me under. All night long, or so it seemed to me, I fought against it, unable to cry for help, and the next day I was not able to walk and so was put in the wagon, which lurched and groaned and writhed over the rough roads.

My head ached and I was very miserable. Every jolt of the wagon increased my pain, although I was packed in between pillows, and everything that could be done for my comfort had been done. I was quite sure my last hour was approaching, and I was going to be buried by the trail, like Linda. We had seen a little grave marked by a board taken from a wagon box, on which the name "Linda," was printed in white chalk on the green paint. A handful of blue fringed gentians, faded and withered lay on the fresh black earth.

I did not mind dying if it would stop my head from beating — I would be glad to die! The ground would be cold, but it would lie still. Maybe they would take me back and lay me beside Linda.

The wagon suddenly stopped and someone picked me up. Maybe I was dead.... Now I thought I must be, for I felt no pain. I had only a great desire to sleep.

"Better let Willie carry her, John," I heard mother say, "she's quite a good weight and your shoulder may ache again."

I felt myself being comfortably laid on my father's broad shoulder.

"Her, is it? A good weight? Poor child! I could carry her to the Tower of Hook. She's just the weight of two dried lamb-skins."

I opened my eyes then, but the light dazzled me and I was too weary to talk. I drifted down into a deep sea of contentment but vaguely through my dreams, I thought of Linda under the blue flowers at the side of the trail. I hoped she liked her grave and did not mind the dark, and I was sure God would send an angel for both of us, before the winter came. If this was dying, it was far nicer than riding in the wagon.

Nellie McClung, *Clearing in the West: My Own Story.*

17

Laura Goodman Salverson

(1890–1970)

Laura Goodman Salverson, née Guðmundsson, was born in Winnipeg to parents who had emigrated from Iceland in 1887 with their four children, two of whom died en route. Her father, Lárus Guðmundsson, was a scholarly man with an adventurous streak. In search of a better life, he restlessly moved the family from farming in Manitoba to ranching in North Dakota, to Duluth, Minnesota, with short stays in Selkirk and a remote part of Mississippi, but always returning to Winnipeg. Because of these constant moves and frequent illness, young Laura did not learn English until she was ten. Her peripatetic life continued when she married railwayman George Salverson in 1913. She is recognized as the first novelist who wrote about the immigrant experience in the West from the insider's viewpoint. The Institute of Arts and Sciences in Paris awarded her an honorary degree for *The Viking Heart* (1923), which deals with the hardships and prejudice that twelve hundred Icelandic immigrants encounter when they move to Gimli in 1876. *Dark Weaver* (1937) won a Governor General's Award, as did her powerful autobiography *Confessions of an Immigrant's Daughter* (1939). Her account of her first visit to a library might well be inscribed in every school: "In this one small unbeautiful room were a hundred empires and a gleaming host of immortals, into which mighty company I might enter at will, thanks to the makers of books."

This soulful portrait of Laura Salvorson "author" was taken "at age fourteen, four years before she started to write" (Laura Goodman Salverson fonds).

Library and Archives Canada, e010767581.

A NIGHT OF EVIL DEEDS

… There was Great-Aunt Steinun, as brave a little lady as ever faced the wilderness. She came to Canada in the first immigration, as we called it. That is to say, with that group of twelve hundred settlers who arrived in 1872, destined for the Gimli and Icelandic River settlements. Through the negligence of the immigration officials in Montreal, these poor, weary home-seekers were made to spend the night in quarters that had housed some Indians polluted with small-pox. Consequently, the immigrants had barely reached their destination when the plague broke out. And, for eighteen months, homeless and helpless, without medical supervision, they were quarantined in the swamps of Gimli.

Now that Gimli has become a favourite summer resort, with railway flier service to Winnipeg, it is difficult to conceive of a time when all the surrounding country was a fly-infested quagmire, through which, in rainy seasons, you had to wade knee-high. Homesteads were often under water for weeks in the spring, the wretched inmates clinging to the damp shelter of their miserable log huts until the water invaded the firebox of the stove, thereby routing the last shreds of comfort.

Great-Aunt Steinun's first shelter in Gimli was a roofless log enclosure, so full of water that her husband had to build a raft on which to lay their beds. A foolish sort of arrangement, you may think, but, to quote the little lady: "It broke the October winds and kept us from floating all over the field."

In such surroundings, the travel-worn immigrants had to meet and suffer the horrors of small-pox, alternating their labours of burying the dead with felling green timber for huts to house the living. Great-Aunt Steinun, though fond enough of reminiscing, did not like to dwell on the epidemic. It was too painful to think of the sodden graves that marked the end of so many fair hopes — and more painful still to remember that one hundred and twenty-five babies literally died of starvation. Poor innocents! How desperately their mothers tried to keep them alive on fish broth and bean stock, the only substitutes available for the milk which could not be had. The Government had intended to supply the settlers with cattle, but all such worthy plans were disrupted and long delayed by the raging pestilence. It was hard enough to get staple foods to the people, to say nothing of livestock and luxuries. Every few weeks the Mounted Police rode up to a specified zone with rations of salt, pork, and beans, food the Icelanders had never before tasted, and, consequently, found indigestible fare in their enfeebled condition.

Terrible though these trials were, the sorest weight upon great-aunt's heart was the uncertainty concerning her eldest daughter. This girl, about fourteen years old, had been sent into service by the immigration authorities, it being their thought she was well able to support herself in the city. In the general confusion of settling so many people, they had, however, omitted to leave the girl's address with her parents, and when the plague set in it was, of course, impossible to communicate this or any other information to the immigrants. During all those frightful months, Great-Aunt Steinun was haunted by the thought that this dearest of her children might have contracted the disease, and perhaps died among strangers indifferent to her suffering and loneliness. Nor was she relieved of this worry when the quarantine was lifted. By that time no one in the immigration bureau even remembered the girl, and it was not until three years later that the family was reunited.

What I like best to remember about Great-Aunt Steinun, however, has to do with an incident which, to my mind, surpasses all others in her hard experience and throws a revealing light upon her forceful character. It happened that, while raising his permanent house Mr Haldorson, her husband, cut his foot rather badly, yet continued his labour, giving slight heed to the wound. An infection set in, which, as the days passed, grew steadily worse, until it was no longer possible for him to keep on his feet, and, as the fever mounted, it was obvious that his condition was rapidly becoming critical. Their homestead, like so many others, was isolated, far from any neighbour. They had no means of conveyance, no draft beast of any kind, and Winnipeg was sixty miles away.

Great-Aunt Steinun was not the sort of woman to sit weeping, waiting for some miracle of grace. What they did possess was a crude hand sleigh for hauling wood. Her mind made up, she poured water on the wooden runners, affixed a rude harness, and, overruling Mr Haldorson's dismayed objections, pronounced herself ready to take him to Winnipeg. But when the sick man had been made as comfortable as the means permitted, Steinun was momentarily panic-striken. She realized suddenly that she had not the slightest idea, beyond an indefinite direction, how to reach Winnipeg. Her husband was no better informed. They had only made the journey once before, in the company of the other immigrants. Besides, the poor man by now was half delirious with fever.

"I thought for a moment that no one had ever been left so helpless," she used to say. "Then I was ashamed of myself. What was the good of having a God you wouldn't trust as well as your neighbour, I asked myself? So then and there I started, and, at the edge of the lake, put it up to the Almighty. Whatever thought He put in my head, I would take for guidance. And that's what I did."

There, according to Great-Aunt Steinun, the tale rightly ended, for she was always loath to delineate personal hardships. Sometimes, however, especially if the listener were sceptical of divine provision, she might supply the remaining details. Drawing that cumbrous sleigh, with its human burden, was in itself a task beyond the normal strength of a little woman scarcely five feet tall, worn with vigils over the sick and dying, and in all probability under-nourished. Yet she trekked on bravely, over the lonely waste of ice, only pausing to rest when the heavy pounding of her heart made her dizzy. Hours later, a wind sprang up, with driving puffs of snow — not the gentle flakes of a milder climate, but the dry, powdered concomitant of a gathering blizzard. No one who has not experienced this phenomenon of the prairie can possibly imagine how quickly a peaceful landscape is changed to an inferno of lashing wind and whirling clouds of snow that sting the eyes and stifle the breath, and obliterate every familiar object.

"Oh, it was a bit of a struggle, to be sure," she admitted. "What of it? I had put myself in God's care. Humanly speaking, I was lost, I suppose, and the strength flowing out of me like water from a cracked crock. But again, what of that? Before I was overcome, an Indian found us, and took us home to his tepee.

"That was a lesson, let me tell you. The young squaw massaged my frozen feet with a mixture of bear's grease and some sort of herb. She fed us from the family pot, and, before I set out once more, dressed me in deerskin leggings and moccasins lined with moss. Ah, they were good, those two brown people. They shared all they had with us and when the storm was over that fierce-looking brave saw me off on the right trail. So you see if my husband was saved, it was not all my doing, but a miracle of God's mercy, working through the simple heart of a savage."

Sometimes these homespun yarns had a humorous twist, even when the undertones were sober. I remember the hair-raising experience of an old charwoman whom the young wags loved to terrorize with tall tales of Indian atrocities. She lived alone in a tiny shanty on Point Douglas, and though her days were devoted to monotonous labour, she was always exuberant in praise of her many blessings. Had she not a cosy shelter for her old bones, food in the larder, and good Manitoba spruce cut to fit her carron stove laid in against the winter? What was more, had not the blessed Lord given her a knack with the little ones, and more than enough strength and patience to struggle with spotted linen and pine boards, so that, whatever the ladies in their big houses required of her, it was always well and respectably done, and she paid with a cheery heart that often expressed itself in a cast-off petticoat or a queerish bonnet, in addition to wages? Blessed she certainly was, and, except for that menace of redskins, found the New World all that one might have expected, since the good God made it.

There came a chill October evening when this fixed obsession was especially rampant. It was cold, with flurries of snow, and shadows long and black on the river bank. A night for evil deeds, thought poor old Ellen, and quickened her stride, despite the crick in her back. On such a night it was good to have a secure shelter, a bit of a place that kept one safe from savage eyes. The sight of her tar-paper shack, hidden in a windbreak of ragged poplars, drew a sigh of happiness from her heart. In no time at all she would be toasting her toes by the stove, and the cat purring his gladness.

She was an orderly soul, and always laid the fire before she went to work in the morning. She had only to drop a match on the kindling to start a cheery blaze, light the wall lamp, and set the kettle on for coffee. This done, she usually called the cat, removing her wraps while Thomas took his time responding, and then shut and barred the door for the night. But now, chilled and blue from the biting wind, she thought of the wood box, and frowned to discover that she had forgotten to fill it. Well, thought Ellen, that's what comes of sleeping in for fifteen minutes! Now she must fetch and carry, though nineteen devils plagued her back. Grumbling, she flung wide the door, "Thomas" framed on her tongue, but neither that nor any other sound came from her lips. As stricken as Lot's sinful wife, she stood there, her horrified eyes fixed upon the road. God and his angels help her! Plain as the nose on her face, the doom she dreaded marched upon her.

Three dusky, buckskinned knaves were striding towards the house, snow whirling round their horrid heads, a long lean hound loping at their heels. She was so frightened, so certain of the inevitable end, that it never occurred to her that she might shut the door, and, by this simple act, escape an unwelcome visitation. Instead, she stood there, too petrified for speech, while the strangers, who, politely enough, asked for shelter, filed in, and with grunts of satisfaction seated themselves on the bench before the table. Evidently they wanted food, as well as shelter, thought the old woman, dim stirrings of rising anger minimizing her fear. The scallawags! Why didn't they kill her and be done! Why must they prolong the agony, the murdering villains! She supposed they would scalp her as a matter of course, for she had long, yellow hair. Just the sort of hair braves love to dangle from their belts, so the wags had assured her. Just the same, there they sat, hungrily, eyeing the kettle. Well, thought Ellen, gathering what wit she had, and hurrying to the cupboard, if she must so shortly meet her Maker, she might as well do it without the sin of inhospitality on her soul. As glumly silent as her company, she laid the supper, which was eaten in typical Indian stolidity, and at its conclusion the trio plunged down upon the floor, prepared to sleep. Even the hound had dropped in a weary loop before the glowing stove.

Ellen was now completely mystified. Was it possible she had misjudged the wanderers? Or were they, perchance, waiting some prescribed ritualistic hour for their evil purpose? Whatever their designs, she had not the heart to let them lie on the cold, bare boards uncovered. Gingerly,

Library and Archives Canada, C-040820.

Peter Rindisbacher (1806–34) painted a Souteaux man travelling with his family in winter near Lake Winnipeg.

she crossed behind the human huddle, and from an old wooden trunk fetched two patchwork quilts for their comfort. A grunt, thoroughly unnerving, was all the thanks she received.

There was nothing more that could be done. She dared not even call the cat. Poor Thomas must take his ease where he found it. Grieved for her pet, whose place was usurped by a smelly mongrel, she restocked the fire, and, musing upon the uncertainty of life, decided that she might as well snatch a wink of sleep to support her through the ordeal to come. With shaking fingers she removed the lamp from its bracket and bore it to the home-made table beside the bed, which occupied the far corner, and was neatly dressed in a cretonne cover and long, frilled valance. Being a modest female, she naturally meant to lie down fully clothed, howsoever her stays pinched. But the fine spread and valance must be removed. This done, she lay down, and then, the breath rattling in her throat, cautiously leaned out and extinguished the light.

Almost instantly hell broke loose. With a savage scraping of nails upon the floor, and hair-raising snarls from a cavernous chest, the great hound came hurtling across the room and dived under the bed. The sleepers sprang to their feet. Some one relit the lamp. Then, to the quaking woman, it seemed that men and dog were inextricably mixed in a heaving, howling *mélée*. A nightmare of fury too swift to follow or comprehend, until the din of battle died away, and there was stamped upon her mind the ineradicable vision of a hulking negro who had been dragged from under her bed, and now hung limply in the iron grasp of the Metis.

Thereupon, realizing the miracle of her deliverance, poor old Ellen promptly fainted. When she regained consciousness the house was sheathed in silence. The red eye of the stove blinked beneficently through the dusk. The dog breathed like a cheerful bellows, and the angels she had entertained unaware snored in solid comfort.

Oh, but she was sore ashamed! Never again would she believe those tales of evil — never, never! In the morning she would open a jar of strawberry jam and fry a batch of flatbread. Other things as well she planned, and, in the midst of it, fell sound asleep — for fear may reign an hour, but old bones require rest. When she wakened the fire was crackling, and the kettle sang, and the bright prairie sunshine was a sunburst of joy on the window-pane. What happiness it now was to hustle up the meal. How glad she was that her bit of cooking was always a matter of pride — her flatbread golden-brown, and her tea hot and fragrant.

This morning she would have welcomed a little chatter to open the way for the question that burned her mind. But the visitors ate all that was set before them in unbroken silence. Not a murmur out of any of them. Not a single reference to the terrible incident of the night before. They behaved just as though nothing out of the ordinary had happened — just as though they had not saved her life.

Not until they were leaving was a word spoken, and then it was an irrelevant question, flung out with a sudden dazzling smile by the youngest of the trio.

"You like moose meat?" he asked. Yes, yes, she did, Ellen acknowledged. "Good," said he, and the others nodded. They would bring her some on their way back from the north.

"But — but —" stammered Ellen, "I want to know — I've got to know —" And there words failed her.

It was then that the nut-brown ancient whose wrinkled face had struck the deepest terror to Ellen's heart spoke for the first time. Drawing himself up to his full, fine height, and swinging his arm in a majestic curve toward the Red River, he said, with proud finality:

"Heap much gone hell!"

Laura Goodman Salverson, *Confessions of an Immigrant's Daughter.*

18

Janey Canuck

(EMILY MURPHY, 1868–1933)

Emily Gowan Murphy, née Ferguson, pen name Janey Canuck, was born in Cookstown, Ontario, into a prominent political/legal family. Educated at Bishop Strachan School in Toronto, she was barely 19 when she married Arthur Murphy, an Anglican minister. His success as a preacher led to missionary work throughout Ontario and two years in England. It was during this nomadic life that Emily began to write. *Janey Canuck Abroad*, a collection of her frank and irreverent impressions of their travels in England and Germany, met with great success following its publication in 1901. Their return to Canada was followed by illness and the death of a small daughter. Doctors ordered an outdoor life for Arthur Murphy, and the family moved west in 1903 to develop his timber limit.

Swan River, Manitoba, was a bleak community of ugly houses covered with "hideous tin," but Emily admired its hardworking inhabitants and soon fell in love with the West. "There is magic in this land," she wrote, "and you can hear unsung things." Described as "sweetly militant," she became active in women's rights and even more politically involved after the Murphys moved to Edmonton in 1907. In 1916 Emily became the first woman magistrate in the British Empire. Like her friend and fellow activist Nellie McClung, she was one of the "Famous Five" who campaigned to have women declared legal "persons." Her political achievements have overshadowed her earlier literary career, but as one critic wrote, "[the] vivid, finely-etched and distinctive sketches [of her youth] catch the West in the very act of bounding forward."

MOSQUITOTIDE

The time of death and the time of falling leaves have been sung; but the time of mosquito is the most serious of all.

Just now we are sore let and hindered by these sanguinary pests. To sit out is literally "the price of blood." It is useless for dwellers in southern cities to scoff and say we exaggerate the evil propensities of these little midgets, for was it not "the little people" who killed the very strong man Kwasind on the river Taquamenaw?

These mosquitoes are ubiquitous, insatiable, and hot-tongued with all the spirit of the furies. They walk, they drop, they fly, they swim, they come up from below, steal rides, blow in; but they are always here. Everywhere you meet them, and are meat for them. Like Pharaoh's frogs, they come up into thine house, and into thy bedchamber and upon thy bed, and into the house of thy servants, and upon thy people, and into thine ovens, and into thy kneading troughs.

They are not only omnipotent, and omnivorous, but omnipresent. You may kill them by bushelfuls, and their phalanxes are apparently undiminished. Insectivorous birds have only to open their mouths to have them filled. The same applies to men and women, for that matter.

I have been keeping a record of the bites I have had since the beginning of the season, also of the mosquitoes killed — a kind of debtor and creditor affair. They balance up thus:

Bites, 583,672,154,871. Deaths, 13.

Stewart Edward White declares that the mosquito is superior to all fly pests in that it holds still to be killed. It is not necessary to wave your arms or slap frantically; all you have to do is to place your finger calmly and firmly on the spot and you get the deliberate brute every time. This sounds well in theory, but it is not always practicable or, for that matter, modest.

When this thrice-accursed insect strikes a trail around your shoulders, or even your ankles, he must be allowed to pursue the even tenor of his way unmolested. It is quite useless to bid him take his beak from out your heart and his form from off your door. He will do nothing of the kind.

Besides, he seldom affects a flippant, racy light heartedness to put you on your guard. As a general thing, he is a procrastinating miscreant, a baritone brute who skulks about you undecidedly to find the most unprotected part of your epidermis. You do not know where his geographical expedition has led him until you feel a puncture, sharp as an electric burn. Or it may be you are wholly unaware of his visit until you see the outward and visible signs of his inward and unspiritual tunnelling.

A man once came to this north country and described the habits of the mosquito thus:

> "He lights upon your head,
> A naughty word is said,
>   As with a rap,
>   A vicious slap,
>
> You bang the spot where he is not.
> He stops and rubs his gauzy wings,
> He soars aloft and gently sings,
>   He sits and grins,
>   And then begins
> To select a spot for another shot."

This man indubitably wrote of hornets. Josh Billings is of my way of thinking, too. He says:

"The hornet iz a red-hot ov nature, ov sudden impreshums, and sharp konklusions. The hornet alwus fites at short range, and never argys a case. They settle all ov their disputes bi lettin their javelin fly and are certain and anxious to hit as a mule iz."

The mosquitoes have no such vagaries. They are epicures, and like to dally with their food before finally tasting.

Edison's Encyclopaedia vouchsafes an interesting piece of information about them. It declares that if you hold your breath when a mosquito has his bill in you, it cannot withdraw till you breathe again. It is seldom an encyclopaedia is humorous at the expense of the public.

But even if you did hold your breath, it would be a mistake to give a mosquito the quietus. It is a mistake at any time. They are only the slow, clumsy ones that get killed. The fittest survive, and so the result cannot fail to be a spryer and more agile race.

If, however, you *are* foolish enough to slaughter them, perhaps there is no way more effective and, at the same time, more amusing, than shooting them with a 32-calibre revolver. You are sure to bore a little hole in them somewhere.

It is a well-known fact, too, that mosquitoes have a passion for black. If you sit beside a fat person dressed in this colour they will leave you happily alone.

Surveyors sometimes lather their faces and necks with a vile decoction warranted to keep off these pertinacious insects. It consists of oil of

Library and Archives Canada, C-033767.

William George Richardson Hind's watercolour of July 1862 demonstrates another method of dealing with the pesky creatures by Setting Fire to the Grass to Drive the Mosquitoes away from the Cattle near Touchwood Hills.

tar, oil of pennyroyal, oil of cedar, and castor oil, in equal parts. But the appetite of a foraging party of mosquitoes is generously uncritical. They find this application highly nutritive above all diet. It is, to them, a sweet savour of Araby the Blest — just a mere tang and sweetness that stimulates them to renewed efforts.

Every Indian has a different story regarding the creation of mosquitoes; but nearly all regard them as agents of an evil spirit.

The Indians in British Columbia have a tradition that a bad woman who lived on the banks of the Fraser River caught young children and carried them in a basket woven of water snakes. One day the children peeped out of the basket and saw her digging a pit and making stones hot in the fire, and they knew she was going to cook them as Indians cook their meat; so they plotted together what they would do. By and by the old hag came to the basket and lifted them out one by one and told them to dance around her on the grass, and she began putting something in their eyes so that they could not open them; but the elder ones watched their opportunity, and while she was putting the hot stones in the pit, they all rushed forward and toppled her over, and piled fire into the pit on top of her till she was burned to ashes. But her evil spirit lived after her, for out of her ashes, blown about by the wind, sprang the dreadful pest of mosquitoes.

In this story the setting is picturesque, the plot good, the action quick, the *dénouement* just.

A certain northern chronicler relates that Kitch Manitou became angry when, one day, all the men married all the women and a universal honeymoon began so that no one would harvest the rice or the corn. At this juncture Kitch created *saw-gi-may*, the mosquito, and sent him forth to work his will and, as the chronicler puts it, "this took the romance out of the situation" so that the honeymoon suddenly waned.

This sounds as if it might be the true story.

The mosquito's very make-up indicates that he means mischief. He breathes from his tail. This is in order that the insatiable little beast may have his bill free to dilute your blood with his yellow poison.

His wings are too swift to be meant for any innocent purpose. The wild duck makes nine strokes a second, but the ordinary mosquito makes 330 in the same period.

I have never been able to examine his body minutely, but I am told — and have no reason to doubt the fact — that his body folds up like a field-glass so that he can elongate himself to take all the blood he can get.

It was Lafcadio Hearn who said he wanted to have the chance of being reincarnated in the form of a mosquito, so that he might sing its pungent song and bite some people he knew. Lafcadio must have meant the missionaries in Japan. He did not approve of them, nor have I ever met a missionary who approved of Hearn.

Speaking of "the thin, pungent sound," it has always been a question in our family as to what the mosquito really *does* sing. Is it a requiem, a lullaby, or merely grace before meat? Perhaps it is all three.

One member of the family declares he is "cussing around promiscuous." It has also been suggested that he sings "Drill, ye tarriers, drill," but it seems to me he is whining an obligato recitative in C minor.

Sometimes he sings "Cuisine! Cuisine!" as through a paper and fine-toothed comb. One thing is certain; his song is the very sound of pain, if pain could speak.

It is said that everything has a use. It is hard to guess the *raison d'être* of this headlong blackguard, unless it is to humble the people of this north country. Speaking metaphorically, there is no other fly in their ointment.

The mosquito has not a single virtue, or if he should have one, like those of Montaigne, it "got in by stealth."

Mr. Punch thinks he found one and penned it thus:

> "I bite to live
> (Some live to bite),
> I sting from sheer necessity
> — not spite."

Being an Englishman, living in England, Mr. Punch can know nothing whatever about the programme of the mosquito.

It is passing strange that the white man, who has conquered rattlesnakes, Indians, small-pox, and various kinds of "varmints," should run and hide from the mosquito. The mosquitoes have come up and possessed the land, and no man is so bold as to say them nay.

Ask a warrior why this is and, likely as not, he will tell you it is useless to reason with a mosquito, for only the female insects bite.

Although scientists have stated this to be a fact, I don't believe a word of it. The horrid lust of food and inordinate craving for variety evidenced by the biting mosquito is, to my mind, a complete refutation of the theory.

When Dolly Winthorpe offered Master Marner some lard-cakes, she said:

"Men's stomicks is made so comical, they want a change; they do, I know, God help 'em."

And what made trouble in Eden? Man and his food. I am not unmindful of the fact that learned commentators have ever laid the evil at the door of woman, but nevertheless it is a true, if not generally understood, fact that the serpent who tempted our mother Eve with the lure of the forbidden, is spoken of in Holy Writ as a male.

Some of us there are who think scientists might be better employed than in gibing at women. We bespeak their efforts on behalf of the stingless mosquito. Luther Burbank of Santa Rosa has, by crossing and recrossing the cactus, robbed it of its stings. It is the mosquitoes' turn now.

Physicians tell us that in the southern states of America, yellow fever, malaria, and elephantiasis (where the victim's legs and arms grow to be the size of grain sacks) are propagated by the mosquitoes. There are also well-authenticated cases where violent insanity has been caused by mosquito bites.

Fifteen thousand deaths were recorded last year in the United States from malaria, showing that the mosquito's bite is by no means a trivial thing. This is one reason the Agricultural Department has sounded the tocsin of war.

The mosquito lays eggs on fresh or brackish water. The eggs are fastened in a sort of raft which swims on the surface. These hatch into "wiggletails" which, like whales, are obliged to come to the surface to breathe.

Professor L.O. Howard has discovered that a film of coal-oil on a breeding pond infallibly kills every wiggletail in fifteen minutes, because it shuts them off from air.

We have been figurating on extirpating the mosquitoes in our neighbourhood, but concluded it would take the whole output of the Standard Oil Company for several years, and at the end of the time we would have no water to drink, wash in, for fire protection, or to float logs. Then we would have to kill all our cattle, for so big a space as a cow's hoof-print would breed a billion mosquitoes. It would cost several million dollars to drain off the marsh lands, and then we still would have our ponds to dispose of.

On the whole, I like best the singularly interesting suggestion that has appeared in the category of vibrations. It is asserted that by sounding a certain note on a tuning-fork these noxious insects may be violently attracted by the sound, and by rigging up a screen through which an electric current can be sent, they may be slaughtered wholesale.

When we get an electric dynamo, and find out what the note is, we intend to kill them.

I could write more about the mosquito, but, to be candid, he is not worth it.

Emily Murphy, *Janey Canuck in the West.*

19

Maryanne Caswell

(1873–1952)

Maryanne Hilliard, née Caswell, was born in Ontario. She was the daughter of a Palmerston storekeeper, James Caswell, who decided to uproot his wife and six children when the family business was severely damaged by fire. He followed his three younger brothers who were homesteading in the Northwest Territories. Letters that 14-year-old Maryanne wrote to her grandmother provide a unique description of the trip west and daily life from April 12, 1887, to New Year's Day 1888. Maryanne married George Hilliard and taught for many years in "Indian" schools around Prince Albert. Her nephew, Lorne C. Paul, who compiled a family history, recalls, "The Hilliards had no children, but Aunt Mary, a strong-willed woman had definite ideas on raising children to which we frequently were subjected." Despite the maturity and vivacity of her letters, as an adult Maryanne turned her attention from writing to painting "very creditably in oils." The letters were published in the Saskatoon *Star-Phoenix* in 1952, adapted for CBC Radio by Mrs. Grace Lane in 1957, and serialized in *The United Church Observer* in 1962; they first appeared in book form as *Pioneer Girl* in 1964. Maryanne, who died before her letters were published, never mentioned them and her family was not aware of their existence. We can be grateful that the letters, with their often poignant evocation of life in "the great lone land," survived.

PIONEER GIRL

[July 1887]

Dear Grandma,

(Our picnic was just over when) Aunt Frankie, who had been in Saskatoon, joined us and to get Jen to stay with her until Uncle Rob returned. We gathered the washed clothes filled the barrel with water in the rays of the setting sun; up the bank for home, herding the cattle along. The sky was memorably beautiful in its orange, crimson, purple and mauve tints of vivid colourings as superb and warlike as the battlefield of Honenlin blending, fading, reflecting to the water of the beautiful, swift Saskatchewan resplendent in the unappreciated silence.

The mosquitoes were terribly vicious and as we neared home Berry became unmanageable, broke from me, upsetting and scattering the pots, pails, laundry and water barrel. So ended our first of July, 1887.

During the night the rain came in torrents. The knot-holes of the roof-boards leaked and rivers flowed inside and out. Mother, as she frequently had to do, put pots and pans on the beds to catch the drips. We dared not move the least bit or water is spilt. The quilts take such a long time to dry thoroughly hanging on poles of the garden fence and this hot, golden sun burns and fades them very much.

The weather is so hot that the heat in the distance dances like wild Indians riding to battle. The prairie is transformed into an enchanted land, inhabited by elves and fairies. If you listen carefully to the whispering of the wind in the grass, the buzzing of the insects about the countless bright, lined flowers, changed by a miracle every few days to another colour and variety, you are in another world.

We have gathered, dried and pressed many of them. A great variety of vetch as in Gray's Botany, which Uncle A.K. gave us years before we left home. The first to show were crocus or mauve anemones in their fur coats. Very much like tulips, then clusters of purple violets, orange cowslips, yellow pea blossoms on a long stem, several kinds of tufts of purple not unlike a thistle, a low vine of coral hollyhock blossoms. Wild

Library and Archives Canada, C-011036.

Maryanne Casswell frequently wrote of her pleasure in prairie flowers, such as this wild floral arrangement being admired by a gopher.

tomatoes, but they taste as if you held a copper penny in your mouth; ground plums, magenta, shooting star, blue gentians, blue stars on the grass, dainty bluebells create a haze of blue all about; roses galore, white and blue asters, golden-rod in three different kinds, wild sage with pur-plish pink burgamot, white yarrow, wormwood, pink, fireweed. Dainty Indian paint-brushes along the river ravines, an occasional Indian moc-casin, yellow and pink ox-eyed daisies here and there interspersed with wild, strongly-scented candytuft.

For future use we gathered wormwood for use as poultices to reduce swellings, wild sage and onions for seasoning, anise with its long, purple licorice-odoured spikes for cough medicine, tansy and yarrow for yeast, golden-rod for dye.

A plant with three stiff silvered leaves — like clover — with pur-plish blossoms, the root of which when dried and cut makes splendid gunwads for the muzzle loaders father uses. The beauty and variety of these, each in their turn make a marvellous dainty and gaudy carpet, very pleasing to the eye, especially when you look to the west about sunset to see the most wonderful colourings of blue, orange, crimson flames splashing across the whole horizon sky from north to south. We marvel at its varying beauties and wish we had paints to try to transfer the vivid and dainty shades to something other than heart's memories.

Mother made cheese this week as it was so hot. We have more milk as the cattle do not wander quite so far away. The milk is warmed, the rennet — a calf's stomach put into it. These we had brought from Palmerston. When the rennet has thickened the milk to junket, it is cut up to drain the whey off, then left to ripen. To test it mother took a heated poker and touched a bit of the curd to it; if it threaded it was ready for salting. Then kneaded and pressed into a cheesecloth sack into a small half-keg with holes in sides and bottom. A plate and stones on top of this keg is put between two planks at either end of which is wrapped a chain. As the cheese is pressed, the hook of the chain is moved to increase the pressure. Occasionally the cheese is turned till drained of whey, then buttered to preserve it till ripened and used.

We have been down along the river for miles, scanning and searching for the body of little Harry Molloy, but did not find it. The Molloy children were playing in bare feet down the river in the sand. On the run home little Harry was last in line. Evidently he was too close to the water-edge for his footprints showed where he had slipped into a large hole. We are very sorry for them. Also for the drowning of the nice Prendergast boy off the scow at Saskatoon. His mother and sisters are on their way here from England. What grief awaits her.

About six miles down and near the river not far from scraggly bushes we know as "the horse," we found several Indian graves. They were heaped with stones, larger and smaller. It must have been hard work to roll and carry these. We peered and pried and tried to move to see beyond down among the stones hoping of course to find an Indian relic.

Nearby were several circles of stones within a large circle. The Indians must have camped here for some time as deep camp-fire spots have burned into the ground almost large enough to crouch into. A few dried twisted poplar stumps remain, which someone twisted while green. Not far away I found a long sharp-pointed peculiar looking knife. The blade and handle appear to have been welded by hand. The handle is of open-work copper with crumbled bone underneath. It has lain there a long time. Looks very much like Grandfather Martin's dirk. Who has been here and lost this knife? Though lying for years it is still very sharp and not eaten with rust, truly a good knife.

We also found several stones with grooves cut all round the centre about three-quarters of an inch deep. Stones are oblongs or ovals about the size and shape of a large, good egg. These are no doubt war clubs or hammers to sling about from a strap. Down by the river, almost screened by the bushes, we found an old scow high and dry on the stones. Evidently it had been carried out from some place and lifted by ice in spring flood, drifting in the lowered water to its lonely fate far from its moorings, possibly Medicine Hat, the nearest ferry or scow place beyond Saskatoon.

It makes you wonder about lots of things.

Love,
from *Maryanne.*

Dear Grandma,

We have been to Molloys (today) for the mail and with eggs, as they are glad to have what we can spare. The yokes are very yellow, not because the fowl are pure Black Spanish but because of the many grasshoppers they feed on. The hoppers have eaten in on the grain about ten to 20 feet, at the edge it is eaten quite clean; though Aunt Patience says it is nothing compared to the hopper destruction in Iowa when she was a girl. We have picked and dried at least a bushel of raspberries and a cotton grain-sack of saskatoon berries. They taste and look like tiny or small purple apples.

The gophers are little scamps. They are about the size of an Ontario rat (of which we have none, thanks be); the colour of the yellowed grass;

not unlike a squirrel, but not such a fluffy tail. They burrow into the ground and have numerous holes or doors into and out of their dens. When startled or you approach they sit on hind legs very still. One could mistake them for a tethering stake. Then they dive into the hole and pop out of another to learn the news.

We have to snare them about the garden as they are too fond of vegetables. We got one that had black barley but there is none that we know of unless 25 miles down and across. They no doubt travel. We use leather shoe strings in a loop or noose; set it over the hole, and as Mr. or Mrs. Gopher pop up we quickly pull the string and there is Mr. Gopher squirming in the loop. John and Jen have become quite expert in snaring. There are plenty of them and no good to us.

Mother made some yeast-cakes before all the cornmeal would be used. These with the berries dried in the sun take some attention and turning to get them just right so they will not mildew.

For the yeast-cakes she boiled buttermilk, and stirred in cornmeal, ginger, and 3–4 yeast cakes from Ontario, kept warm, and then more meal to roll, cut and dried in the open air.

It is haying time, so out into the great, unbroken, western expanse of prairie for ten or 12 miles father and I started with our ox-team hitched to the wooden-legged wagon, with mower knives, rake, forks, camp equipment and food for a week's stay. Father had not been very well. I was to be company and cook for the camp. This did not seem enough for me in the loneliness so after cutting some of the hay I was shown how to turn the winnows with a long pole that the other side of the cut hay might be exposed to the sun to cure. Then how to smooth the rake heaps into rainproof haycocks. It was unbearably lonesome, hot work by myself with father cutting or raking in other dry sloughs. If only mother with Mabel would come over the rise in some magical way, how relieved with happiness I would be. But no!

I amused myself one evening by imitating the cries of coyotes on the ridge. I did so well that father hurried to me in fear I was being attacked. Lifting their heads to the sky their cry is weird, very like a heart-broken abandoned or grief-stricken woman's cry. So I imagine mine would be if I were left alone without any hope in this great emptiness.

The afternoon air was scorching hot, stiflingly oppressive, the sky a shimmery blue with a dark copper fan cloud gathering in the west. Suddenly a strong, roaring wind came at us out of the vastness. Anxiously we ran for the shelter of a load of hay, driving the oxen with difficulty, father at their head, I prodding the rear. The storm of hail broke in mad fury as if the pent-up anger of the gods were wreaking vengeance at our invading of the undisputed territory. When we arrived at camp, father was minus his hat, with a red handkerchief tied under his whiskers, two large lumps on his head from the hail, my sunbonnet battered to pulp and a bruised shoulder; a sorry sight we were, yet we laughed and gathered large hail stones to eke out our water supply, spreading our bedding to dry in the warm sun as it returned, chasing the storm war-horses before its beams.

Early in the morning before sun up, and that is early, father arose to attend to the oxen. He returned shortly with consternation in every fibre to tell me the oxen were gone, "to hasten breakfast." In the clearer light of sun-up we found their tracks in the wet grass toward the east. We traced them through long, grassy miles home. Mother had them in the kraal. Startled by a noise she found Berry standing looking in at her. They had tasted a bit of everything in the garden before making their presence known. How very contrary oxen can be!

After a lunch we prepared to return to the haying, Martha accompanying us this time. We were to ride ox-back. Martha chose Berry placing a mat on his back on which to sit. I elected bare-back. Father followed shouldering another pitchfork to show how hay fields were mown. In a few miles I found myself slipping forward. Suddenly over onto Bright's neck, grabbing his horns, I yelled. Father, prodding with a fork behind, sent Bright off on a wild run. Finally in much merriment we halted and I again adjusted on ox-back. Bright's horns were so wide that I, astride, could not have jumped clear of him, so it is well I stuck to his horns and to him.

When we reached camp the sun was setting in mighty splashes of purple crimson flames lengthening the light to make camp. Martha and I slept on the load of hay away from the buzz and torment of constant mosquito hosts. We sang "The Spacious Firmament on High" for worship and so to rest after a long, tiring day.

Next morning we moved camp. While I was making the fire Martha unloaded the camp equipment, throwing the lid of the tin trunk (which held our food) on my head. As if there was no other spot in all this lone land for a lid to be hurled! With camphor to disinfect, the bleeding was stopped. Father lectured on carelessness, that nearly all accidents were from carelessness. Before the sun went down we remembered mother's oft-repeated, "Never let the sun go down upon your wrath." So peace reigned supreme in this ageless, vastest, limitless, space.

Sometimes we do get lonesome, Grandma.

Our love,
Maryanne

Dear Grandma,

… We had a pleasant treat when a number of red-coated North-West Mounted Policemen came galloping to our domain on their way to Saskatoon for some military manoeuvres to keep them fit. They are nice, polite Englishmen looking smart on their beautiful mounts with fresh accoutrements and trappings. Their commander and father drank the health of "Her Gracious Majesty, Queen Victoria" in buttermilk. The wagons and their dunnage came altogether too soon for us as we were enjoying the novelty of the brilliant company, and the superb symmetry of the well-groomed, prancing horses of the North-West Mounted Police.

The first of July, Dominion Day, dawned bright and gay. So were we, for had we not been promised a holiday with mother at the river? Quickly the chores were done. Harnessing Berry ox to the stone-boat, leaving Bright for Uncle Joe and father at the well, we loaded the big iron pot, wash-tub, soiled clothes, pails and barrels with our lunch aboard and off we happily set to the foot of our place at the river to fish, wash and play.

Queen's University Archives, Shortt-Haydon Collection, Locator #V009-Pgc-1412.

What lonely fourteen-year-old girl would not have admired dashing young men like these "Riders of the Plains" shown here during a morning drill at Regina.

We built a fire between the stones, set the pot on it full of water to heat while we scampered about. We found a great pile of buffalo bones where the bank drops steeply to the river, stones, trees and shrubs below. Long ago there must have been a stampede for the countless buffalo skeletons heaped high as ten-twelve feet from a mad headlong rush over the sharp bank indicates this is how they met their death, or the earth gave way under them. There are lots of buffalo paths to the river.

In a thorn bush nearby we found a hawk's nest with two young ones in it. Carefully we picked them up by the wings. Jen, being too close to peek into the nest, got her face scratched from their claws as they swooped toward her. While playing in the coarse gravel we were richer by pieces of petrified wood and a bit of petrified fish about two inches long. I have it yet.

When we returned, the water was ready so we helped wash the soiled clothes, and the sheep's wool for carding, later had a bath, hung the clothes to dry on the bushes while Jen and John attended to the fish lines. After a bit of lunch we hunted for berries, hopped on the stones and occasionally ran to the top of the bank slope road to keep an eye on the cattle which we had driven with us. We caught seven small fish, keeping two for father and Uncle Joe. We cleaned and fried the five for our picnic supper with cookies with a raisin in the centre for a treat.

Love from us all,
Maryanne.

Maryanne Caswell, *Pioneer Girl.*

20

Maria Adamowska

(1890–1961)

Maria Adamowska, née Olynyk, was born in the village of Mykhalkove in Western Ukraine. Her family immigrated to Saskatchewan in 1899 in search of liberty and land. They homesteaded in the Canora district for 11 years before moving to a farm at Hyas, Saskatchewan. In 1923 she began submitting poems to the *Ukrainian Voice* in Winnipeg. She lived for her last 20 years in Melville, Saskatchewan, where she was active in the Ukrainian community. The two articles about her early experiences, from which this excerpt is taken, were published in the *Almanac of the Ukrainian Voice* in 1937 and 1939. Although life improved significantly — and she was only nine when she came to Canada — her verses reflect a profound longing for her lost village. "Is the green maple tree / Still standing by the gate? / Has my young orchard / Grown up more beautiful?"

UKRAINIAN PRAIRIES

It is now forty years since my parents and I left our native village of Mykhalkove, the familiar thatched cottage, the beautiful orchard, and all those lovely scenes of my early, carefree childhood. Inexpressible grief seized my young heart when all our relatives and everyone from the village met in our yard to wish us Godspeed into the faraway, unknown world. The parting and the mournful keening were heartbreaking. Old and young wept as they bade us farewell, perhaps forever. And little girls, my schoolmates and girlfriends, wept with me.

The mere mention of school broke my heart. It was as if my soul presaged the loss of the most valuable treasure in my life, one which I would never recover. I loved school and learning as I loved my dear mother. But cruel fate had decreed against me.

...

My father was a man of firm resolve. He was glad to tear himself away from the Polish yoke once and for all. Hence, having temporarily borne the pain of parting with his homeland, he began to take an interest in the beautiful scenery as it flashed past the windows of the train and began to weave golden visions of that fabulous land, Canada.

Mother, on the other hand, was tender-hearted. Of all the trials that had been her lot in life, this one was the most bitter. Whenever father had mentioned going to Canada, she had started to cry. And she cried all the way on the train and missed seeing the lovely sights in God's good world.

We arrived in Hamburg. Here we had to wait a few days for our ship. My childish fancy was captured by the sight of huge dogs hitched to carts full of large milk cans. The milk vendors shouted as they went about making their deliveries.

Finally, our ship arrived. It anchored some distance away from the shore, and we were transported to it in a small boat.

Aboard the ship, we met more of our countrymen from Galicia and Bukovina who were also on their way to Canada....

Finally, we sailed into port at Halifax. On the shore, a crowd of people stared at us, some out of curiosity, some out of contempt. Our men, particularly those from Galicia, were dressed like gentlemen for the voyage, but the women and children travelled in their everyday peasant costumes. The older men from Bukovina attracted attention to themselves by their waist-length hair — greased with reeking lard — and by their smelly sheepskin coats. Perhaps that was the reason why the English

*A group of Galician immigrants arriving in Quebec circa 1911 looks understand-
ably apprehensive about what faces them in a strange new land out west.*

people stopped their noses and glued their eyes upon us — a strange
spectacle, indeed.

In Halifax, we boarded a train and continued on our journey. As
we sped across Ontario with its rocks, hills, and tunnels, we were afraid
we were coming to the end of the world. The heart of many a man sank
to his heels, and the women and children raised such lamentation as
defies description.

At last we arrived in Winnipeg. At that time, Winnipeg was very
much like any other small farmers' town. From the train we were taken
to the immigration home....

...

[From Winnipeg, we went to Yorkton, Saskatchewan. There we hired
a rig which took us more than thirty miles farther north. At long last,
after a miserable trip — we were nearly devoured alive by mosquitoes
— we managed to reach our destination, the home of our acquaintances.

Our host, who had emigrated to Canada a year or two before, had written us to boast of the prosperity he had attained in such a short time. He said that he had a home like a mansion, a large cultivated field, and that his wife was dressed like a lady. In short, he depicted Canada as a country of incredible abundance whose borders were braided with sausage like some fantastic land in a fairy tale.

How great was our disenchantment when we approached that mansion of his and an entirely different scene met our eyes! It was actually just a small log cabin, only partly plastered and roofed with sod. Beside the cabin was a garden plot which had been dug with a spade. The man's face was smeared with dirt from ear to ear, and he looked weird, like some unearthly creature. He was grubbing up stumps near the house, and his wife was poking away in the garden. She reminded us of Robinson Crusoe on an uninhabited island. She was suntanned like a gypsy and was dressed in old, torn overalls. A wide-brimmed hat covered her head.

When mother saw this scarecrow, she started crying again. Later on, father reprimanded the man for writing us such nonsense. But his only answer was, "Let someone else have a taste of our good life here." ...]

Our troubles and worries were only just beginning. The house was small, and there were eighteen of us jammed within its four walls. What was one to do?

My father had brought some money with him, and with it he bought a cow and, later, a horse. Needless to say, I was the cowherd.

One day, as I was herding the cow some two miles away from home, I unexpectedly came upon a tent. In front of it was a bonfire, and in a circle around it, several elderly Indians were squatting. A couple of them were busy skinning some animals, and a squaw was stringing the flesh on a stick and roasting it over the fire. At this sight, I froze on the spot. I felt the urge to run, but my feet refused to obey me. What's more, I could tell that these strange people had spied me, though all they could see was my head, poked above the grass. To my bewilderment, the woman started to move towards me with a piece of her roast. Its appetizing aroma tickled my nose. She offered me the meat, gave me a pat on the back, and rejoined her group. How I enjoyed that meat — as though it were some rare delicacy! I discovered afterwards that it was roasted gopher.

...

Winter was setting in. Dreading the idea of having to spend the season in such cramped quarters, my father dug a cave in a riverbank, covered it with turf, and there was our apartment, all ready to move into. Oh, how fortunate we felt! We would not have traded that root cellar for a royal palace. [To this spot, we carried hay in bed sheets on our backs and stacked it. We also dragged firewood on our backs and made other preparations.

Day by day, our provisions ran lower and lower. The older folk were able to put up with hunger, but the famished children howled pitifully, like wolves.

One day I sneaked into our hostess's garden and pulled a turnip. Then I slipped out of the patch and ran as fast as I could into a gorge where I planned to hide myself in the tall grass and enjoy a real treat. Unfortunately, our hostess spied me, grabbed a club, and chased after me with the speed of a demon. To escape, I hid in some tall grass, but this heartless woman searched until she found me. There she stood over me and, as she raised her club, hissed, "You detestable intruder! One blow with this, and you'll be dead like a dog."

...

And so, for a piddling turnip, I almost paid with my life.]

Came winter. Our cow stopped giving milk. Aside from bread, there was nothing to eat at home. Was one to gnaw the walls? One time I happened to notice tears rolling down mother's cheeks as she sipped something from a small pot. We children began to weep with her. "Mother, why are you crying? Won't you let us taste what you're eating?"

Mother divided the gruel among us. She tried to say something, but all she could manage was "My chil —"; further words died on her lips. Only a moan of anguish escaped from her breast. We learned afterwards that, late in the fall, mother had visited the garden of our former host and painstakingly raked the ground for potatoes that had been too small to be worth picking at potato-digging time. She had found a few tiny ones, no larger than hazel nuts. From these potatoes, she had made a gruel that tasted like potato soup, and it was this gruel which we children shared, tears flooding our eyes. Who knows how we would have managed if father had not brought his gun from the old country. With it he went hunting, and we had game all winter.

Before spring arrived, father went to look for a farm. He found one some fifteen miles to the west of us, and we began to build a house. [We dug a round pit in the ground about five yards in diameter, just deep enough to scrape the black earth off the top and reach clay underneath, We mixed hay and water with the clay and kneaded it with our bare feet. With this clay, we plastered our house. In the spring, we moved into it. By that time, all our provisions had run out.]

And so it was that father left home one day, on foot, prepared to tramp hundreds of miles to find a job. He left us without a piece of bread, to the mercy of fate.

While father was away, mother dug a plot of ground and planted the wheat she had brought from the old country, tied up in a small bundle. Every day, she watered it with her tears.

That done, there was no time to waste; every moment was precious. Mother and I began to clear our land. But since I was hardly strong enough for the job, I helped by grabbing hold of the top of each bush and pulling on it while mother cut the roots with the axe. Next we dug the ground with spades. How well did I do? At best, I had barely enough strength to thrust half the depth of the blade into the ground, no deeper. But that did not excuse me from digging. Where the ground was hard, mother had to correct my work, and thus the two of us cleared and dug close to four acres of land.

We lived on milk. One meal would consist of sweet milk followed by sour milk; the next meal would consist of sour milk followed by sweet milk. We looked like living corpses.

[In the beginning of our life in Canada, old and young alike had to work grievously hard, often in the cold and in hunger. The effects of this hard work can now be painfully felt in even the tiniest bones of our bodies....]

Our Rumanian neighbour, who lived a mile from our place, had made himself a small handmill for grinding wheat into flour. In the fall, when our wheat was ripe, mother reaped it very thoroughly, every last head of it, rubbed the kernels out, winnowed the grain, and poured it into a sack. Then she sent me with this grain — about eight pounds of it — to have it ground at our neighbour's mill.

It was the first time I had ever been to his place. As soon as I entered the vestibule of the house, I could see the hand mill in the corner. Now a new problem faced me: I had not the faintest idea how to operate the mill, and there was no one around to show me. I sat down and began to cry. After a while, the neighbour's wife showed up and spoke to me, but I could not understand her so I just kept on crying. I had the feeling that she was scolding me for sneaking into her house. I pointed to the bag of wheat. She understood what I wanted, pointed to the hand mill, and went inside the house, leaving the door open. She sat down at the table, picked up a piece of bread which was as dark as the ground we walked on, dipped it in salt, and munched away at it.

As I watched her, I almost choked with grief. Oh, how strong was my urge to throw myself at her feet and plead for at least one bite of that bread. But, as she obviously was not thinking of me, I got ahold of myself. That piece of bread might well have been the last she had in the house. That experience gave me the most profound shock of my entire life. No one can fully appreciate what I went through unless he has lived through something similar himself.

Continually swallowing my saliva, I kept grinding the wheat until I had finished. Then I ran home with that little bit of flour, joyfully looking forward to the moment when we, too, would have bread.

But my joy quickly evaporated. Mother pondered a moment and said, "This will make two or three loaves of bread, and the flour will be all gone. Not enough to eat and not enough to feast our eyes upon. I'm going to cook cornmeal for you; it will last longer." And so we teased ourselves with cornmeal for some time.

On his way home from the other side of Brandon, where he'd been working, father stopped at Yorkton and bought a fifty-pound sack of flour. He carried it home on his back every inch of the twenty-eight miles. When we saw him coming home, we bounced with excitement and greeted him with joyous laughter mixed with tears. And all this excitement over the prospect of a piece of bread! Father had not earned much money, for he had lost a lot of time job-hunting. Then, at work, he had fallen from a stack onto the tines of a pitchfork and been laid up for a long time. But he had managed to earn something like twenty dollars, enough for flour to last us for a time.

The coming of winter presented new problems. We had nothing to wear on our feet. Something had to be done about that. Mother had brought a couple of woollen sheets from the old country. From these she sewed us footwear that kept our feet warm all winter.

That winter our horse died. We were now left with only one horse and he was just a year-old colt, though he looked like a two-year-old. Father made a harness from some ropes, and a sled, and began to break him in.

[… Even in winter we had no rest. We had settled in a low-lying area. In the summertime, water lay everywhere, and the croaking of frogs filled the air. And it never rained but poured in those days. Often the downpour continued for two or three weeks without a letup. In the winter, the water in the lakes froze up, the wells — always few in number — dried up, and there was nothing one could do about it. We were concerned not so much about ourselves as about our few head of livestock, which would have no water. We could not let them die; a way had to be found to obtain water for them.

Father found a piece of tin somewhere, shaped it into a trough, built an enclosure out of stones, placed the trough over it, built a fire in the enclosure under the trough, kept the trough filled with snow, and, as the snow melted, collected the water in a tub at the bottom end of the trough. But this was not the best way to water cattle. A cow could drink up a couple of tubs of water at a time and then look around and moo for more.

As a result, we messed around with snow all winter long, until at times the marrow in our bones was chilled. And talk about snow in those days! Mountains of it! Your cattle might be lowing pitifully in the stable, and you could not get to them because heaps of snow blocked your way. It might take a hard morning's work before a tunnel could be dug to the stable, and the cattle fed.]

During Lent, we ran out of flour. Although there were still a few cents in the house, it was not easy to get to Yorkton because of snow-drifts. One evening, father decided to call on our Rumanian neighbour and borrow some flour to tide us over until we could buy our own. He was gone a long time. We waited until midnight, but still no father. And so we went to bed thinking that perhaps the two men had had a lot to talk about for the Rumanian spoke a little Ukrainian. Then, too, maybe father had decided to stay overnight.

In the morning, father dragged himself home, more dead than alive. Without suspecting anything wrong, mother asked, "Did you have to stay there overnight? Was it so far to come home?"

Then father began to explain. "What I lived through last night, I would hate to see happen even to my worst enemy. When I got to the neighbour's, I only stayed for about an hour. I explained why I had come, he let me have half a bag of flour, and I left for home. But the blizzard was so fierce that I strayed from my path and went God knows where. I tramped all night with the bag of flour on my back. I was so exhausted that several times I felt like sitting down for a rest. However, I had enough presence of mind to realize that if I did, I would never get up again. So I summoned all my strength and trudged on.

"Came dawn, I looked about but in no way could I get my bearings. Not far off I saw a house. Worn down by exhaustion, I proceeded to crawl toward it. Even as I got closer to the house, I still could not recognize it. It was a strange house. I had never seen it before. I concluded that I must have wandered a long way during the night. But there I was. I knocked at the door. A man answered and came out. Horrified to see me in this plight, he clutched his hair and exclaimed, 'Oh, dear! You didn't get home last night, Mr. Oliynyk? Oh, you poor soul!'

"It was then that I got my bearings. I recognized the man — he was the same one I had visited last night. He took me in. I got warmed up and recounted my unfortunate experience. The man then dressed up, put the sack of flour on his back, took me to within sight of our house, and went back home."

...

Father's mishap was not without its harmful effect on his health. He was confined to bed for over a month. His fingers were frozen, and all the skin on his feet peeled off. We barely escaped becoming orphans, and father barely escaped ending up as an invalid for the rest of his life.

[Ours was a life of hard work, misery, and destitution. Things got a little better only after we acquired a yoke of oxen to work with. But when we first got them, we experienced some unhappy and frustrating moments.

The first time that we harnessed the oxen, we hitched them to the plow. As soon as the plowshare dug into the ground, presto! our oxen balked and refused to budge. Then, as if acting on command, they both lay down. Try as we might to make them get up on their feet — pleading as best we knew how, then persuading them with the switch — the dumb beasts would only lie down again.

We had a spirited but hair-brained young horse which was causing us a lot of grief. Father turned to me: "As the last resort, let's have that confounded creature here."

We hitched the horse in front of the oxen and — "Giddap!" The horse tugged with all his might but the oxen would not budge. It was as if they were under a curse. The plow jerked forward just far enough to shear the heel piece of the ox on the right. Then the horse gave another tug, and the traces snapped. This time the horse whirled around in a flash, reared on his hind legs, and lunged at the horns of the oxen. One of them pierced his shoulder blade. It all happened so suddenly — like the crack of a whip.

We were all in tears. Father cursed. We unhitched the injured creatures and went back to digging with our spades until the animals had licked at their wounds and regained strength.

...]

That autumn father's earnings were a little more substantial. He was able to buy another cow and another steer. And he bought me a pair of shoes and material for a skirt. Those shoes meant more to me than any ordinary ones. It seemed as though they came right out of Ivan Franko's tale about Abou-Kazem's slippers. They were about the size of a medium-sized sled. They were made from leather that was no more pliable than tin, and for lacing each had six eyes as large as a cow's; you could not have missed them on the darkest of nights with an inch-and-a-half thickness of rope. They pinched and burned my feet badly enough to bring tears to my eyes.

As for their durability, suffice it to say that when one of us girls got married, she handed the shoes down to the younger sister, and the process was repeated until four of us had worn them, each for a few years. And who knows how many more generations those shoes would have survived if it had not been for mother. She got so disgusted with them that she threw them into the stove one day and burned them....

Year by year the cultivated area of our farm grew in size. And when the field got too large to be harvested with sickles, father had to buy a binder. For the first couple of years we used it, we hitched our oxen to it. That was a miserable experience. Cutting grain of medium height posed no problem, but if it was heavy or lying flat and you had to give the binder a little more speed, you could not make the oxen move faster even by lighting a fire under them. They kept to the same slow pace no matter what. The only way to cope with this problem was to buy another horse. A team of horses made harvesting so much easier.

During the long winter evenings, I taught younger children to read in Ukrainian. Among my students were a girl of non-Ukrainian descent and an elderly gentleman. There were no schools anywhere around in those days. Children grew up like barbarians....

A cheerful harvesting scene from a Ukrainian farm circa 1918 suggests that early difficulties have been triumphantly overcome.

[We had quite a few books at home. Father had brought a lot of them from the old country, all on serious subjects. Later on, when Ukrainian newspapers began to be published, none of them escaped father's attention. Even if he had to go without food and live on water for a whole week, he found the money for newspaper subscriptions. Since there were several literate people in our community, they used to get together at our home on the long winter evenings, to read the papers and discuss their contents. Many a sunrise found these men, though weary from the previous day's hard toil, going without a wink of sleep to forge a happier lot for themselves and their children.

…]

As for churches or Ukrainian priests, you could not have found one if you'd searched the country with a fine-tooth comb. Occasionally a priest would stray our way, but he was what we called an "Indian priest," and we could not understand him, nor he us. Our poor settlers consulted among themselves and decided to meet every Sunday and sing at least those parts of the liturgy that were meant to be sung by the cantor. Since our house was large enough, that was where the meetings were held. On Sunday morning, everyone hurried to our house the way one would to church. The late Fedir Stratychuk … was an excellent cantor. Even yet I can hear his voice in my mind. W. Gabora and my father harmonized with him, and all the others followed them. And so it was that we were able to gratify, at least partially, the longings of our souls.

In due course, the Bukovinians built themselves a church in which services were at first conducted by a visiting Russian priest. Often we were invited to attend but we could not understand their service, which was in Rumanian.

Later, other priests, the so-called *Serafymtsi*, made their appearance. [One of them, Julian Bohonko, announced the first blessing of the *paska* at the home of Tserkowniak, ten miles away from our place. What rejoicing! Mother began to bake *paska* and to decorate *pysanky*, and tears of joy rolled down her emaciated cheeks.

That year Easter came very early. It was the Saturday before Easter, but only here and there was the snow beginning to melt. The day before, a severe blizzard had piled up banks of snow and drifted over all the roads. But there was no power on earth which could have stopped us from carrying out our plans.

Mother wrapped the Easter goodies in an immaculately white tablecloth, and in the afternoon father and I set out on foot toward Tserkowniak's. At first everything seemed to be going fine, and I managed to keep up with father, but as we got farther along — good Lord! I sank into snow up to my waist and did not have the strength to get out. Father had to help me, though not without a few harsh words. With great difficulty, we reached our destination.

Although we were dead tired, our souls were heartened early Sunday morning by the glad Easter hymn, "Christ is Risen from the Dead." Immediately after the service, we hastened to return home. It was already dark when we got back. We had fasted all day long, not only father and I, but also those at home, waiting with deep reverence for the gifts from God which had been blessed by the priest....]

...

In 1908, father traded farms with an Englishman, and our family moved thirty miles farther north, to the Hyas district. [The origin of the name "Hyas" goes back to the time when our people used oxen for driving and urged them on by shouting "*Heys, ta heys!*" That *heys* appealed so much to the English people that they named the district "Hyas." Before that, it was called "Ulric."

By moving to Hyas, we had to start all over again and suffer the same hardships as in the beginning. But hope of better times lifted our spirits and gave us courage and strength to face future labours.]

Maria Adamowaska, "Beginning in Canada" in Harry Piniuta, editor and translator, *Land of Pain, Land of Promise: First Person Accounts by Ukrainian Pioneers 1891–1914.*

21

Mary Schäffer (Warren)

(1861–1939)

Mary Townsend Schäffer Warren, née Sharples, was born into a cultivated and affluent Quaker family in West Chester, Pennsylvania. A precocious child, she shared her father's passion for natural history, learning much about "the story of stones, grasses and the small things people pay no attention to." In 1889, she married Dr. Charles Schäffer of Philadelphia, a physician and amateur botanist who was 23 years her senior. That summer she saw the Rockies for the first time when they travelled from Montreal to Vancouver on the new CPR train. In 1891 the Schäffers began over a decade of summer visits to the area, gathering specimens and then retreating to a comfortable CPR hotel to dry and press them.

By 1903, Mary had lost her husband, her parents, and fortune. With the guidance of a family friend and future prime minister, R.B. Bennett, she recouped her financial losses and undertook further expeditions. Despite the fact that she had not learned to make a bed until the age of 18 and was terrified of horses and bears, she learned to camp, travel on horseback, explore caves, and climb mountains. *Alpine Flora of the Canadian Rocky Mountains* (1907), with a text by Stewardson Brown, based on Dr. Schäffer's collections, was illustrated with her watercolours and photographs. (A skilled artist and photographer, she had studied with a famous American flower painter.) Expeditions in 1907 and a trip to the forgotten Maligne Lake in 1908 ("Lake Louise is a pearl; Lake Maligne is a whole string of pearls") led to *Old Indian Trails*, of which *The New York Times* wrote, "it is difficult to decide just what impresses us most: the excellence of the writing, the picturesqueness of the country described [or] the personality of the author herself."

Eventually, Mary settled in Banff, furnishing her mountain bungalow with eighteenth-century family antiques and artworks, Aboriginal artefacts, and a parrot. In 1915 she married her long-time mountain guide, William "Billy" Warren (many years her junior), who became a successful businessman. Mary wrote numerous articles for newspapers and scholarly journals, gave lantern slide lectures to learned societies, and lobbied for the protection of her beloved Rockies. Known to the Stoney as *Yahe-Weha* (Mountain Woman), she aptly summed up her life when she wrote, at 72, "I hate doing the ordinary thing."

EXPLORATION IN THE ROCKIES

And now with all necessary things gathered together, with trunks packed, not with frills and furbelows, but with blankets and "glucose," air-beds and evaporated milk, with "Abercrombie" shoes and dried spinach, we were off across the continent by the first of June, 1907. At Winnipeg we picked up some highly recommended tents, made of "Egyptian sail-cloth," exceedingly light weight and small bulk, though later we found they had their faults — "but that is another story." Our trunks had been checked at Montreal to the little station of Laggan [Lake Louise Station] on the Canadian Pacific Railway — our point of departure into the mountains, and in calm faith we dropped down the hill to Field, to get our breath and bearings, and wait for the bad weather to clear. This seemed likely to occur at any moment; for a fiercer winter than that of 1906 and '07 had not been known in the memory of the "oldest inhabitant"; the spring had been equally bad, and our reception was enough to cool even greater ardour than ours. We decided on June 20th as the latest day for the start; if the snows were not off the Bow Pass by that time, they should be, and even though it was so cold and chill, it was time by the calendar for the

Saskatchewan to rise and on this point we meant to take no chances. Our entire outfit of horses and saddlery were for the time being in Banff, so we hied ourselves hither, primarily to investigate the "grub-pile," but in reality to behold the gathering of the new family. Why try to sketch our opinion? There were but two members on exhibition, one was "Buck," the sight of whom was enough to kill the most deep-seated case of horse-pride. Long and gaunt, with a hide of yellow tan, a mane and tail of black, dragged in from his free open life on the plains where he had never known a care, shod under the bitterest protest, he was a depressing-looking beast to us who had no idea where to look for the best points of a trail-horse. If we had been guilty of speaking in an off-hand, nonchalant way of "our" horses, we stopped right there and engaged our minds with bacon and beans. The future, however, proved the homely and unpopular Buck to have been made of sterling stuff; strong and willing, he had but one fault, a pair of violently active heels. No one ever received greater respect behind his back than Buck, and it soon became second nature to make a wide detour when passing him. His companions were not always as cautious as we, and I have never seen him forget a slight, or fail to punish it, not once but many times, by a resounding, sickening thud in the ribs of the offender when off his guard.…

...

As I have said previously, our plans were to leave civilisation on June 20th. Our troubles, however, began on the eighteenth, at the awful discovery that our most valuable trunk, containing bedding, clothing, and photographic material for the expedition, was not at Laggan, to which point it had been shipped the week before. It is here that I start the record.

June 20th — The day has come but not as we had planned. Two days ago it was discovered that a precious trunk was lost, and the agent comfortingly told us: "It must be somewhere between Montreal and Vancouver, if it has not been shunted off to Seattle." This gave us at least a wide field for imagination, and a fit of the horrors at the same time, as we saw a long-planned trip dissolving into nothingness for the want of a few necessary articles, while we could but gaze upon and admire the stony indifference of the four or five agents, to whom we had confided our troubles in all their harrowing details, yet remained so sublimely impassive. With determination born of despair, we hastened to Calgary and repurchased the few articles possible, though valuable photographic plates and a precious air-mattress were not to be replaced for love or money.

Incidentally we poured our woes into the ears of the baggage-master-in-chief at Calgary, not because we really expected sympathy, but more as a safety-valve to our pent-up despair. His actions astonished us quite as much as those of his subordinates. In ten minutes reports were overhauled, and messages flying over the wires in every direction; the trunk had passed through Calgary and the baggage-master was confident it lay between there and its intended destination. In two hours that executive and energetic gentleman was aboard the west-bound train with us, and rigorously inspecting the baggage department of every little wayside station along the line to Laggan. At last our poor little tragedy had touched a railroad heart, and even were that trunk never found, we would have with our new and ill-assorted garments a comforting sense of sympathy from one human soul. Our newfound friend's kindness and energy were rewarded. The trunk was calmly reposing at the Lake Louise chalet, where proprietor, baggageman, teamster, and station-agent had all vowed it was not, and at least there was one cause for thankfulness, that none of the searchers had fallen over it and broken a bone, as it was found in a most dangerously conspicuous place. At sight of it, all sorrow fled, and we could have hugged that dirty, travel-worn object with joy, whose every scar was by this time a point of beauty.

As for that baggage-master, he will live in our hearts as long as the memory of the trip remains. It is not time but circumstances which make us our friends; this total stranger had stood by us in our hour of need; through him the missing valuables had come to light, and were shortly distributed upon the backs of the horses. The duffel-bags fell into line, sugar and bacon joined hands, and with a wave of good-bye and a cheery *au revoir* from our new friend, we set our faces to the north and the fire-swept hills of the Bow Valley. A brand new Waterbury watch said it was high noon. The low clouds, laden with sleet and snow, intimated that it was already far in the day, but there was emphatic reason for choosing a camp-ground far from the railroad track where the constant shifting of engines was liable to bring an untimely end to some of our family.

It seemed, as we wound slowly through the sparsely standing, burnt timber, that we had not left all calamity behind, but that it stalked beside us, hurling defiance in our faces with each gust of wind that swept angrily by, and reminded us of its power as the gaunt black trees crashed down about us. The new horses, accustomed to the open prairies, and nervous with the great packs they had never known before, erratically tore here and there in their endeavour to avoid the falling trees, and many times came very near to being struck. The fearful storms of the winter of 1906 and '07 had strewn the trail with timber, so that between jumping logs, chopping those we could not jump, and ploughing through the most disheartening muskeg, we at last, at nightfall, threw off the packs on a knoll with muskeg everywhere. Our first camp-fire was built in mud, we ate in mud, slept in mud, and our horses stalked around in mud, nibbling the few spears of grass which the late cold spring had permitted to sprout. The new air-mattresses came well into play, for we felt a comforting certainty that if we broke through the muskeg we would at least float. It did seem a rather dreary breaking-in for a whole summer's camping trip and, if it was to continue, somewhat of a trial to both spirit and flesh, but tired as we were, we crawled into our sleeping-bags saying, "It might have been worse!"

The next day was Friday. A superstitious person would have revelled in our woes. Clouds were hanging ominously low, a sickly sun tried hard to shine, gave it up in despair, and sank into oblivion. Beds were rolled up and tents folded, while hail struck contemptuously at us. Only too thankful to leave that marsh behind us, we rushed into worse troubles. Not a hundred yards from camp we plunged into the worst muskeg we had so far encountered. Our horses, as yet untrained, recognised no leader, and went down one by one; heavily laden, they were helpless in that fearful quagmire. Buck, who was loaded with about two hundred pounds of bacon and flour, was soon under water, pack and all, and was only saved from a watery grave by a quick application of a knife to the ropes, when down went the cargo and up came Buck. Both were quickly landed on more substantial soil, and the bacon had had its first bath, but never its last. I have been asked frequently the definition of "muskeg." The most lucid one I could think of would be, "get in a bad one, and you will see that there are no words adequate to its description." It is not a quicksand, it is not a marsh. In many instances, it looks like a lovely mountain stream flowing between banks rank with a rich growth of waving grasses; again, it is a damp-looking spot, but still overgrown with the same attractive, waving green. If not yet thoroughly acquainted with the signs, just watch your horse, he will begin to snuff the ground beneath him, and if there is any way around, it is well not to force him through that which his own judgment tells him to avoid.

...

Bow Park was our stopping-place for the night, a fine camp-ground for man and beast after the trials of the two previous days. For a number of years it has been a favourite resting-place for hunters and the few travellers who have been in that vicinity, and consequently porcupines are numerous. Poor little fellows! With not a hard thought in their hearts for a soul, gentle and almost tame, they are the bane of the camper's existence. Like other animals I could mention, they are fond of good living, but unlike some people, if good things are not to be had, they will fill up with what is on hand. The consequence is that bacon and saddlery, shoes and ropes, soap and tent-skirts are all grist for their insatiable little mills. Our sleep at Bow Park was broken by ominous rustlings of stiff quills dragging on the ground, gentle squeaks, then a sortie, a dull thud, and the listeners knew one more poor creature had come to his death because of an ungovernable appetite. Then we would turn over with the virtuous thought that we had made pillows of our shoes, that the cameras were under the bed, and other valuables hung from the ridge-pole, so that dozens of the enemy could do us no serious harm. My heart felt a little sad the next morning, there were so many inanimate bodies lying about who would never chew straps any more, and even a great corner out of a slab of valuable bacon failed to leave me with a hard thought for our amiable, neighbourly little enemy, the porcupine.

The day was Sunday; for the first time during the trip the sun rose warm and bright over the great crags hanging above us. Up and off beside the sparkling Bow River the foot-way improved, but the sun grew hotter and hotter, and we knew it meant but one thing — the snow-fields so long locked by the tardy winter would be pouring their torrents into the large river (the Saskatchewan) we must soon cross.

...

Never have I seen the lake look more beautiful than on that fair morning in June. It was as blue as the sky could make it, the ice reflected the most vivid emerald green; in the distance a fine glacier swept to the lake-shore, whose every crevasse was a brilliant blue line; the bleak grey mountains towered above, at our feet the bright spring flowers bloomed in the green grass, and over all hung the deep blue sky. Around us hovered the peace which only the beauty and silence of the hills could portray.

From the summit of the Bow Pass (6800 feet high) we gazed to the north on as fair a picture as dreams could suggest. Winter was reluctantly loosening its hard grasp upon those open meadow-like slopes; the snow lilies (*Erythronium grandiflorum*), the pale pink spring beauties (*Claytonia lanceolata*), and the bright yellow violets (*Viola sempervirens*), were flirting with the butterflies and bees, pretending to be utterly oblivious to the mountains of snow all about them....

Camping on the far side of the pass in a stretch of burnt timber, we shook ourselves into camp routine. Not so with our horses, they were to be cajoled with no such thought that their keepers had chosen the best there was in that section of the country for them; and if there is one thing a trail horse possesses, it is a clear recollection of the place he stopped in "last night." ...

It was this evening that we had our first glimpse of mountain-goat. While waiting for the coffee-pot to boil, one of us picked up a very strong pair of binoculars, and stood gazing into the pocket which we knew held

Peyto Lake, wondering what life there was in the hollow of those hills. The westering sun was drawing long purple shadows in sweeping lines into the valleys, a tiny chirp from the almost silent birds of the north, and we felt the coming slumber of night in the atmosphere. Suddenly a moving white spot far on the mountain opposite, then a second, then a third, caused the eye to steady and the hand to grow rigid. "A bunch of goat!" she gasped, and oh! what beauties they were! Strolling out on the impassable grass-grown cliffs after the heat of the day, with no fear in their movements, they were taking their own bacon and beans before the sun set in that sea of mountains. The coffee was forgotten, the bannock burned, and by the time the men and the truants had returned we were still able to point out "our" goat through the evening haze, with far more pride than if we had shot them.

The trail down Bear Creek is one of beauty from its very inception. We were up and off with the sunrise the next morning; it grew hotter and hotter, and in our minds we were watching the steady rise of the Saskatchewan River, still a day's journey off. There could be little hurry with such heavily loaded horses, so we camped that night at the lower end of the second Wild Fowl Lake. Lying as it does under the shadow of Pyramid Peak, the view was superb, while the music from the falling avalanches left no words for our thoughts. Just as the purple shadows fell, a silvery crescent stole into the deepening sky, and by its soft light we could still catch the outline of the avalanches as they fell with reverberating roar down the precipices opposite our tents. The camp-fire crackled, on the soft breeze came the distant tinkle of the horse-bells, a mosquito hummed, a night-hawk with his raucous cry swept past, the moon's rays filtered through the Spruce boughs, the fire died down and the camp slept. And they ask if one grows lonely. Lonely? How can one, when all Nature sings the evening hymn?

A third day now added its heat to the other two, and the chief topic of conversation was the rising waters of the Saskatchewan. About noon we met a bunch of horses, fully sixty head, coming in from the Kootenai Plains where they had wintered. Tying up our own horses, we watched the procession headed by Tom Wilson, their owner, pass by. Then came the flower of the band, "Nibs," who was to leave his chums and follow the vicissitudes of his mistress for the next four months. Just an Indian-bred pony, with a coat that only one who loved him could say was beautiful, he proved himself a perfect trail-horse. The saddle was soon transferred from the reliable old Pinto, and Nibs was presented to his new rider.

...

Having caught Nibs, we waved a last "good-bye" to Tom who now started ahead with his huge band, he for Laggan and the tourists, we for the unknown north. Singing out, "Sorry for you going through the Bow muskegs with all those horses!" — he called back, "Sorry for you crossing the Saskatchewan!" and our hearts went flop as we realised the time for that crossing was almost with us. For Tom, who had both wintered and summered on the Saskatchewan several years, knew the power and the danger of those rapidly rising waters and we knew that he knew. By 3:30 in the afternoon we had crossed Bear Creek at its mouth. The water was boiling and plunging over the huge boulders and warned us that there

Mary Schäffer Warren astride the faithful Nibs. He shared her adventures for four months and although not beautiful except to those who loved him — as she clearly did — "he was a perfect trail-horse."

was no time to lose. All got over that small stream safely which is not always the case, as the great force of the water is apt to cause a horse to stumble in so rough a river bed. One mile to the west of the entrance of Bear Creek into the Saskatchewan, there is one of the best fords on that river if you are bound for the north. On the ocean-like beach we took our stand, while "K,." mounting the only horse of the bunch which we knew could take care of himself in the great river (Nibs, of course), struck into the stream. The little fellow showed not the slightest hesitation as he took to the water but seemed rather proud than otherwise of showing off his ability to his new acquaintances.

Those were anxious moments as we saw "K" cross branch after branch of the great river. He slowly waded in, the water would creep higher and higher about the plucky pony's shoulders till horse and rider almost disappeared from view; they would then back out and try it farther up or down, then emerge to a bar and work over the next channel in the same way. At last after fifteen minutes, we saw him, a distant speck in the brilliant setting sun on the north shore. He waved his hand, and we knew that our yet untried horses could be got over without much danger of being washed down-stream.

Yes, we got over without having to swim, but one never wants to take those large rivers, which are fed by the great ice fields, other than seriously; the power of the water is that of the avalanche from the mountain-side, and it sweeps along throbbingly, intermittently, cruelly, and relentlessly. The horse, his head facing up stream a little to avoid the full blow of the onrushing waters, bends his whole body to the force; the rider, to help him in the balance, leans in an opposite direction; and as the water rises higher and higher, the feet have an inclination to fly up and the body to float out of the saddle. The temperature of all the rivers in that section of the country is about 42°, and as the water creeps to the waistline one longs for the courage to turn back. As the deepest point is reached, all sensation of movement and advance ceases, every thought but that of self-preservation has gone bobbing down with the river which is flashing by, and it is then that you think of your guide's words of caution: "If your horse rolls over, get out of your saddle, cling to his mane, tail, or any thing you can get hold of, but *don't let go of him altogether*! He may get out, you *never* will, alone." These are of course first sensations. Eventually when one has learned to trust his horse, becomes accustomed to knowing what to do, realises that caution and judgment mean safety, much of the danger is cancelled, but I should never advise a belittling of the possibilities for accidents in these mountain streams. It is the very contempt for danger which has caused so many of the accidents which are recorded.

Three days' easy travel brought us out on the Emerald Lake road near Field. Special toilets had been arranged on the previous afternoon; sundry grease-spots had been removed from our skirts, a scarlet neckerchief had been washed, some wool shirts ditto, two or three pairs of shoes, with toes and heels intact, came up from the depths of the duffel-bags, and shaving soap had been liberally laid on. A smile of sincere admiration went round when we collected to behold our united elegance of appearance on the morning we started on our last ride. As for the horses, every one bore his inspection well, not one missing, and all in far better

Courtesy of Whyte Museum, b527-na-78.

Mary Schäffer Warren's name is permanently linked with her historic trip to the mystical Maligne Lake in 1908. In 1911, she returned with her young nephew Paul Sharpless and sister-in-law Caroline for a surveying expedition on behalf of the Parks Department.

condition than when we left Laggan in June. Is it any wonder their master was proud of their appearance and we proud to be in such company as I am sure we were?

And then we struck the highway and on it a carriage with people in it! Oh! The tragedy of the comparison! The woman's gown was blue. I think her hat contained a white wing. I only saw it all in one awful flash from the corner of my right eye, and I remember distinctly that she had *gloves on*. Then I suddenly realised that our own recently brushed-up garments were frayed and worn and our buckskin coats had a savage cast, that my three companions looked like Indians, and that the lady gazing at us belonged to another world. It was then that I wanted my wild free life back again, yet step by step I was leaving it behind.

We entered the little mountain town of Field just as the whistles shrieked out the noon hour. How garish it all sounded to ears that had for months heard nothing but Nature's finer notes. Then we grasped the hands of waiting friends (who told us it was Mr. and Mrs. Rudyard Kipling we had passed on the road), and fled from the eyes of the curious tourist to that civilized but perfect luxury — the bath-tub.

"Trouble at the Start" in E.J. Hart, ed., *A Hunter of Peace: Mary Schäffer's Old Indian Trails of the Canadian Rockies.*

22

Ella C. Sykes

(1863–1939)

Ella Constance Sykes, born in Devon, was known in her day as "the brav-
est woman in Europe." She was the daughter of a clergyman who had
been honorary chaplain to Queen Victoria. From 1881 to 1883, Sykes
attended Lady Margaret Hall. (She and her sister Edith were among the
earliest women Oxford graduates.) In 1894 her brother Percy, a soldier,
diplomat, and explorer, asked her to accompany him as he set up a consulate at Kerman, in what is now Iran. She accepted joyfully. "I had been
civilized all my life," she later wrote, "and now I had a sense of freedom
and expansion which quickened the blood and made the pulse beat high."
She acted as hostess at the consulate, learned the language and history of
Persia (she wrote a book for children based on Firdausi's *Book of Kings*),
and was the first woman to ride from the Caspian Sea to India, a journey
of two thousand miles by side-saddle.

In 1911, on behalf of the Colonial Intelligence League for Educated
Women, she toured Canada to learn about opportunities for educated
women who migrated there. Perhaps in emulation of her brother, who
was also a spy, she posed as an indigent gentlewoman looking for work.
In 1915, she travelled with her brother on a marathon wartime journey to
Kashgar in Chinese Turkestan, where he served as consul and she handled
difficult circumstances, including wild mountain journeys by yak, with

characteristic aplomb. She lectured to learned societies and was secretary of the Royal Asiatic Society (1920–26) and one of the earliest women Fellows of the Royal Geographical Society. Her books include *Through Persia on a Side-Saddle, Persia and Its People,* and *Through Deserts and Oases of Central Asia* (with Sir Percy). *A Home-Help in Canada,* a balanced, informative, and amusing record of her experiences in Canada, (chiefly in the West), marks a radical departure from the colourful scenes and high adventures in the East.

Dairy Farm

I well remember how I arrived at my destination, a large dairy-farm, after ten o'clock on a June night, and wondered whether anyone would meet me at the station.

As I stood by my things on the platform, a man stepped forward from among a group of working men, and, with the kindness that I have encountered everywhere in Canada, asked me whether he could carry them for me. I said that I was bound for Mr. Brown's farm, and was engaged as home-help by his wife. "Oh, that's all right," was the answer. "Over there are two of Brown's boys. I'll tell them that you are here, as most likely they have come to meet you." This, as it happened, was the case, and I shook hands with two taciturn yokels in "Buffalo Bill" hats, who volunteered a timid remark or two as they picked up my "grip" and hold-all and marched me off between them into the darkness. After a while we turned in at a gate and stumbled along a track among pines, where we seemed in danger of colliding with cows, their bells sounding on all sides of us as we picked our way as best we could over the tree-roots on the path. Though I had only engaged myself for a fortnight, yet I was not quite easy in my mind, for I knew that my success in this venture depended almost entirely on whether my new "missus" and I took to one another; and I should have liked to have questioned my guides about her, but of course that would not have done at all. By this time we were approaching a white-painted, log-built house, with green doors and windows, and a woman, with one of the kindest faces I have ever seen,

Library and Archives Canada, C-011024.

This idyllic portrait, A Ranch in the Rockies *by Edward Roper (1857–91), suggests a very different existence from the exhausting life of the estimable Mrs. Brown on a large dairy farm.*

came out with a light and shook hands with me. I liked and trusted her on the spot, and next day she told me that she had had the same favourable opinion of me, so our acquaintance had an auspicious beginning....

Mrs. Brown asked me to be in the kitchen next morning by seven o'clock, in order that she and I might get breakfast ready for her husband, his three hired men, and the three children. Mr. Brown always quietly crept down the staircase at five o'clock, roused his men sleeping in a shack close by, and he and they started to milk forty cows before the eight o'clock breakfast. This began with porridge, eaten with new milk, the staple dish throughout Canada; and then would come fried bacon or boiled eggs, and plenty of hot toast and butter, with, of course, the inevitable tea, usually too potent a beverage for my taste. Mrs. Brown and I used to have our breakfast alone if the men were late, as was often the case, and this arrangement I liked, for directly they appeared our work was cut out in waiting upon them. We all ate in the dining-room, and had a good deal of running into the adjoining kitchen to fill their plates, and those of the children, from the porridge-pot, to bring in the eggs, bacon, and toast kept hot in the oven, to pour out their tea, and so on. During the progress of breakfast, the children would begin to straggle down in stockinged feet, and would hunt about in the kitchen for their boots....

I do not wish to run down the youth of Canada, but certainly in the three situations in which I encountered children I found them rough, mannerless, and unruly, a great contrast to their courteous parents: they were always undisciplined, and completely lacking in deference to their elders.

The young Browns did not go to school, but hung about all day, and not having enough vent for their energies, used to squabble constantly, the one who was worsted in any encounter, howling so vigorously, that at first I used to rush to the spot, feeling sure that some fearful accident had occurred. One reason of this was that the parents were far too busy to bring up their children in the way they should go, and Mrs. Brown, who was under no illusions as to her noisy family, used to lament to me that she, who had been a school-teacher, could not keep her own treasures in better order.

...

She told me that the moment she saw the word "educated" in my "ad," she longed to secure my services, more as a companion than as a home-help, and I felt that first day as if I had anchored my bark, for the present, in calm water. My new mistress was most easy to get on with, and did not make me nervous or find fault with me....

My first task after breakfast was to sweep out the men's shack and make their beds; then there were the two bedrooms upstairs to be done, the dining-room and kitchen to sweep out, water to fetch from the well close at hand, and wood from the wood-pile near by; the fowls also had to be fed and watered. When these "chores" were done, it was time to peel a bowl of potatoes, the only vegetable used in many parts of Canada, and then I laid the table for the one-o'clock dinner, and put the potatoes on to boil, and began to turn pieces of steak in the frying-pan. Canadians have a perfect horror of meat being "rare," as they call it, and so the steak had to be cooked until it was almost of the consistency of leather. We women waited on the men as soon as they appeared and had taken their seats, and we ate our own meal in the intervals of supplying them with meat, bread, and potatoes, pouring out big cups of tea for them, and dispensing slices of rhubarb-pie. This differs from our English fruit-pies, as the rhubarb, sliced small, is placed on one round of pastry and covered by another, and then baked. Though nice when freshly made, the lower crust soon becomes sodden as the juice oozes through it. Meat and "dessert," which answers to our pudding course, were served on the same plate; but considerate Mrs. Brown produced another one for me, saying, "I expect that Miss Sykes is accustomed to have two plates." Of course I declined a privilege shared by none of the family, and indeed, so many ways are there of looking at things, I soon got to approve of the "one-plate" system, as it meant nine plates less to wash up after the meal!

Mr. Brown was a good-looking, intelligent young man, and often talked well when he had got accustomed to me, but at first the three hired men were very "bashful," as Mrs. Brown expressed it. She told me later on that since my advent they spent twice as much time as formerly in washing themselves and brushing their hair before meals, at which they always appeared in their shirt-sleeves. Poor fellows! They had a hard life, I thought. Master and men were up at five o'clock, and would drive the forty cows into an enclosure and milk them. Some sixty gallons of milk had then to be strained twice, the pails well washed, and the milk put into cans, which were half sunk in the water of the "milk-house," a wooden building that floated on the stream close by.

. . .

Later on, when the weather became sunny, I produced my camera, and took snapshots of one and all. Fortunately most of my portraits turned out well, and gave great pleasure to my sitters, who in time got less tongue-tied.

. . .

Certainly Canadian air, as a rule, is most invigorating; and I worked sometimes from half-past six to half-past four without a pause (barring meals), and did not feel the slightest fatigue. But personally I could not have borne to have lived my whole life in this way, so much housework and so little relaxation; and if I found the life monotonous in lovely summer weather, what would it have been in the winter, with the house probably over-heated, the windows hardly ever opened, and the minimum of out-door exercise?

. . .

It always seemed to me that I got through very little in the morning, though I was down at seven o'clock. Breakfast would be ready by eight; but often the men did not get in till half an hour later, and the porridge, bacon, toast, and eggs had to be kept hot for them.

. . .

The two boys were rather a trial to me, as they were in and out of the kitchen all day long, drinking water at frequent intervals, with the dip-per, out of the pails. The habit prevails throughout Canada of using the tin dipper as a drinking-cup. The men, after drinking, toss away the rest of the water, but the children, unless my eye were on them, would drink and put what they did not finish back into the bucket. Kitty, an intelligent child, began the rudiments of the three R's in my spare moments, and got on quite nicely; but the boys, who never left the enclosure, seemed to be in mischief every few minutes, as an outlet to their bubbling-over energies. There were so many "dont's" in their lives that I had an involun-tary sympathy for them in spite of the way they bothered me.

(1) The fence bordering the railway track must never be crossed.

(2) The creek by the milk-house (the most temping spot in the whole domain), must never be approached.

(3) The pump must not be touched.

(4) They must not play in the wheat-shed.

(5) They must not chase the hens.

To this long list I added a few "dont's" of my own as to teasing the dog and keeping grasshoppers and toads imprisoned in their hot little hands.

...

I was with the Browns on Coronation Day, and to mark the event I gave "Coronation" post cards all round at breakfast. Mr. Brown said that he thought he ought to run up a flag to show his loyalty, and of course I applauded the idea warmly, but nothing was done — we were all far too busy. It was washing-day for us women, and directly we had cleared away breakfast and had swept the rooms, we began, Mrs. Brown rocking the "cradle," and I turning the wringer. She did not make nearly as toilsome a business of the whole operation as I found prevailed elsewhere in Canada, and we got the family washing all hung out to dry soon after midday. On the other hand, it was by no means as snowy white as when I saw it done by other housewives, though probably the sand that got into everything may have been the cause of this. Certainly I have never been in a place where so much sweeping was required, every breath of wind seeming to cover the kitchen floor with sand in spite of all our care.

Mrs. Brown had had a hard life since her girlhood, and, though a comparatively young woman, looked far older than her years, worn out with ceaseless work. Like the great majority of Canadian women, she was extraordinarily quick and capable, and, as I told her, would have concocted a cake and put it in the oven, and perhaps baked it, before I had collected the materials to make mine. But the Demon of Work had got her in its clutches, as it seems to get so many Canadian women, and she *could* not rest or take things easily.

She had been for four years on a ranch — completely bare of crops, as it was a cattle-range — and she said that the great expanse got on her nerves, and she hated it, save when in the spring the ground was starred with myriads of tiny flowers. Her husband and the other men were off with the cattle during the greater part of the day, and she told me that without her children she thought that she would have gone mad.

In summer the heat was great, and the mosquitoes were so bad that she hardly ever left the house, but lived behind the wire screens, which were in front of all the doors and windows; and she often watched her husband riding off, looking as if he and his horse were in a mist, so dense was the cloud of these pestilent little insects. The men all wore veils and gloves, and covered their horses as much as possible with sacking. The poor cattle, however hungry they might be, dared not feed when the air was still, but lay in the barns to get refuge from the mosquitoes, waiting there until a breeze sprung up, when they would hurry out to the pasture. Sometimes the winters were terrible, so severe that the cattle died on the ranges, and she was kept indoors for weeks at a time. Mr. Brown, most fortunately, had a great store of hay, and once fed his sheep, over two thousand in number, daily, and he and his partner had a snow-plough that tossed away the snow, and enabled the animals to feed on the grass underneath. They got to understand the purpose of this plough very soon, and the whole flock would follow it in a straggling line, perhaps a mile long, browsing as they went.

Canadian as she was, Mrs. Brown had ever a good word for the English, who, she said, were considered to make the kindest husbands of any, in the way of helping their wives, though the Canadians were supposed to give money more freely for household expenses. Again and again on the prairie an Englishman would give her a hand with the interminable dish-washing, and would sometimes be sneered at by the other men for so doing. The rough old Scotchman, her husband's partner, would never help her in any way, and she quoted to me more than once the remark of a Scotchwoman on the prairie, who said to her, "My countrymen seem to think that there is no limit to a woman's strength."

Day after day she rose to a round of unending toil, and during all the incessant work her three children arrived. The second came before his time, and as a snowstorm was raging, it was impossible to go for the doctor; so she and her husband had to do as best they could. Usually the women go into the nearest town for their confinements, every hospital in Canada having large maternity wards for the purpose; and as all Canadian men are as handy at household "chores" as their wives, they can look after themselves and the children very well for a time.

My employer and her husband were a thoroughly united couple, yet she assured me that had she had a vision of what her early married life would be, she would never have linked her fortunes with his.

"I haven't a single good word for the prairie," she would say, "and I got to hate the very sight of a man when I was there." I was surprised at this, and inquired why.

"Because a man meant preparing a meal. Our ranch was on a main trail, and man after man as he came along would drop in and ask for food, as a matter of course, and very seldom did he give me a word of thanks for it."

"How horrid! I should have felt inclined to refuse to cook for such ungrateful creatures," I remarked.

"Oh, well, I felt like it very often," was her reply; "but if I had done so, we should have got a bad name in the district, and I had to think of my husband. It was a life of slavery. Just imagine it! In shearing-time I had to cook for fifteen men, and they needed five meals a day, and I couldn't get a woman to help me for love or money. I was too busy to go and see my neighbours — the nearest lived four miles off — and I just got into the way of thinking of nothing but how to get through the day's work."

"Don't you think that the men would have helped you if you had asked them?" I said. "I met a girl who told me that her husband had a ranch, and that she rode half the day and 'jollied the boys,' who did her work for her."

"Yes, there were women in our part who went on like that, but," and Mrs. Brown's voice had a tragic note, "they could never get free of the prairie as we have done. They took their freedom while they were there, wasted the time of the hired men, and there they will have to stay all their lives," and she shuddered at the mere thought of it.

"But aren't there some women who love the life? In England we hear so much of the 'call of the prairie.'"

My mistress looked dubious. "There may be some," she conceded, "but I never met them. All my friends hated the loneliness and the lack of amusement and the same dull round day after day. Do you know, if ever I sat down and wrote, or did some sewing, Kitty would come up to me to ask whether it were Sunday, so astonished was she to see me resting, as on the week-days I was on the 'go' all the time. I have heard since from two or three of our neighbours, and they are all suffering from 'nerves,' and I myself am worn out and old before my time with the life."

This was true; but I pointed out to her that now, as they were so well off that Mr. Brown need not work at all, she ought to rest every afternoon, or go out and see some of her neighbours. But this was a counsel of perfection. She saw its wisdom, but said sadly that she was so wound up, as it were, that she positively *had* to keep going all day, and that she had now lost all desire for social intercourse. And this I found to be the case with many Canadian women. The habit of work was so deeply ingrained in them that they went on when there was no necessity for it, and far too often broken health and mental derangement stop this activity. From the Atlantic to the Pacific the women in country districts, as a rule, wore far worse than the men, and the monotonous work, too much tea, little outdoor exercise, and few neighbours or amusements appeared to me to be the causes of this. The men have a far better life, though the extremes of heat and cold must be very trying. They work with other men, and have the animals to look after, and, best of all, are in the open air most of the day. As Mr. Brown remarked to me when talking of their life on the ranch, "The prairie is no 'snap' for a woman."

The isolation makes men and women shy and nervous, and I had an example of this when three smartly dressed ladies turned up at the kitchen door one wet afternoon, asked to buy eggs, and requested glasses of water. Mrs. Brown had a fit of shyness, and her home-help had to give the ladies water and tell them where to go, as they wished to interview Mr. Brown about supplying them with milk. Poor things! They had to wait a long time in the rain near the cow-house before one of the four men summoned up sufficient courage to emerge from it and confront them. Mrs. Brown chaffed them about their cowardice when we were all sitting at tea afterwards, and her husband turned to me and explained the matter thus, "You see, Miss Sykes, those ladies were real 'toney' folk. They weren't in our class, and so we didn't feel comfortable with them."

They were all quite "comfortable" with *me*, but this state of things was nearly destroyed one day, when in the course of conversation at table I carelessly dropped the information that I spoke French. There

Ella Sykes visited the National Park at Banff on her way from Calgary to British Columbia. Despite previous wild adventures in India and Persia, she wrote that she "had a distinct pang of apprehension when my companion and I found ourselves close to the great animals, which were feeding quietly among the short scrub."

instantly ensued an uneasy silence, and the faces of the grown-ups wore a look almost of dismay, until I explained that owing to the nearness of England to France this accomplishment was naturally far commoner than it would be in Western Canada.

This leads me on to make a few diffident remarks on the subject of class distinctions in the Dominion. It struck me again and again that the difference between England and Canada in this respect was that England acknowledged these distinctions, and Canada pretended to ignore them. In the big towns, where I had introductions, things seemed to be very much as they are in the Old Country; but on the prairie, and in small towns, where everyone is "on the make," all are on an equality, and one realizes that one is in a land developed by the pluck and energy of self-made men and women. It is a kind of paradise for the labouring classes, and, as a working woman remarked later on, "I call upon people here who would not have taken any notice of me in England." Culture and refinement, art and literature, are not much wanted as yet. The ideal side of life is left out; the material side is often too much in evidence, as money is the criterion of success, and a man wins respect according as he "makes good."

All this is inevitable in a new country, a land full of such splendid opportunities and possibilities that even a traveller feels exhilarated by the atmosphere of optimism, and I longed again and again for British women with high ideals to come out and do their part in building up the Empire.

At last the time came for me to leave Mrs. Brown, and though I had only engaged myself to her for a fortnight, yet I had a sense that I was deserting her, so often had she said that my presence made the work a pleasure to her instead of a toil. All were sorry to say good-bye to me, and though the three men had an access of shyness as I shook hands with them, they managed to stammer out good wishes for my success. Mr. Brown invited me to stay as a guest at any future date, and Mrs. Brown came to see me off at the train, the tears in her eyes as we embraced at parting.

"You *have* been a good 'missus' to me," I exclaimed gratefully.

"I have only treated you as I should like anyone to treat me," was her reply, but it was typical of the whole woman, and I knew that I should have to travel far before I met her like again.

Ella C. Sykes, *A Home-Help in Canada.*

23

Monica Hopkins

(1884–1974)

Amy Monica Hopkins, née Maggs, the daughter of a Wesleyan minister, was born in Dorset, England. Despite the strictures of a Victorian Methodist household, "neither her exuberant personality nor her delightful sense of humour" were stifled, although a hearing problem, not discovered until her teens, led to a certain lack of success in school. In 1900 her father was appointed Principal of Wesleyan Theological College at McGill. During the trip out, Monica met Francis W.R. ("Billie") Hopkins, an adventurous if not robust young man who had lived in Argentina in the 1890s. The youthful shipboard romance led to marriage in 1909.

Although Monica's parents had reservations about their gently reared daughter living on a ranch in the foothills of Alberta, she adjusted to the frontier society with grace and enthusiasm. She became active in church and community and developed a deep fondness for animals, as well as a passion for literature and letters. "It is a glorious life," she wrote to a friend in Australia, "even if we don't make our fortunes." In 1943, the devoted pair moved closer to the city for medical help for Billie's worsening arthritis. During this time they rewrote and expanded the letters which were eventually published by the Glenbow Museum. After Billie's death in 1948, Monica returned to Ireland. At the age of 72, with no immediate family left, she returned to Alberta, cheerful and involved as ever, until her death in Calgary in 1974.

HOUSEKEEPING

Enmore,
Priddis,
March, 1910.

Dearest Gill:

Helene is busy writing to her beloved Dan so I'll follow her example and start my letter to you. Billie and Joe have their pipes going and a book each. All is peace inside, but oh my dear, outside it is somewhere around 20 degrees below and I just hate to poke my nose outside. They all tell me I'll not feel the cold much for the first year or two. All I can say is if I'm going to feel it much more I'm going home to England.

Helene has been here over three weeks now, quite settled down and is, I think, enjoying all the new experiences and revelling in the snow. The only snow she has seen before was when she was staying in Leeds, and as you can imagine, Leeds' snow does not look quite like the snow out here. It takes on a grimy look very quickly while here it remains dazzlingly white all the time.

...

Helene is taking over the washing department and Billie, who has helped me up to now, has retired thankfully....

... We decided to soak everything. "Soaking," said Helene, "is the only way to get clothes a good colour. Rub them well with soap, roll up and leave them to soak overnight." As soaking was about the only thing that Billie and I hadn't done I decided that that was where we had made our mistake and asked Billie why he hadn't suggested it. "I did suggest it,"

Despite even more primitive conditions than those amusingly described by Monica Hopkins, laundry day on Wyman's Farm, near Bon Accord, Alberta, circa 1916–19 seems relatively cheerful.

Glenbow Museum, na-2041-1.

indignantly said my husband. "I told you to soak them in the creek and you wouldn't," and walked out of the house for once having the last word!

We had so much laundry that we decided the only place to soak it was in the bath. The room was rather cold — it was ten degrees below zero outside, but we rubbed the clothes with soap, rolled them up and placed them in rows in the bath. There were about three layers of things; we covered them well with water and left them, planning to start very early next morning.

The temperature went down to 30 degrees below zero that night and the next morning it was clear and bright, but still very cold. Billie went down to the stables so Joe brought us the water and helped us get the washing machine and other things ready. We hurried with our housework and when the water was hot we went to fetch the clothes. We found them incased in a solid block of ice as if we had placed them in the middle of an iceberg in the Atlantic. We decided to thaw them out and poured on a kettle of boiling water. Huge columns of steam arose and there was a crackling of ice so in our innocence we said, "We'll give them ten minutes," and went back to a warmer clime. We returned in ten minutes to find that all we had done was to add another inch of ice to the top layer of our washing. We then poured another kettle of boiling water and added a pailful as well. Again there were the ominous cracks and much steam, and we returned to huddle over the kitchen stove. When we next returned we found we had increased the depth of ice by another two inches and if we continued at the rate we were going we should soon leave have a good indoor skating rink. So we decided we would chop the clothes out and were each armed with an axe and a meat chopper when Billie came in.

"What on earth are you going to do now?" he asked.

"Chop our washing out of the ice," we told him and led him into the bathroom.

Billie gave a whistle when he saw the block of ice with a few patches of colour showing through. "What the dickens made you put them in there?" he wanted to know. "They are there until the spring thaw."

We asked him if there was anything we could do.

"Not a thing. You'd have to thaw them out from the bottom and if you put a lamp under the bath you'd burst it. Even now it's probably cracked with all that ice in it."

"But we need some of the things!" we wailed in chorus.

"You won't get them this side of Easter unless there is a chinook; then you might be able to thaw them out. So you might as well make up your minds about that and let's get out of this morgue and get warm."

Every hour or so one of us would look into the bathroom to see if a miracle had happened and the ice turned into water, but no luck.

Three days later there was a chinook arch and I thought it would probably be warmer as towards evening a nice west wind sprang up. Before going to bed I went into the bathroom and opened the window; at any rate the ice couldn't get any thicker and it might start to thaw a little. I didn't tell anyone what I had done as I knew exactly what would be said about opening a window wide in the middle of winter....

The boys are hauling hay from a stack several miles up the creek so they are away three or four hours at a time. Billie came in just before he left and told us "not to go monkeying around with that ice; you'll only crack the bath. Just let it thaw out gradually." "Of course," we said, and went on with washing up the breakfast things, but as soon as they were out of sight we started our operation. We made up a huge fire in the kitchen stove and got the kettles boiling. The ice was beginning to look a little watery around the edge and we chose a spot where some clothes were nearer the surface and the ice thinner. We poured boiling water on this particular place. There were some harrowing cracks and we jumped with guilty fear at each one for we couldn't tell whether it was the ice or the bath that was cracking, but hoped for the best. We got quite a nice little hole at one end and then we started on the other. Still not a budge, so I went for a couple of Billie's tools — screwdrivers I think they are called — and we heated them on the stove and when they were good and red we prodded away and joy! The whole sheebang moved. We shoved the iceberg up the sloping end of the bath and with thick mitts on our hands we managed to lift the whole thing out. It weighed tons. Between us we carried the corpse out and reverently laid it on a sheet that we had spread on the floor before the stove and it wasn't until then that we began to breathe normally again. Helene produced a strong cup of hot tea and we drank a toast to ourselves. I carefully put away Billie's tools; there's a bit of a curve to the screwdriver that wasn't there before so I'm hoping he won't be needing it for some time.

We chipped away the ice very carefully and soon had the clothes separated and thawing out in boiling water. The next day we washed. I'm sure that already my things are a better colour for their soaking and you will be glad to hear that the bath is still intact.

...

We have been taking Helene around to meet some of our neighbours — a neighbour is anyone within a radius of 20 miles. We both love sleighing and of course it's a novelty to me as well as Helene. This year the snow is deep; in places the drifts are several feet high and the trail runs between banks of snow two feet deep. There is no chance of straying off the straight and narrow path, except that our path isn't straight. It winds around in some places so that I wonder we don't tie ourselves in knots.

One of our visits was to the Mitfords who live about ten miles away. We arrived there in time for lunch. They are a most hospitable family and always insist on us having a meal whatever time we get there, so we decided it would be less trouble for them if we reached there at noon which is the time for the mid-day meal for people who breakfast at six o'clock. …

The Mitfords are a large family — mother, father, five boys and two girls. They were all at home and it seemed to us that the table was simply covered with food, but Mrs. Mitford kept saying that she wished she had known we were coming as she would have cooked something up for us. Still we managed quite well with what there was. We had fried home-cured bacon, an enormous omelette which must have contained well over a dozen eggs, potatoes, turnips and carrots, while spread about the table were the usual little dishes of pickles and the weirdest thing called "sauerkraut." It is cabbage that has fermented; it is a pale yellow and has a salty taste. I didn't care for it very much but Helene and Billie tucked into it. I might grow to like it. I imagine it is an acquired taste, like olives, but I don't think I shall make it. For one thing you have to keep it behind the stove to ferment and the back of our stove is packed with dogs. They all squash behind it and the cats may be on top of them. There certainly would be no room for a barrel of sliced cabbage going bad as well; personally I would much prefer the dogs to the sauerkraut.

…

Enmore,
Priddis,
Alberta,
May, 1911.

Dearest Gill:

I was dashing off to pack our bag for Calgary when I ended my last letter to you. We had a glorious three days' holiday; the drive both in and out

Glenbow Museum, pa-2336-3a.

Perhaps Monica Hopkins was getting ready to visit Calgary when this picture of her wearing a fur stole and muff was taken at the ranch, circa 1912–13.

was lovely, neither too hot nor too cold, and without any very disturbing actions on the part of the team....

...

There is quite a nice lot of grass and the trees have a grey green tint which means they will be in leaf soon. The spring flowers are out, although there are very few of them in the hills. But on the way to Calgary we passed one hillside on the Sarcee Reserve that was simply covered with crocuses of a pale helio and in the distance it looked as if the whole hillside was covered with heather. It made me feel homesick for a sight of the Ilkley moors. Flowers and trees on the prairie around Calgary are three weeks ahead of ours in the foothills and all the grass is green whereas here only the hillsides have grass on them and that's spotty....

...

The last few weeks have simply flown. I couldn't keep up with them at all. I staggered along in the rear trying to do my spring cleaning, looking after my setting hens, helping Billie at times, churning every week, putting in the garden with Billie, and a dozen other odd things kept me busy all day long. I fell into bed every night, tired but happy, slept like a top and woke up next morning to start another day which would be full of interest. Billie is just as busy so at least we have no time to be bored with each other or with our way of life.

One day Billie and Joe cut up a pig we had bought, 240 pounds. I had a hectic time trying to use up the scraps. I rendered down all the lard and have tins and crocks full enough to last me for months to come. I made brawn with the head and we ate at it until we were sick of the sight of it. I gave away a lot to Joe and Harry; the liver, kidneys and tender loins I fried and I wonder Billie and I didn't die of biliousness. But it didn't upset us at all; we must have insides like rhinoceros — at least I have. Billie's is apt to protest at times but mine, never!

The hams and bacon pails are in brine and I hope they will stay there for some time. I'm tired of anything appertaining to a pig and hens are rapidly going into the same category. Hens are such utter fools; I wouldn't believe that any creature could be so stupid. I have looked after the miseries for months, waited on them hand and foot, fetched and carried for them, fed and watered them, and wiped their beastly little noses if they had colds. Mothered them as if they were my own children and what thanks do I get? None! I have a dozen broody old brutes shut up in a shed sitting on eggs; each has its own nest and you would think they would know their own beds, wouldn't you, but do they? Hardly a one of them. I creep into the shed as if I had a dozen babies asleep there that I did not wish to wake. Immediately every head is raised and as I put the feed and water down a muttering under their breath starts. As I lift the first old Biddy off her nest she either lets out a yell as if I was murdering her and flies to the other end of the shed, screeching at the top of her voice, or else she huddles on the ground grumbling away to herself and cussing me for all she is worth. When I have got the dozen off their nests and they all act in a similar manner, I tiptoe out and shut the door carefully behind me.

If I go back in about 20 minutes I generally find that about eight have managed to get back on a nest — their own or someone else's — the other four are probably all trying to sit on one nest or they are sitting on the top of the box, anywhere but on their eggs. I gently lift one back and she either dances the can-can and breaks a couple of eggs or else she refuses to stay at any price; the others all act in the same maddening way. Sometimes I'm down there an hour before they are all settled and if you could only see the leer in their eyes as I finally go out, you'd wonder, with me, why I don't go back and wring their necks. One day I shall. I have a few chicks already hatched out; there should have been more but after seeing the many dangers that beset a chicken the minute it comes out of its shell and indeed before it comes out as well, I'm surprised I have any at all.

I've come to the conclusion that I'm no poultry woman. I have no love for the creatures at all. You can't pet them, they refuse to be friendly, and they look down their noses in such a superior manner. I detest them!

The house looks nice and fresh with all the summer curtains and clean cushions out. I'm not fond of spring cleaning, especially alone, but I am thoroughly enjoying the results of my hard labour. I wander from one room to the other sniffing the nice clean smell of scrubbed boards and paint, and wishing that Mother could see it for I'm quite sure she will never believe it until she actually sees it....

It was Billie who rather hurried me on my spring cleaning. I really had no intention of doing it quite so early. I had simply been talking about it and gently intimating to Billie all the different little odd jobs that I should expect him to help me with. I usually approach him on subjects like that of an evening when he is settled in his chair, pipe going full blast and deep in a book. After telling him all my plans I say, "Is that all right, Billie?" Usually I get, "Yes, quite right," in a voice that tells me he hasn't listened to a word I have said; so that when I again introduce the subject nearer the time when I want the little jobs done, I'm able to say, "but you *said* you would." Billie generally does it though he probably has no remembrance of ever saying anything. But this time he evidently had remembered, for one morning bright and early he announced that he had decided to clean the stove pipes.

I was in bed, having spent a couple of days there with one of my wretched colds in the head. Billie had brought in my breakfast and I was toying with the idea of getting up after lunch when Billie mentioned the stove pipes and said he was going to do them right away. I was horrified, to say the least, for cleaning stove pipes is almost as bad as having the chimney sweep at home and you know what preparations are made for his visit? And here was Billie, acting as if it was mere child's play to clean those stove pipes when he ought to know that it takes two people — and more if they are available — to tackle the job. In spite of all my protestations he airily started in while I listened to his preparations with dismay.

Billie started with the sitting room stove. The pipes of this stove come through a hole in the wall, into our bedroom, stretch across the room and go into a cement chimney built on the opposite wall. There is about ten feet of stove pipe and each pipe length is about 18 inches. One person stands at the end by the stove while the other gently wriggles it out of the chimney. The main thing is to see that the lengths don't come apart because if they do quantities of soot fall out and our coal has particularly filthy soot. Miraculously, Billie managed to get the entire stove pipe out without any accident at all and so puffed up was he with his success that he decided to clean the chimney as well. I advised strongly against this but he wouldn't listen and went ahead gathering his implements. He tacked a piece of strong cardboard over the whole in the cement chimney to stop the soot coming through and then clambered on to the roof armed with a pole that had a sack tied around the end of it.

I heard him scrambling up to the chimney and then heard the pole being pushed down the chimney. At the first whack off fell the cardboard and flew across the room to be followed by a cloud of soot that simply covered everything. I heard Billie draw up the pole with a sort of sucking sound and then down it came again, and another large cloud of soot shot out into the room. I yelled my loudest to Billie to try and tell him what was happening, but I couldn't make him hear. He was making such a row himself, whistling away and having a glorious time. I hated the idea of getting out of bed to shout to Billie from the window for I would have had to pass right through the cyclone that was pouring out of the chimney and I didn't want to get covered too. I needn't have bothered about that however. Soon I heard Billie slide down the roof and clamber down the ladder, presenting himself at the bedroom door with a cheery "Well that's done!" Then he stopped suddenly and *roared with laughter*. He said afterwards he couldn't have stopped if his life had depended on it. The sight of me sitting up in bed with an absolutely black face — eyes rolling — speechless — was just too much for him. But when he saw the awful mess that everything was in, he soon stopped. I was too mad to speak and just cried with rage; you can imagine the awful effect that had on my face....

I forgot all about my cold and we took everything out of doors, and washed them all. The next day Billie colour washed the room all over again in a pale green while I washed the white paint. The white bedspread and other white things after a couple of boilings are still rather grimy looking. Wasn't it fortunate that I had put the satin eiderdown away? It would have been absolutely ruined. Billie is allowing me to help when he does the kitchen stove and has decided not to clean the chimney.

I repeat again that I wish only at times, but only at times, that we lived where there were a few conveniences, and on the day of the stove pipe episode I would willingly have exchanged our log cabin for a house in a terrace with neighbours on either side of us and some at the front and back of us as well. Billie would be going out every day to the bank or office arrayed in a blue serge suit and bowler hat while I had fireplaces, electric light and all the other joys of a town house. But now that my little house is sweet and clean again I wouldn't exchange it for Buckingham Palace while neighbours any nearer than three miles seem like over crowding. Any thought of Billie in anything else but his overalls, coloured handkerchief, and Stetson hat is quite repulsive. How the precious lamb would loath any other way of living but this!

It's nice being by ourselves — the first time we have actually been alone since we were married and we are enjoying it immensely. I am afraid that I am rather inclined to spend more time than I should outside with Billie, helping him when I can. I find that another pair of hands can be very useful around a corral, not to mention a pair of legs to "run and fetch things." It's a case of "Hold this halter while I tie Buck's feet," or "Can you steady the log while I hang this gate?" I have heated branding irons in a fire while Billie has roped and tied a calf that he is turning out on the range with its mother. I have also helped Billie brand Buck, that is, Billie did the branding; I handed the red hot iron to him and felt like the Lord High Executioner in doing it. Billie says it doesn't hurt the animal very much if the iron is good and red, but I don't know, I'd hate to have it done to me. But I must confess that it doesn't seem to bother the animal very much after the first jump; just as soon as they are let out of the "squeeze," their first idea is to nibble at the grass.

So you see I'm quite useful. Generally these jobs, according to Billie, only take "two minutes" but I usually find that 30 minutes are nearer the mark. I suddenly realize that it is getting on to lunch time and nothing is ready so I dash to the house to catch up with my own work....

Monica Hopkins, *Letters from a Lady Rancher.*

PART V

British Columbia and Northern Regions

24

Susan Allison

(1845–1937)

Susan Louisa Allison, née Moir, was born on a coffee plantation in Ceylon but returned to England at the age of four after her father's death. She received an excellent education, becoming familiar with Greek, Latin, and French. Her mother married a charming wastrel who deserted the family in 1864, four years after they immigrated to British Columbia. In 1868 Susan married John Fall Allison, a prospector and rancher who discovered Allison Pass. They moved first to his ranch in the Similkameen, then to "Sunnyside" on Lake Okanagan in 1873. Nine years later, the Allisons returned to the original ranch at Princeton, British Columbia.

Susan's serenity and resilience stood her in good stead through the difficulties and disasters of pioneer life: a plague of grasshoppers, isolation, and the destruction of their homes by fire and flood. Between 1869 and 1892, she bore 14 children, virtually unaided. In the cabin at Sunnyside, there was no potable water, rattlers lurked in the walls and among the pots and pans, and there were incursions by the murderous McLean boys.

During her years in the wilderness, Susan studied Chinook, educated her children, caught and cured fish, dried venison, and learned to make moccasins, straw hats, and braid for lariats. She also collected the lore and legends of the Similkameen Indians and wrote a long poem about their customs; her paper on the tribe was published by the British Association for the Advancement of Science in 1891. She moved to Vancouver in 1928 and was persuaded to write *Recollections*, based on stories written years before. First published in the *Vancouver Sunday Province* in 1931, these settlement narratives have been edited and annotated by Dr. Margaret Ormsby. Known as the Mother of the Similkameen, Susan Allison is an appealing example of the pioneer gentlewoman.

The family was living in a house near Princeton when this portrait of Susan Allison was taken with eight of her 14 children — and a dog.

FLOOD

I think it was in the middle of June 1894 after a cold and backward spring that there was a sudden change in the weather, the night frosts suddenly ceased and it set in unbearably hot.

Then both the Similkameen and the Tulameen rose at once, and the Similkameen from a small wasted stream became a roaring, raging flood tearing on, gathering all the flotsam and jetsam within its reach — great logs and slender saplings — eating away the banks, and moving huge boulders that we had for years considered landmarks.

Our house was standing on the river's bank, but not on the brink. There was a sugarbeet patch of rich deep soil and a storehouse between us and the river, so at first we had no fear of the flood. Mr. Cawston had come up a few [days] before the one of which I write, and we sat on the kitchen steps which led down to the river where we got our water. We were all as usual enjoying the shade after the burning sunshine of the day, and discussing the cause of Mr. Cawston's visit, the shape of the road over the Mountain, which he wanted to ascertain in order to drive a bunch of beef steers to Hope, when we noticed some very large logs floating down. The bank seemed to be hit by them as they passed. Mr. Cawston made some joking remark about the sugarbeets. He decided to hold his drive for a few days until the river fell.

Our bridge had gone out the year previous. After Mr. Cawston started for Keremeos the river continued to rise. Mr. Allison and I sat and watched the sugarbeets going down the river as it ate away the soil of the bank — we sat and watched as long as we could see; but could not stop the damage. When we did go to bed the river was at least twenty feet from the house, but the whole patch between seemed to be saturated with water. All night long we could hear the roaring of the river, and once or twice there came a shock that seemed like logs bumping against the corner of the house. After a while, tired out, we slept the sleep of the just.

We woke next morning with the daylight. My husband said, "It sounds funny; I will just get up and look." In a few moments he was back. He told me quietly that he thought I ought to get up and dress, adding quite calmly that half my bedroom was undermined and would soon have to be cut adrift from the house.

I got up at once and made the children get out of their beds. Then I went out to take a look round. The river was running under both my room and Louisa's. There were two rooms above these, and it seemed as if that part of the house was doomed. I saw my husband and the boys coming with two long saws. I asked what they were going to do and was answered, "Saw the house in two — and try to save half. Get out the bedding and furniture and store [them] near the side hill."

So to work we went taking all our things out of the doomed part of the house while the boys sawed manfully to split the house in two. We had most fortunately built a new stable to accommodate ten horses and a harness room over near the side hill. The horses had not been occupying it for more than a week, and my husband said rather grimly that if we could not save half the house, we could turn the horses out and live in the stable. The boys did turn the horses out, for they had not time to feed them.

The river was still rising. At noon we moved the cook-stove out to a shed near the stable. When my husband and boys had sawed off four rooms from the house and lowered them into the river, I gave them a lunch under the old shed and went with Grace and Carrie to see what was going on.

We found that the dairy was gone, the calves' shed, the blacksmith's shop and the slaughter-house and numerous other buildings. There was yet a small chicken-house clinging to the bank and the door was swinging open. Grace cried out, "I am going in there." I begged her not to try, but she ran on and jumped in and as she did so the chicken-house began to float downstream. She jumped quickly back and fortunately landed on solid ground. Next we inspected the garden. It was going quickly. The asparagus bed we had planted twenty-five years before was rapidly disappearing. Some of the asparagus roots were 17 feet long; we measured them afterwards. The young fruit trees had gone and now the currants and gooseberries were going. Rose and Carrie sat on a dry spot and watched the demolition. "The Lord giveth and the Lord taketh, blessed be his name," said Rose. Carrie jumped up, seized a shovel and cried out, "He shan't get away with the currants and gooseberries if I can help it," and set to work digging them up.

By this time some people from the new town of Princeton had come to see what was going on. They offered help, but that was out of their power, for who can curb a torrent. When night came we had most of our effects out of the house except books and papers. We hoped to save the nursery, sitting room and Mr. Allison's office and half the dining room. We thought that it would be safer to sleep in the stable.

The small children had had a glorious day, wading in the puddles and using our wash tubs for boats, and little Alice was paddling a tub for her own canoe when Jack Pioto, an Indian friend, rode up and splashed into about two feet of water, grabbed her by one arm and, swinging her up onto his saddle, brought her to the stable and said the ground was too rotten near the river for children to play there.

When we were ready to retire for the night, we looked from our stable at the house and thought that though much smaller than in the morning, we still had a pretty good house left. So we went to bed tired out and thankful.

When we arose next morning and looked, the house was gone and the river flowing where it had stood. So for the second time we lost our home and most of our possessions.

Our loss when the river rose was serious. We had altogether lost fourteen buildings including the house, our garden and a lot of good ground. The girls' flower garden alone was left with its bright flowers.

We made the big stable comfortable and even managed to entertain such of our friends as passed our way. Soon we had another garden started, though we missed our well established asparagus bed. But the currants and gooseberries flourished as well as ever.

"When the River Rose" in Margaret A. Ormsby, editor, *A Pioneer Gentlewoman in British Columbia: The Recollections of Susan Allison.*

25

Emily Carr

(1871–1945)

Emily Carr was born in Victoria on the year British Columbia entered Confederation. From the start, she chafed at the restrictions of a conventional household and society. She trained at the California School of Design in San Francisco from 1890 to 1893, returned to Victoria and taught art to children in a barn studio on the family property. She then studied in England at the Westminster School of Art and the art colony at St. Ives in Cornwall for five years, working in the English landscape tradition. During this period, she suffered a breakdown and spent more than a year in a sanatorium in East Anglia. During a 1907 visit to Alaska and the Yukon, she was inspired by the totem poles and carvings of the Northwest Coast tribes and decided to document them before they were lost forever. From 1910 to 1911, she studied in France, where she was influenced by Post-Impressionism.

Back in British Columbia, she continued to visit Aboriginal settlements and by 1913 had produced almost two hundred paintings. After an exhibition of these works was greeted with indifference, she spent the next 15 years running a boarding house, raising sheepdogs, and making pottery for tourists. In 1927, for the first time, her work was included in a major exhibit at the National Gallery in Ottawa. At the opening, she met members of the Group of Seven, most significantly Lawren Harris, who became

Little Emily Carr at the age of four or five.

a friend and correspondent. She began to paint again — in a different style — and slowly gained critical recognition for her powerful evocation of the B.C. landscape and native culture. In 1937, after suffering a heart attack, she turned to writing. *Klee Wyck* (1941), which received a Governor General's Award, was followed by *The Book of Small*, about her childhood, and *House of All Sorts*, about her unhappy life as a landlady. Her journals, written between 1927 and 1941, were published under the title *Hundreds and Thousands* after her death. A complex woman, often more at home with "the dogs and the monkey and the rat" than with people, she is a unique figure in the Canadian landscape.

BC Archives, H_033313.

Childhood in Victoria

Beginnings

VICTORIA, on Vancouver Island, British Columbia, was the little town; I was the little girl.

...

My father did not come straight from England to Victoria when, a lad of nineteen, he started out to see something of the world. He went to many countries, looking, thinking, choosing. At last he heard of the California gold rush and went there. He decided that California was a very fine country, but after the rush was over he went back to England, married an English girl and brought his bride out to California in a sailing ship, all round Cape Horn. Intending to settle in California, he went into business but after a while it irked Father to live under any flag other than his own. In a few years, having decided to go back "home" to live, he chartered a vessel and took to England the first shipment of California wheat. But, staunch Englishman though my Father was, the New Land had said something to him and he chafed at the limitations of the Old which, while he was away from it, had appeared perfect. His spirit grew restless and, selling all his effects, he brought his wife and two small daughters out to the new world. Round the Horn they came again, and up, up, up the west coast of America till they came to the most English-tasting bit of all Canada — Victoria on the south end of Vancouver Island, which was then a Crown Colony.

Father stood still, torn by his loyalty to the Old Land and his delight in the New. He saw that nearly all the people in Victoria were English and smiled at how they tried to be more English than the English themselves, just to prove to themselves and the world how loyal they were being to the Old Land.

Father set his family down in British Columbia. He and Mother had accepted Canada long before I, the youngest but one of their nine children, was born. By that time their homesickness was healed. Instead of being English they had broadened out into being British, just as Fort Camosun had swelled herself from being a little Hudson's Bay Fort, inside a stockade with bastions at the corners, into being the little town of Victoria, and the capital of British Columbia.

Father bought ten acres of land — part of what was known as Beckley Farm. It was over James' Bay and I have heard my mother tell how she cried at the lonesomeness of going to live in a forest. Yet Father's land was only one mile out of the town....

As far back as I can remember Father's place was all made and in order. The house was large and well-built, of California redwood, the

This impressive house in Victoria is where Emily grew up amidst her father's dreams of England.

garden prim and carefully tended. Everything about it was extremely English. It was as though Father had buried a tremendous homesickness in this new soil and it had rooted and sprung up English. There were hawthorn hedges, primrose banks, and cow pastures with shrubberies.

We had an orchard and a great tin-lined apple room, wonderful strawberry beds and raspberry and currant bushes, all from imported English stock, and an Isabella grape vine which Father took great pride in. We had chickens and cows and a pig, a grand vegetable garden — almost everything we ate grew on our own place.

Just one of Father's fields was left Canadian. It was a piece of land which he bought later when Canada had made Father and Mother love her, and at the end of fifty years we still called that piece of ground "the new field." The New Field had a snake fence around it, that is, a zigzag fence made of split cedar logs or of young sapling trees laid crisscross, their own weight holding them in place so that they required no nails. Snake fences were extravagant in land and in wood, but wood and land were cheaper in Canada in early days than were nails and hinges. You made a gate wherever you wanted one by lowering bars to pass through and piling them up again. The only English thing in our new field was a stile built across the snake fence.

The New Field was full of tall fir trees with a few oaks. The underbrush had been cleared away and the ground was carpeted with our wild Canadian lilies, the most delicately lovely of all flowers — white with bent necks and brown eyes looking back into the earth. Their long, slender petals, rolled back from their drooping faces, pointed straight up at the sky, like millions of quivering white fingers. The leaves of the lilies were very shiny — green, mottled with brown, and their perfume like heaven and earth mixed.

James' Bay and Dallas Road

JAMES' BAY DISTRICT, where Father's property lay, was to the south of the town....

James' Bay was the part of the town to be first settled after Victoria had ceased to be a fort. Many Hudson's Bay men built fine homes across the Bay — Sir James Douglas, Mr. Alexander Munroe, Mr. James Bissett, Mr. James Lawson, Senator Macdonald, Bishop Cridge and Dr. Helmcken.

...

... When you climbed to the top of Beacon Hill and looked around you knew that the school geography was right after all and that the world really was round. Beacon Hill seemed to be the whole top of it and from all sides the land ran away from you and the edges were lost. To the west lay the purple hills of Sooke; to the south were the Straits of Juan de Fuca, rimmed by the snowy Olympic mountains, whose peaks were always playing in and out among the clouds till you could not tell which was peak and which sky. On the east there were more sea and islands. The town was on the north, with purple Cedar Hill and green Mount Tolmie standing behind it. Our winds came from the Olympics in summer and from the icy north in the winter.

... In the woody swamps of the Park millions and millions of frogs croaked all through the Spring nights. They sounded as if all the world was made of stiff paper and was crackling up.

Dallas Road was the first pleasure drive made in Victoria. Everyone drove along it to admire the view. The road ran sometimes close to the edge of the clay cliffs and sometimes there were thickets of willow and wild rose bushes between. The trees and bushes were so waved by the beating of the wind that they grew crooked from always being pushed north when they were really trying to poke south into the sun. There were stretches of fine, soft grass on the cliffs and great patches of camass and buttercups. As the wind swept over these they looked as if they, too, were running away from the sea. How the petals of the wild roses managed to stick to their middles I can't think, but they did and the bushes were more pink than green in June. Their perfume, salted by the sea air, was the most wonderful thing that ever happened to your nose.

...

Most of the beaches below Dallas Road were pebbly and had rough, rocky points jutting out into the sea and dividing the long beaches and the little bays one from another. All the beaches were piled with driftwood — great logs bruised and battered out of all resemblance to trees except that some of them still had tremendous, interlocked roots tough as iron, which defied all the pounding of the waves, all the battering against the rocks to break them. The waves could only wash them naked and fling them high up on the beach to show man what he had to wrestle against under the soil of the Canadian West. But the settlers were not stopped. They went straight ahead taming the land. It took more than roots to stop those men.

The waters of the Straits were icy. Occasionally we were allowed to put on white cotton nightgowns and go bathing in the sea. Your body went down, the nightgown stayed up, icy cold bit through your skin. At the first plunge you had no breath left; when it came back it was in screeches that out-screamed the seagulls.

Silence and Pioneers

THE SILENCE of our Western forests was so profound that our ears could scarcely comprehend it. If you spoke your voice came back to you as your face is thrown back to you in a mirror. It seemed as if the forest were so full of silence that there was no room for sounds. The birds who lived there were birds of prey — eagles, hawks, owls. Had a song bird loosed his throat the others would have pounced....

When we were children Father and Mother occasionally drove out beyond the town to Saanich, Metchosin or the Highland District, to visit some settler or other carving a home for his family in the midst of over-whelming growth — rebellious, untutored land that challenged his every effort. The settler was raising a family who would carry on from generation to generation. As he and his wife toiled at the breaking and the clearing they thought, "We are taming this wilderness for our children. It will be easier for them than for us. They will only have to carry on."

They felled mighty trees with vigour and used blasting powder and sweat to dislodge the monster roots. The harder they worked with the land, the more they loved these rooty little brown patches among the overwhelming green. The pioneer walked round his new field, pointing with hardened, twisted fingers to this and that which he had accomplished while the woman wrestled with the inconveniences of her crude home, planning the smart, modern house her children would have by and by, but the children would never have that intense joy of creating from nothing which their parents had enjoyed; they would never understand the secret wrapped in virgin land.

...

The first Victorians could tell splendid stories of when Victoria was a Hudson's Bay Post, was called Fort Camosun and had a strong blockade about it with a bastion at each corner to protect the families of the Hudson's Bay men from Indians and wild beasts.

Though my parents did not come to Victoria till after the days of the Fort and I was not born for many years after that, still there were people in Victoria only middle-aged when I was little, who had lived in the old Fort and could actually tell you about it. Nothing delighted me more than to hear these "still-fresh-yesterday" stories, that were not old "once-upon-a-timers!" You could ask questions of the very story people themselves and they did not have to crinkle their foreheads, trying to remember a long way back.

There was a childless couple with whom I was a favourite — Mrs. Lewis and her husband, the sea captain. Mrs. Lewis had been Miss Mary Langford before her marriage. Her Father was Captain Langford, a naval man. I am not certain whether the Langfords ever actually lived in the Fort or not but they came to Victoria at the very beginning of its being. Captain Langford built a log farmhouse six or seven miles out from town. The district was named for him.

...

Mrs. Lewis was a good teller. She was pretty to watch. The little bunch of black curls pinned high at the back of her head bobbed as she talked and her eyes sparkled. She told how young Naval officers used to take the pretty Miss Langfords out riding. When they came to Goldstream and Millstream, which were bubbling rivers with steep banks, that crossed the Langford trails, the men would blindfold the girls' horses and lead them across the river, using as a bridge a couple of fallen logs. One night as they were hurrying along a narrow deer trail, trying to get home before dark, they saw a panther stretched out on the limb of a tree under which they must pass in single file. The bushes were too dense for them to turn aside, so each rider whipped his horse and made a dash along the trail under the panther.

Mrs. Lewis told, too, of the coming of their piano from England. It sailed all round Cape Horn and was the first piano to come into the Colony of British Columbia. It landed at Esquimalt Harbour and was carried on the backs of Indians in relays of twenty at a time through a rough bush trail from Esquimalt to Langford. The tired Indians put the piano down in a field outside the house to rest a minute. The Langford girls rushed out with the key, unlocked and played the piano out there in the field. The Indians were very much astonished. They looked up into the sky and into the woods to see where the noise came from.

. . .

I was a very small girl when the business men of Victoria chartered a steamer and, accompanied by their families, made a tour of Vancouver Island. It took the boat, the *Princess Louise*, ten days to go all round the Island. My Father and two of my sisters went. I was thought to be too small but I was not too small to drink in every word they said when they came back.

Father was overwhelmed by the terrific density of growth on the Island. Once when they were tied up for three hours he and another man took axes and tried to see how far they could penetrate into the woods in the given time. When the ship's whistle blew they were exhausted and dripping with sweat but their attack on the dense undergrowth scarcely showed. Father told of the magnificent trees, of their closeness to each other, of the strangling undergrowth, the great silence, the quantity of bald-headed eagles. "Really bald, Father?" I asked, but he said they were a rusty black all over except for white heads which shone out against the blue sky and the dark forest. Great white owls flew silently among the trees like ghosts, and, too, they had seen bears and whales.

. . .

Saloons and Roadhouses

ON ALMOST every street corner in Victoria there was one saloon or more. There were saloons in the middle of every block as well.

I used to think that every saloon belonged to the Navy because sailors, wearing little boys' collars and wide trouser legs that flapped round their feet, rolled in and out of saloon doors at all times. These doors swung to noiselessly. They were only pinafore doors, made of slats and flapped to so quickly when a sailor went in or out that you never got a chance to see what it was they hid, not even if you were right in front when one was pushed open and nearly knocked you over. We were strictly forbidden to look at a saloon in passing. Grown-ups dragged you quickly past and told you to look up the street though there was nothing whatever to see there.

This made me long to know what was inside saloons. What was it that we were not supposed to see? Why was it naughty to twist your neck and look? You heard laughing and singing behind the swing doors. What did they do in there?

...

Goodacre, the butcher, had a slaughter-house out on Cadboro Bay Road. Cattle and sheep were brought from the Mainland by boat and landed at the wharf in front of Father's store. They were then driven straight through the centre of the town, up Fort Street which, after it had gone straight in the town, wiggled and twisted and called itself "Cadboro Bay Road".

The wild range cattle were crazed with fright. They bellowed and plunged all over the sidewalk, hoofing up the yellow dust. Women ran to shut their gates before the cattle rushed in and trampled their gardens. All the way up the street doors banged and gates slammed as everyone hurried to shelter.

I had been to visit my sister who lived on Fort Street. I was to go home by myself as there was no one to fetch me that day. It was the first time I had been through town alone. When I was just opposite the Bee Hive Saloon a drove of these wild cattle came tearing up the street. They were almost on top of me before I knew what all the dust and shouting and bellowing was about. Men with long whips whooped, dogs barked, the street seemed to be waving up and down with the dull red movement of beasts' backs bumping through the dust. Suddenly I was snatched up in a pair of huge black arms, a black face was near mine. It had grinning white teeth. We backed through the swing door and I was inside a saloon at last. The big black man set me down on the bar. The barkeeper and the negro ran to the window to look over the painted green glass at the boiling tumult of cattle outside. I could only hear their bellowing and scuttling.

I looked around the Saloon. Shiny taps were beside me and behind the long counter-bar ran shelves full of bottles and sparkling glasses; behind them again was looking-glass so that there seemed to be twice as many bottles and twice as many glasses as there really were, and two barmen and two negroes and two me's! In the back half of the saloon were barrels and small wooden tables; chairs with round backs stood about the floor with their legs sunk in sawdust; bright brass spitoons were everywhere. The saloon was full of the smell of beer and of sawdust. There was nothing else, nothing that I could see to make anyone sing.

...

Ways of Getting Round

BEYOND the few blocks of Victoria upon which the shops stood the roads were of dirt and had sidewalks of one, two or three planks according to the street's importance. A great many people kept cows to supply their own families with milk. When their own pasture field was eaten down they turned the cow into the street to browse on roadside grass along the edges of the open ditches, or to meander out to the grassy land on top of the cliffs off Dallas Road. Victoria cows preferred to walk on the plank sidewalks in winter rather than dirty their hooves in the mud by the roadside. They liked to tune their chews to the tap, tap, tap of their feet on the planks. Ladies challenged the right-of-way by opening and shutting their umbrellas in the cows' faces and shooing, but the cows only chewed harder and stood still. It was the woman-lady, not the lady-cow who had to take to the mud and get scratched by the wild rose bushes that grew between sidewalk and fence while she excursioned round the cow.

...

There was no way to get about young Victoria except on legs — either your own or a horse's. Those people who had a field, a barn, and a cow usually kept a horse too. The horses did not roam; they had to be kept handy for hitching. All the vehicles used were very English. Families with young children preferred a chaise, in which two people faced the horse and two the driver. These chaises were low and so heavy that the horse dragged, despondent and slow. The iron tires made such a rumbling over the rough stony roads that it was difficult to hear conversation while travelling in a chaise especially when to the rumble was added the rattle of wheel spokes that had got over-dry and loosened. What you did then was to drive as deep as you dared into the first stream you knew of and let the chaise wheels soak, all the while encouraging the horse to go forward and back, turning the wheels in the water until they swelled again. You could not go into very deep water for fear of drowning the driver for the chaises were set so low that the driver sat right down among the wheel hubs....

Men preferred to drive in high, two-wheeled dogcarts in which passengers sat back to back and bumped each other's shoulder blades. The seat of the driver was two cushions higher than that of the other passengers. Men felt frightfully high and fine, perched up there cracking the whip over the horse's back and looking over the tops of their wives' hats. There were American buggies, too, with or without hoods which could be folded back like the top of a baby's pram.

...

In town there were lots of livery stables where you could hire horses or could board your own. The smell of horse manure was so much a part of every street that it sat on your nose as comfortably as a pair of spectacles. Of course there were no livery stables among the drygoods, food, and chemists' shops. Everywhere else you saw "Livery Stable" printed above wide, cool entries and heard horses chewing and stamping, and saw long rows of tails swishing out of stalls on either side of a plankway while ugly, square vehicles called hacks stood handy waiting for horses to be hitched to them. These hacks for hire were very stuffy. The town had one imported hansom-cab which thought itself very smart, and there was Mr. Winter's picnic carriage, a huge vehicle that held as many children as the Old Woman's Shoe. When its wide, circular back seat was crammed and more children were heaped on top of Mr. Winter up on his high driver's seat, and they were all yelling, and yellow dust rolling, and wheels rumbling, it looked and sounded like a beehive swarming. For immense affairs like Sunday School picnics and excursions there were yellow buses with long rows of windows, long wooden seats, uncushioned except for strips of carpet running from driver to door. They had no springs to speak of, and were so noisy that you could not hear your own groans being bumped out of you.

Victoria's baker and butcher boys delivered meat and bread on horse-back, carrying their loaves and joints in huge wicker baskets rested against their hips. As soon as they had one foot in the stirrup and while their other leg was still flying in the air over the horse as he galloped off, they shouted "Giddap!" It was a wonder the boys did not grow crooked balancing such heavy baskets on their hips, but they did not — they were straight and strong. I used to wish I were a delivery boy to throw my leg across a horse and shout "Giddap!" to feel myself rush through the air, but I should have preferred bread to meat in my basket.

The first time I knew that Victoria was slower than other towns was when, at the age of twelve, I was recovering from typhoid fever and a lady whom Mother knew, and whose two children had had typhoid in the same epidemic as I, took me along with her little girls for a trip to Puget Sound. It was my first visit to an American city and I felt giddy in the head from its rush. I heard Americans laugh and say "slow as Canadian" and call my town "sleepy old Victoria."

I heard one man say to another, "Went across the line this summer."

"Did eh? What sort of a place is Victoria?"

"Sleepiest ever!" laughed the first, "Every place of business had a notice up, 'Gone to lunch. Back in a couple of hours.'"

This was the first time I knew we were slow.

...

Americans dashed across the line sometimes to look at us Canadians and at British Columbia as if we had been dust-covered antiques. They thought English and Canadian people as slow and stupid as we thought the American people uncomfortable rushers — makers of jerry-built goods that fell to pieces in no time. We preferred to wait ages for our things to come by sailing ship round the Horn from England rather than to buy American goods. This annoyed the American manufacturers.

Emily Carr, *The Book of Small.*

26

Charlotte Selina Bompas

(1830–1917)

Charlotte Selina Bompas, née Cox, was born into an established musical family in London, England, but because of her physician father's asthma the family spent many years in Italy. At her first ball given by the British ambassador, she danced with the King of Naples. This artistic young woman, who wrote for magazines and spoke Italian, initially had little interest in religion (she described missionary meetings at her brother's vicarage in Devonshire as "the dullest affairs"). But that changed in 1874, when she married her second cousin, William Carpenter Bompas ("The Apostle of the North"), who had been consecrated bishop of the newly formed diocese of Athabasca. Five days after the wedding, they set off on the arduous journey to Fort Simpson, a Hudson's Bay Company post in the Northwest Territories. Charlotte Selina Bompas was to spend most of the rest of her life there, interspersed with long stays in England and Montreal for the sake of her health. Although life was primitive and lonely, with precarious supplies, she learned the Slavey language, enlivened church services by playing the harmonium, supported the Northern mission field by raising much-needed funds, and created a centre for miners during the Yukon gold rush. After her husband's death in 1917, she lived with two nieces in Westmount, Quebec, where she is buried.

Extracts from her journals and letters were published in *A Heroine of the North: Memoirs of Charlotte Selina Bompas* (1929), compiled by S.A. Archer. An earlier work, *Owindia: A True Tale of the Mackenzie River Indian North-West America* (1886), was a tribute to one of two small children she had informally adopted — both died young — and an attempt at publicity for the missions.

GOLD RUSH

[1892]

You know that the exact position of my husband's diocese is between the Rocky Mountains and the United States Territory of Alaska, extending from the Arctic Ocean on the north to the boundary of British Columbia on the south. The diocese contains 200,000 square miles; the population is now only about 5,000, including some hundreds of miners.

...

The mission centres now established consist of one at Rampart House on the Porcupine River, St. John's Mission, Buxton, and at Selkirk, both these latter on the Upper Yukon. Intermediate mission stations are greatly needed, and work amongst the miners is most important.

At present the only certain communication with the outer world is by steamers from San Francisco in May or June, or occasionally in August.

The great drawback to this position is that we are not far from the gold reefs to which the miners come in crowds from all parts of the world, and they intend making our station their headquarters during the winter months, when they cannot work the mines. We have every reason to fear that their goings on will be very sad and distressing, and to the ruin of our poor Indians. I want to try and open a sort of club-room for the miners with magazines and paper and occasional music, and to get a few of the men to join the "White Cross Army."

...

We have been working very hard ever since I arrived, and what has been accomplished is really marvellous. The house here was scarcely finished when Mr. Ellington left on account of failing health, and Archdeacon Macdonald put one of the native catechists in charge, who allowed a number of Indians to have free run of the house, and the state of filth and disorder when we took possession was really terrible. However, with much hard work and patience, a good cleaning has been effected, many repairs carried out, partitions made in the rooms, besides tables and benches, and hanging up the school bell. I have taken up my quarters for the present in a good-sized loft, which is divided into three rooms by means of curtains. I have my own furniture round me, which came quite safely, my chairs and little tables and carpet and mats, all the dear home treasures of pictures and photographs, with my bookshelves which are quite full, so you may think of me as very snug and comfortable, although with only sloping rafters. I sit at my window and look at the beautiful Yukon flowing by so stately and yet swiftly, and at the Eastern mountains which I tell myself lie towards Salisbury! The quiet life and mountain air suit my health. There is no bustle or excitement here, but yet I have so much to do that I never feel dull. God has granted me the desire of my heart in bringing me back to my husband and my work amongst the Indians. My life henceforth is doubly consecrated to Him in humblest service.

...

BUXTON (ALSO CALLED FORTY MILE), ST. JOHN'S MISSION

August 1892

In vain I look and long for tidings from my dear ones. One realizes now our immense distance from civilization. Not only is there no Government mail, but this is the first year that any stamps have been in the country, and there has been such a rush for them by the miners, that they are all sold already, so we have to trust to a happy chance of someone stamping and forwarding our letters from St. Michael.

...

November 6

... My life here is a very busy one, but just such a one as I love, with plenty to do for the hands and heart, and not overtaxing the brain. Of course, some things one would wish very different, but apart from this, one has such store of mercies as one could hardly deem possible to be vouch-safed to one so utterly unworthy. My dear husband is in so much better health since he came to this side of the Rockies.

...

In these regions winter sets in very early. We seem more thoroughly Arctic than at Fort Simpson, and everyone dresses accordingly. We wear such beautiful fur boots made of fur and deer-skin, or Russian shoes made of sheep-skin with the wool inside. They are warmer than moccasins, but still one has to wear warm stockings and blanket socks inside the shoes.

...

January 20, 1893

We have been here six months. It seems much longer, for we have got into regular routine, and the weeks fly by only too quickly. The little Mission House is very plain and homely, and very small, as, especially in the winter, we have to live in the smallest space possible to economize fuel, as, of course, we burn only wood here. We have a good outer kitchen, but we can only use it in summer, as the air comes in between the logs at every chink, so, with the four Indian girls, we are confined to the three rooms, and they none of the largest, and I find it difficult to keep them all in order. For the most part our days run thus:

William is up between five and six and kindly sees to the starting of the three stoves. I have a short, quiet time and then call up the girls, who dress and proceed to their different duties. "Tosca," whom I have made the cook, a fine handsome girl of fifteen, gets the breakfast, usually dried fish (always salmon here), tea, bread and butter. The latter, and flour, we get from the traders, and I make — myself — all the bread for the household. Before breakfast we go into the Bishop's study for prayers. I have a nice harmonium there and play a hymn when the keys are not too hard frozen.

The school bell rings at 9:30, and then comes a scramble to finish washing up, sweeping rooms, etc., and each girl comes to me for inspection before going in to school. Then Baby Mary and I have the house to ourselves. I make arrangements for dinner and then, if it is not too cold, take a short walk with baby, wrapped in her "parka," as it is called here — a pretty deer-skin coat with a hood coming over the face. It is very warm, and she looks so quaint and pretty in it. I shall try to send you home a parka to see. It is very merciful of God to let me have charge of another little Indian child. It was very painful at first, as she is just the age of my dear little Lucy the year we went to Fort Norman, and one seemed living over the past again, and at times almost forgot the interval of deep sorrow. But she is quite unlike my little "Owindia," except in some of her quaint Indian ways. She is really a lovely child with passionate black eyes. Her mother was a Chilkat Indian — a tribe which has always been very warlike, and given at times a great deal of trouble. Mary's fits of passion are fearful. I was quite frightened the first time I saw her in one of them, when the small creature threw herself on the floor and rolled backwards and forwards across the room, roaring as loudly as she could. She clings to me with great affection, and if she wants anything coaxes very prettily by putting up her mouth to "kuss." One day last autumn she was thirsty, so with the pluck and independence of her nation and tribe, she toddled alone down the bank to the river's brim and there lay down and drank, sucking up the water with avidity. It was such a pretty picture! The great Yukon River rolling on its turbulent course of more than 2,000 miles, and

A miner pans for treasure during the Gold Rush.

Library and Archives Canada, C-005389.

the tiny child quenching her thirst out of it as if it had been only a saucer.

We are here in the centre of a large gold-mining district. Fresh creeks are constantly being prospected and found to be rich in ore and gold dust. These are most of them on American territory, but the access to the mines is from the British side. Miners are arriving every year in increasing numbers. About 350 are now stationed at Birch Creek, some 100 miles from Fort Yukon. They are already building houses, and have named their new settlement Circle City, being situated close to, if not within the Arctic Circle. The miners make this, Forty Mile Creek, their headquarters during the winter. They have built themselves neat, comfortable cabins, some of them with kitchen gardens. Many of them are well-educated men, far ahead of the low average level of the mining camps. But others, again, are of a very different type, and these come from their mines flush of money, ready to spend it in any way that will furnish them with comforts, luxuries, and amusements. And two first-class traders are here, with well-equipped stores, containing every article that heart could fancy, from a flour-bag to a wedding ring (which latter article, alas, is perhaps the one least frequently asked for in the whole colony). Here is a good lending library and billiard-room. Here at least six saloons, several restaurants, and a theatre. We can also boast of two doctors, two blacksmiths, one watchmaker, and one dressmaker, with the latest fashions from Duncan. And, worse than all these, there are several distilleries where rum or whisky is made and sold to the Indians, and they have learned to make it for themselves, and that other highly intoxicating spirit called "Hoochino." Thus our Indians, being brought into contact with the white man, fall in only too easily with his taste for luxury, love of gambling, coarse, vile language, and for the miserable and ruthless degradation of women. Our American citizen would scorn to marry an Indian; indeed, by an iniquitous law of his country he is forbidden to do so; but the higher law of God he can set aside and ignore. The sweet, oval face and laughing eyes of our Indian girl please him; he knows that she can be made as deft with her hands, as tidy and orderly, as skilful with her needle as any white woman. She is sadly, deplorably vain, poor child, and a gay shawl or two, a pair of gold ear-rings, will sorely tempt her, as the bag of flour has tempted her father to wink at the transaction.

Yet even we are not without some gleams to cheer us, some light amid the clouds to whisper hope and comfort. We have, thank God, a few, too few, yet each time an increasing number of Indian communicants. There are some of our men making strenuous efforts to keep from drink. We have heard of some leaving this neighbourhood and going off into the woods to be out of the way of temptation. Throughout the last winter, with a temperature as low as 55° and 64° below zero, when the lamps would hardly burn from the frozen oil, we never failed to have our little band of worshippers at Evensong; men holding their ears from the cold, women wrapped in their blankets, little ones toddling along in their rabbit-skin coats, would hasten in at the sound of the mission bell, and join reverently in the prayers and singing.

...

The Bishop contemplates opening another mission beyond Selkirk, where are a number of heathen Indians who have never yet heard the sound of the Gospel.

EXTRACTS FROM JOURNAL

January 29, 1893

It is a strange state of things here, for there is no law and no magistrate. The miners have their own code of laws, which are, for the most part, pretty fair, and they often do most generous acts among themselves and to others also. By-the-by, on Christmas Day a deputation of miners came up to see us and presented me with a gold nugget worth about £10 in honour of my being the first white lady who has wintered so far north.

As to my health, this last and closing chapter of my life exhibits quite a new condition of things. I am wonderfully stronger and able to get through a very tolerable amount of work in the day, feeling none the worse at night, except natural tire.

...

May 22, 1893

By the great mercy of God I have been greatly comforted and refreshed by four of your letters brought over from Juneau, on the Pacific coast, by the first miners. I must begin by saying, in answer to your cravings for news of us, that we are quite well, thank God, having all of us, including Mr. Totty, Bishop, and myself, with the Indian girls, now seven number, passed through the eight months' winter without one day's illness, or any sufferings to speak of from the cold.

It was comforting to feel the sun, which we had not seen at all for six weeks, gaining daily, and the days lengthening. The snow melted gradually, and little bits of green grass appeared from time to time. Then a fly upon our window, which caused great excitement to little Baby Mary, then came snow-birds, and ducks and geese and snipe and the dear swallows. Large spaces of open water then appeared upon the river, growing larger and larger, and last Friday (May 12) at 10:30 pm came the sound of rushing wind or water, and behold! all the river was in motion, the great mass of ice moving along suddenly, while huge blocks five or six feet thick were tossed up on the banks as if they were only foam. It has been interesting to watch the disappearance of the ice. As soon as the great Yukon was clear of its own share, down came the Pelly River ice, and then that of the White River and more from the lakes north of this.

. . .

Our short summer is drawing to a close — there are already many signs of autumn coming on. Our winter store of wood is lying near the house on the bank, in the shape of great trees which were cut down and brought here on a raft. A man is engaged to cut them into small logs and faggots to fit each stove. It has cost us £60 to get all this done, but it is a splendid lot of dry wood, and will, I hope, last throughout the winter.

. . .

Our Sundays are very peaceful. The Indian service at ten o'clock, and we have a good number at it. The English service immediately afterwards, when some of the miners come, and we hope the number will increase. The singing is very nice and hearty, especially at the Indian service. The Indians are very musical and have good voices. I enjoy teaching them, and they so respond to all one's efforts and take a real interest in the service. Some of them are fine manly fellows, beside whom a great proportion of the miners look small and pitiful. If we could only get more clergy out here!

August 30

The steamer just come in and all is bustle and confusion. We have a large mail of letters and newspapers, but your package is not come, and I wanted many of the things I sent for. Never mind! I must wait patiently and hope for it in another nine or twelve months!

A Mrs. Beaumont, wife of one of the traders, came up from St. Michael to have her first baby baptized. "Mary Yukana" behaved very prettily, and is said to be the first white child born within the Arctic Circle.

...

December 1893

... We are weathering the winter, which is pretty severe just now, without suffering or any great hardship. By dint of constant effort during the last two months W. has got our house into a far more warm and comfortable condition than it has been before. He has had all our rooms lined with what is called here "drill," a coarse strong calico, and then covered with a thick coating of red paint. The schoolroom was the last to be papered, but we fear it will be lost labour here, for the cold was so severe (that is, 50° below zero) that the paste froze on the wall before it could dry (in spite of a large fire), and all the paper is cracking.

Our great business of the day is getting in our wood and water. It is so picturesque a scene that I must describe it.

At twelve o'clock Miss M. and the children come out of school and the five elder mission girls muster on the bank — all wrapped up to their noses and with their fur mittens on — and run down to the water hole, which is some short distance out on the river. The girls all carry pails, and the Bishop precedes them with an ice chisel and axe to open the water hole, which has to be done anew every day. Then he bales out the water and the girls run up to the house, where there are one or two large water-kegs close to the stoves. It takes three or four pails to fill the two kegs, at each of which Miss M. stands to empty the pails into them, or the children are sure to spill the water, which immediately becomes ice.

After this they are all summoned to get in wood. Our firewood is now chopped and piled on the top of the bank, extending for fifty or sixty yards, and is six feet high. The girls put the billets of wood into a neat little sledge which the Bishop has had made and haul it in, and then carry them in to the wood boxes in the different rooms.

Although it was taken in Montreal in 1896, this Notman Studio photograph of Mrs Bompas with Snowshoes *captures her indomitable spirit.*

McCord Museum, ii16337.

It is wonderful how much wood we consume this weather. I fear that our large pile will hardly carry us till spring.

It is a comfort that the children all like the wood and water business and think it high fun. Yesterday, with glowing cheeks, they assured me it was not at all cold. At that time in the middle of the day, with a bright sun, the thermometer was 50° below zero.

Our greatest trials just now are the very short days. Miss M. says she is quite out of breath trying to catch up her time. We shall lose the sun now for some weeks. He has been rising later and later and describing a smaller arch each day, but one has still most lovely colouring at the time of rise and set, and then the gloaming is so passing beautiful.

I often think when I turn out in the morning at eight o'clock it must be like the light on the first day of creation, when God said: "Let there be Light."

I have been so mercifully kept in health, hardly ever a headache, and my digestion is so much stronger that I can live on the porridge and dried fish, which is now our principal food, without suffering as I did at first. In spite of all this, however, I feel the infirmities of age coming rapidly upon me. My hair is growing grey, and I have had to take to spectacles, when I can get them, but alas! according to the invariable practice of old ladies, I am for ever losing them! And yet one's inner man is still youthful enough.

Our household goes on very peacefully and happily. Miss Millett is a real blessing to us. She is a thorough Irish girl and a good churchwoman. She gets on well with everybody. The children are devoted to her, and she keeps them in first-rate order. One comfort is that she has good health and is not troubled with nerves. She bears the cold manfully, and was only a little startled lately when her blanket at night was fringed with icicles from her breath freezing....

...

January 16, 1894

The letters which were to have started ten days since are still delayed, our good miner having been forced to postpone his start in consequence of a severe spell of cold. How severe you will understand when I tell you that for some days our thermometer ranged between 60° and 70° below zero, and for two days went down to 73° and 75°. It was a very sharp experience, such as I had never before undergone, and certainly was trying enough, but God's hand sustained us and we were kept in health and in good spirits all the time. Even this low temperature is endurable so long as the air is still, but, if the least wind rises, it requires very strong courage and resolution to take a walk. But our North-West attire is such as to render us almost impervious to cold and our "brave northeasters," and even 100° of frost fail to penetrate our seal-skin, long-legged boots, and deer-skin "parquets," which parquets are a coat and hood all in one, the latter completely covering the head and forehead, and is edged with a thick fringe of grey wolf fur. One night during the intense cold we had a most glorious aurora and were obliged to stand outside and watch it, with only our eyes uncovered in spite of everything. I cannot describe to you the beauty of the colouring which shot across the sky. The very heavens seemed to open in a beauty which one cannot describe.

Can you imagine the cold of the handle of a kettle on the fire being so intense that one cannot touch it, while the kettle itself is boiling? The temperature has now moderated and we can breathe more comfortably, although you will not think 46° (below zero) very mild.

We welcomed the first disc of the sun back on January 7. We had had no sun above our horizon for nearly six weeks, and so we hailed his return almost with shouts and acclamations. Yet in these snowy regions our winter nights are by no means of pitchy darkness. Even had we no aurora to shed its consecrated gleams upon our sky, the reflection from our bright carpet of snow is enough to make visible most of the surrounding landscape. Our twilight also is so long that, even when the sun does not rise at all, there are lovely streaks of day-dawn in the south-east in the early morning, and the last streak will not expire till nearly 5 pm.

It is very pretty to see one of our Mission children often seated on the ground with a group of Indian women around her, showing and carefully explaining Scripture prints. The exclamations of amazement and admiration are wonderful, and the intelligence and interest they evince are very interesting....

But I must not say more. W. protests against every letter I write. In truth, my brain is weak. I feel writing at all an increasing difficulty. I have to write a little and then run out for a breath of air. I fear that my various falls on the ice have certainly injured my spine and this tells upon the poor brain. Still I plod on in hope. I cannot tell you how precious some of the books that you have sent are to me. Of the large parcel that you speak of nothing has been heard as yet. Maybe it will arrive in July after two years' wandering!

"Forty Mile Creek" in Selina Bompas, *A Heroine of the North: Memoirs of Charlotte Selina Bompas*.

27

Letitia Hargrave

(1813–1854)

Letitia Hargrave, née Mactavish, granddaughter of the chief of the Tavish clan, was to experience a very different life in the North after her proper Victorian upbringing in Scotland. Her family was of great significance in the Canadian fur trade: the famous Nor'wester Simon McTavish was a relative, and her uncle and three brothers were also involved with what later became the Hudson's Bay Company. She was educated at a ladies' finishing school and in 1840 married James Hargrave, chief trader at the main supply depot on Hudson Bay. After several months in London, the Hargraves sailed for York Factory. Her detailed, perceptive, and entertaining letters home provide a remarkable portrait, first of Dickensian London, then of mid-nineteenth-century life in a remote post in which, James Hargrave wrote, there were "nine months of winter varied by three of rain and mosquitoes."

"My 1st exploit on being lowered into the yawl," his wife confessed, "was to turn my back on the company & cry myself sick." Life was difficult — both Hargraves suffered from ill-health — but this kind and witty Scotswoman did have a comfortable house with a handsome piano "seasoned for any extremes of climate," and her fashionable gowns were a subject of amazement. The women of the area brought Hockimaw Erqua (Chieftainess) flowers and berries, and she was impressed by their care

A spirited rendering of The Governor of the Red River, Hudson's Bay, Voyaging in a Light Canoe *in 1825 by Peter Rindisbacher.*

for their children. For the Hargraves, there was the birth of five children, painful separation for the sake of their education, a few trips home, and eventually a longed-for transfer to Sault Ste. Marie, Ontario. Tragically, this more pleasant life was to last only two years. Letitia Hargrave died suddenly of cholera in 1854.

TRAGEDY

TO MRS. DUGALD MACTAVISH

York Factory 1st April 1843

My dear Mama

When I closed my letter on the 9th Decem altho' anxious & uneasy, I had little idea of the pain I now feel in writing to you again. Hargrave wrote papa the moment that my poor baby was born, wch was about 2 on the 10th, & died on the 27th — I will try & tell you its sad history. Altho I think of it constantly I will never be able to write with composure. I became ill about midnight but was not regularly so till 8 in the morning, and till 12, was no worse than I had expected. After that, the suffering was fearful & almost continuous till, after what seemed to me some difficulty on the D^{rs} part, the child was born. The delay had been caused by the navel cord being twisted round his neck, & when I looked the D^r was working with him & he was blue & had not breathed. When I saw the little chest move, I never as completely forgot myself, nor felt any thing like the gladness I did. It was very large & strong, much more so than Joseph was. I fear that my trials began with myself for my breasts got so sore that the irritation brought on a feverish attack & we had to get a nurse for awhile, for he drank so constantly that I c^d not get them properly treated. The girl had a thriving baby of her own wch she left with her sister. I was nervous about it, but they assured me there was no danger. After the 2nd day I nursed him at night myself but from having been ill & leaving off had not enough of milk & kept her. He continued well till the 24th when he kept wailing all day. The D^r thought there was nothing the matter as his pulse was good & he drank as usual. Next day he was better till night when I found that there was something fearfully wrong. The D^r came & said it was rupture. He reduced it easily & comforted me by saying that it was not dangerous in an infant. He said shortly after that there seemed to be a little inflammation & after a little hesitation put 2 leeches on his hand, he remained watching all day till 5 when he said the pulse was much calmer, breathing better, & bid me offer him a drink in a little, & call him if there was any change as he was tired from being up all night & w^d take a rest. Willie came in & assured me that the complaint was so rapid that he must be recovering & told me that it was very common here that Munroes whole family were born with hernia & that men & boys of them were strong. He left me along with Hargrave quite satisfied that danger was over. The child on my knee, Marg^t lay down to hush Joseph & they fell asleep together — I felt babys hands rather cold about 9 & rose from the stove to get some more to put round him when shortly after he gave a sharp cry & Marg^t awoke. It was the first time he had cried for 8 hours & was so peculiar that she ran for Harg^{ve} & the D^r. I soon found that there was no hope. They took it from me & I only recollect thinking of every thing in the world but it

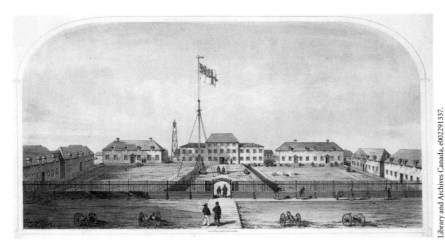

York Factory in 1853, ten years later than when Mrs Hargrave was wrestling with a garden which "only produced a few very small red cabbages about the size that cresses are & of course quite green. Mary made 6 pickle bottles full with chili vinegar & that was all we had except for a few miserable lettuces."

till I saw Willie carry him out of the room, I dont know when. I asked the D^r next day if I had been too late of sending for him but he said no, he had done all he could, & hoped from several symptoms particularly by its bowels being very open, that it would have recovered.

Poor Hargrave was terribly distressed, but he soon got well again. I thought I never [would]. The first thing that roused me was an attack of pains in the nerves like Tic Doloureux. I have lain for 36 hours without stirring or drawing my breath further than was absolutely necessary. This remained for a month & went off gradually. We have all been perfectly well for 6 weeks past, Beppo growing in mind & body. He has known all his large letters since the end of January and recites with great emphasis all the nursery rhymes he has an opportunity of acquiring. Poor thing he was so frightened & perplexed by the disappearance of his little brother. He used to come looking so bewildered to my bed side & look anxiously for it — None baby, none baby, poor Mama.

Letitia Hargrave, *The Letters of Letitia Hargrave.*

28

Mina Hubbard

(1870–1956)

Mina Hubbard Ellis, née Benson, was born on a farm near Rice Lake to parents whose families had immigrated to the area in the 1840s. After an education that began in a one-room schoolhouse, she moved to New York and graduated as a nurse in 1899. After nursing journalist Leonidas Hubbard, Jr. through typhoid fever, she married him in 1901. Hubbard, who wrote for an outdoor adventure magazine, dreamed of a great adventure, and persuaded his editor to let him make an ambitious expedition through the barren lands of Labrador. The territory was unmapped and virtually unknown to the outside world. With his friend Dillon Wallace, a lawyer, and George Elson, a Scottish-Cree woodsman from northern Ontario, the group sailed for Labrador in June 1920. Due to their inexperience and virtually every mishap possible, they turned back before reaching the halfway point. Hubbard died of starvation in his tent while the others sought help. They returned with his body to New York in May. Wallace wrote a book about the ill-fated venture, but the young widow was displeased with his portrayal of her husband and withdrew her support for the project. Nevertheless, *The Lure of the Labrador Wild* became a perennial bestseller, going through many editions.

In 1905, Wallace planned to return to Labrador to complete the journey. Mina Hubbard secretly planned an expedition of her own

— the press joyfully chronicled the contest. George Elson joined her with three other guides. The two groups departed a day apart, following different routes. Mina Hubbard, who had learned from the mistakes of the first trip, took proper supplies and reached her destination six weeks earlier than Wallace, thus winning the race. *A Woman's Way Through Unknown Labrador* (1908), first published in *Harper's*, is considered a more valuable guide than Wallace's more popular *The Long Labrador Trail* (1907). After her return to the United States, she lectured widely on her Labrador experience. In 1907 she met Harold Ellis during a speaking tour in England and married him a year later. She stayed in England following their divorce in 1926, but returned often to Canada and remains an inspiration to those who continue to explore this beautiful and untamed land.

CARIBOU

TUESDAY morning, August 8th, dawned clear and calm, and Gilbert came forth to light the fire, singing: "Glory, glory, hallelujah! as we go marching along." Yet before the tents were taken down the wind had sprung up from the southwest, and it was with difficulty that the canoes were launched and loaded.

A short distance above our starting-point, we were obliged to run into a sheltered bay, where part of the load was put ashore, and with the canoes thus lightened we crossed to a long, narrow point which reached half-way across from the other side, making an excellent breakwater between the upper and lower parts of the lake. The crossing was accomplished in safety, though it was rough enough to be interesting, and Job and Joe went back for what had been left behind.

The point terminated in a low, pebbly beach, but its banks farther up were ten to twelve feet high, and above it was covered with reindeer moss. Towards the outer end there were thickets of dwarf spruce, and throughout its length scattered trees that had bravely held their heads up in spite of the storms of the dread northern winter. To the south of the point was a beautiful little bay, and at its head a high sand mound which we found to be an Indian burying-place. There were four graves, one large one with three little ones at its foot, each surrounded by a neatly made paling, while a wooden cross, bearing an inscription in Montagnais, was planted at the head of each moss-covered mound. The inscriptions were worn and old except that on one of the little graves. Here the cross was a new one, and the palings freshly made. Some distance out on the point stood a skeleton wigwam carpeted with boughs that were still green, and lying about outside were the fresh cut shavings telling where the Indian had fashioned the new cross and the enclosure about the grave of his little one. Back of this solitary resting-place were the moss-covered hills with their sombre forests, and as we turned from them we looked out over the bay at our feet, the shining waters of the lake, and beyond it to the blue, round-topped hills reaching upward to blend with exquisite harmony into the blue and silver of the great dome that stooped to meet them. Who could doubt that romance and poetry dwell in the heart of the Indian who chose this for the resting-place of his dead.

Walking back along the point we found it cut by caribou trails, and everywhere the moss was torn and trampled in a way that indicated the presence there of many of the animals but a short time since. Yet it did not occur to me that we might possibly be on the outskirts of the march of the migrating caribou. Ptarmigan were there in numbers, and flew up all along our way. We passed a number of old camps, one a large oblong, sixteen feet in length, with two fireplaces in it, each marked by a ring of small rocks, and a doorway at either end. Near where we landed, close in the shelter of a thicket of dwarf spruce, was a deep bed of boughs, still green, where some wandering aboriginal had spent the night without taking time or trouble to erect his wigwam, and who in passing on had set up three poles pointing northward to tell his message to whoever might come after.

The wind continued high, and squalls and heavy showers passed. Nevertheless, when lunch was over we pushed on, keeping close to the west shore of the lake. Little more than a mile further up the men caught sight of deer feeding not far from the water's edge. We landed, and climbing to the top of the rock wall saw a herd of fifteen or more feeding in the swamp. I watched them almost breathless. They were very beautiful, and it was an altogether new and delightful experience to me. Soon they saw us and trotted off into the bush, though without sign of any great alarm. George and Job made off across the swamp to the right to investigate, and not long after returned, their eyes blazing with excitement, to say that there were hundreds of them not far away.

Slipping hurriedly back into the canoes we paddled rapidly and silently to near the edge of the swamp. Beyond it was a barren hill, which from near its foot sloped more gradually to the water. Along the bank, where this lower slope dropped to the swamp, lay a number of stags, with antlers so immense that I wondered how they could possibly carry them. Beyond, the lower slope of the hill seemed to be a solid mass of caribou, while its steeper part was dotted over with many feeding on the luxuriant moss.

Those lying along the bank got up at sight of us, and withdrew towards the great herd in rather leisurely manner, stopping now and then to watch us curiously. When the herd was reached, and the alarm given, the stags lined themselves up in the front rank and stood facing us, with heads high and a rather defiant air. It was a magnificent sight. They were in summer garb of pretty brown, shading to light grey and white on the under parts. The horns were in velvet, and those of the stags seemed as if they must surely weigh down the heads on which they rested. It was a mixed company, for male and female were already herding together. I started towards the herd, kodak in hand, accompanied by George, while the others remained at the shore. The splendid creatures seemed to grow taller as we approached, and when we were within two hundred and fifty yards of them their defiance took definite form, and with determined step they came towards us.

The sight of that advancing army under such leadership was decidedly impressive, recalling vivid mental pictures made by tales of the stampeding wild cattle in the west. It made one feel like getting back to the canoe, and that is what we did. As we ran towards the other men I noticed a peculiar smile on their faces, which had in it a touch of superiority. I understood in part when I turned, for the caribou had stopped their advance, and were again standing watching us. Now the others started towards the herd. Emboldened by their courage, and thinking that perhaps they held the charm that would make a close approach to the herd possible, I accompanied them. Strange to relate it was but a few minutes till we were all getting back to the canoes, and we did not again attempt to brave their battle front. We and the caribou stood watching each other for some time. Then the caribou began to run from either extreme of the herd, some round the south end of the hill, and the others away to the north, the line of stags still maintaining their position.

After watching them for some time we again entered the canoes. A short paddle carried us round the point beyond which the lake bent to the northwest, and there we saw them swimming across the lake. Three-quarters of a mile out was an island, a barren ridge standing out of the water, and from mainland to island they formed as they swam a broad unbroken bridge; from the farther end of which they poured in steady stream over the hill-top, their flying forms clearly outlined against the sky. How long we watched them I could not say, for I was too excited to take any note of time; but finally the main body had passed.

Yet when we landed above the point from which they had crossed, companies of them, eight, ten, fifteen, twenty in a herd, were to be seen in all directions. When I reached the top of the ridge accompanied by George and Gilbert, Job and Joe were already out on the next hill beyond, and Job was driving one band of a dozen or more toward the water at the foot of the hill, where some had just plunged in to swim across. Eager to secure a photo or two at closer range than any I had yet obtained, I handed George my kodak and started down the hill at a pace which threatened every second to be too fast for my feet, which were not dressed in the most appropriate running wear. However the foot of the hill was reached in safety. There a bog lay across our way. I succeeded in keeping dry for a few steps, then gave it up and splashed through at top speed. We had just hidden ourselves behind a huge boulder to wait for the coming of the herd, when turning round I saw it upon the hill from which we had just come. While exclaiming over my disappointment I was startled by a sound immediately behind me, and turning saw a splendid stag and three does not twenty feet away. They saw us and turned, and I had scarcely caught my breath after the surprise when they were many more than twenty feet away, and there was barely time to snap my shutter on them before they disappeared over the brow of the hill.

The country was literally alive with the beautiful creatures, and they did not seem to be much frightened. They apparently wanted only to keep what seemed to them a safe distance between us, and would stop to watch us curiously within easy rifle shot. Yet I am glad I can record that not a shot was fired at them. Gilbert was wild, for he had in him the hunter's instinct in fullest measure. The trigger of Job's rifle clicked longingly, but they never forgot that starvation broods over Labrador, and that the animal they longed to shoot might some time save the life of one in just such extremity as that reached by Mr. Hubbard and his party two years before.

The enjoyment of the men showed itself in the kindling eyes and faces luminous with pleasure. All his long wilderness experience had never afforded Job anything to compare with that which this day had brought him. He was like a boy in his abandon of delight, and I am sure that if the caribou had worn tails we should have seen Job running over the hills holding fast to one of them.

The caribou painted by Dennis Gale (circa 1860) were less fortunate than those observed by Mina Hubbard — who hunted with her kodak.

Before proceeding farther we re-ascended the hill which we first climbed to take a look at the lake. It could be seen almost from end to end. The lower part which we had passed was clear, but above us the lake was a network of islands and water. The hills on either side seemed to taper off to nothing in the north, and I could see where the land appeared to drop away beyond this northern horizon which looked too near to be natural. North of Michikamats were more smaller lakes, and George showed me our probable route to look for "my river."

Squalls and showers had been passing all the afternoon, and as it drew towards evening fragments of rainbow could be seen out on the lake or far away on the hills beyond it. Labrador is a land of rainbows and rainbow colours, and nowhere have I ever seen them so brilliant, so frequent and so variedly manifested. Now the most brilliant one of all appeared close to us, its end resting directly on a rock near the foot of the hill. George never knew before that there is a pot of gold at the end of the rainbow. I suspect he does not believe it yet for I could not persuade him to run to get it. Gilbert, more credulous, made a determined attempt to secure the treasure, but before he reached the rock the rainbow had moved off and carried the gold to the middle of the lake.

Camp was made a little farther up. When it was ready for the night Job and Joe were again off to watch the caribou. They were feeding on the hills and swimming back and forth from islands to mainland, now in companies, now a single caribou. Job was so near one as he came out of the water that he could have caught him by the horns. Now and then a distant shout told that Job and the caribou had come to close quarters.

. . .

For fifty miles of our journey beyond this point we saw companies of the caribou every day, and sometimes many times a day, though we did not again see them in such numbers. The country was a network of their trails, in the woodlands and bogs cut deep into the soft soil, on the barren hillsides broad, dark bands converging to the crossing place at the river.

At the time I made my journey the general movement of the caribou was towards the east; but where they had come from or whither they were going we could not tell. Piles of white hair which we found later at a deserted camp on Cabot Lake where the Indians had dressed the skins, and the band of white hair clinging to the west bank of the George River, opposite our camp of August 15th, four feet above the then water-level, pointed to an earlier occupation of the country, while the deep cut trails and long piles of whitened antlers, found at intervals along the upper George River, all indicated that this country is favourite ground with them. Yet whether they had been continuously in this territory since the spring months or not I did not ascertain. The Indians whom we found at Resolution Lake knew nothing of their presence so near them.

Towards the end of August the following year Mr. Cabot, while on a trip inland from Davis Inlet, on the east coast, found the caribou in numbers along the Height of Land, and when he joined the Indians there, though the great herd had passed, they had killed near a thousand. It would therefore seem not improbable that at the time I made my journey they were bending their steps in the direction of the highlands between the Atlantic and the George.

The movements of the barren ground caribou of Labrador have never been observed in the interior as they have been in the country west of Hudson Bay. So far as I can learn I alone, save the Indians, have witnessed the great migration there; but from such information as I was able to gather later at the coast, their movements appear to be as erratic as those of the caribou of northern Canada.

From Mr. John Ford, the Agent of the Hudson's Bay Company's post at the mouth of the George River, I learned that they cross in the neighbourhood of the post at different times of the year. He has seen them there in July and August, in October and November, in January, February, and March. They are seen only a few days in the summer time, but in winter stay much longer — sometimes two months. In 1908 they were near the post all through February and March. On one occasion in the summer one of Mr. Ford's Eskimo hunters went to look for caribou, and after walking nearly all day turned home, arriving shortly before midnight, but without having found a trace of deer. The next morning at three o'clock they were running about on the hills at the post in such numbers that without trouble as many could be killed as were desired.

From the George River post they hunt west for the caribou, which are more often found in the vicinity of Whale River post than at either George River or Fort Chimo to the west. For the five years preceding my visit the caribou had crossed regularly in November at Whale River. That is to say they were seen there in great numbers, but no one knew whence they had come, or whither they went. Their coming cannot, however, be counted upon every year.

In September 1889 the whole band of George River Eskimo went for the annual hunt, by which they expect to supply themselves with winter clothing. Day after day they travelled on without finding the deer. When provisions gave out they were so far away from the post that they dared not turn back. One family after another dropped behind. Finally, the last little company gave, up, one young man only having the strength to go any farther. He, too, was about to sink down, when at last he came upon the caribou. He went back to help the others, but in spite of their best efforts twenty-one of the band perished from starvation.

That the caribou of Labrador have greatly decreased in numbers seems certain. Mr. Peter M'Kenzie, Chief Factor of the Hudson's Bay Company in the east, who was a fellow-traveller on my return journey, told me that many years ago while in charge of Fort Chimo he had seen the caribou passing steadily for three days just as I saw them on this 8th of August, not in thousands, but hundreds of thousands. The depletion of the great herds of former days is attributed to the unreasoning slaughter of the animals at the time of migration by Indians in the interior and Eskimo of the coast, not only at Ungava, but on the east coast as well, for the caribou sometimes find their way to the Atlantic. The fires also which have swept the country, destroying the moss on which they feed, have had their share in the work of destruction.

Only twice during the journey did we find trace of their enemy — the wolves. These hunt the caribou in packs, cutting out a single deer, and following him till his strength is gone, when they jump on him and pull him down. Mr. M'Kenzie tells how, when on one of his hunting trips at Fort Chimo, a caribou came over the ridge but a short distance from him followed by seven wolves. The animal had almost reached the limit of his strength. He ran with head low and tongue hanging out. From cover of a boulder Mr. M'Kenzie waited for them to pass, and one after another he dropped four of the wolves. The others taking the hint altered their course, and the victim escaped.

Mina Hubbard, *A Woman's Way Through Unknown Labrador.*

29

Lydia Campbell

(1818–1905)

Lydia Blake Campbell, née Brooks, the descendant of one of the earliest settlers on Hamilton Inlet, was born in Labrador. Ambrose Brooks fled the press gangs during the English–French wars, came to Labrador, married an Inuit woman whose ancestry went back thousands of years, and produced three daughters. The Reverend Arthur Waghorne sent seventy-five-year-old Lydia Campbell "an exercise book" and begged her "to write me some account of the Labrador life and ways." Although she had never left the coast, or gone to school, and had endured great hardships, "her life had its absorbing and varied interest and pleasures." Her memoirs appeared in 1894 in *The St. John's Evening Telegram*. *Sketches of Labrador Life was* published in booklet form in 1980 by the magazine *Them Days*, whose editor, Doris Saunders, was Campbell's great-great-granddaughter. Lydia Campbell's brave, touching narrative is "full of wisdom, wit and grace," wrote Tony Williams in the introduction. "She represents the beginning of a literate, independent and self-sufficient group of pioneers who made their home in Labrador."

Peter Rindisbacher's Labrador Eskimo in his canoe drawn from nature *(circa. 1821) paddles calmly through the ice floes. A timeless figure, he could belong to the "Eskimaux" Noah fable described by Lydia Campbell.*

BUT THAT HAS ALL CHANGED NOW

THE ESKIMAUX'S NOTION ABOUT THE FLOOD, HANDED DOWN FROM GENERATION TO GENERATION MAY 24, 1894

They had it to say that once upon a time the world was drowned and that all the Eskimaux were drowned but one family, and he took his family and dogs and chattles and his sealskin boat and kayak and komatiks, and went on the highest hill that they could see, and stayed there till the rain was over, and when the waters dried up they descended down the river and got down to the plains. When they could not see any more people they took off the bottoms of their boats and took some little white pups and sent the poor little things off to sea, and they drifted to some islands far away and became white people. Then they done the same as the others did, and the people spread all over the world.

Such was my poor father's thought — the poor people can read it for themselves in the Bible what few there are in this bay.

They say that the thunder came about after an old woman was replening [working, or rubbing dry seal skins to make them supple] a seal skin, and the skin did rattle so like all sorts of seal skin will after they are dry, and rubbing and tramping on them will get apt. So they said that the seal skin blew away up to the clouds and began to rattle and that it has been thundering ever since be-times.

There is a big rock about half a mile from our summer house with a large crack in it, and the natives here about said every time that they passed that rock there would be a little woman looking out of the rock or standing by it, and that, the rock goes by the name of Angnasiak, meaning pretty woman. We pass that rock every day in the summer, for our salmon nets is alongside of it. The only thing alive that is of any consequence was a deer standing by that rock about sixty years ago and my poor husband came out of the woods and shot it, and it howled past and lodged against the rock, and we saw it for years after it was done....

... The first time that my dear old father came from England, what few whites was here they was scattered about here and there. It was lovely, he said often about here, no one to see for miles but Eskimaux and Mountaineers and they was plentiful. He said that dozens of canoes of Mountaineers would come down out of the Big Bay as it was called then, what is now called Hamilton Inlet or the Large Lake. They used to come skimming along like a flock of ducks, going outside egg hunting on the island. Well, I know it is a pretty sight to see a lot of birch canoes shining red in the sunshine. I have seen them paddling along, I have, men steering, the women paddling and the children singing or chatting ... where are they now? Hardly ever see a family now except in winter when we will, now and then, get a visit from a family or two. Oh, our Indians have been killed with drink, the dirty tobacco and strong tea, how few they are now.

AUGUST 3, 1894

I have seen fifteen, as far as twenty, Eskimos seal skin tents in my time scattered here in little groups not far from each other, five or six tents together and such a bustle, women cleaning seal skins and covering kayaks, their little boats. The men out on the water after a large school of seals, throwing their darts at the end of their houliack harpoon strap. They use a bladder, mostly young seal skin skinned on the round and made tight, to float a seal after being harpooned. What work to kill them then. I do not know when I saw the last seal skin tent — the few that is left is living in wooden houses, and I seen one kayak this summer, only one now! There was only three or four small families before but the World's Fair people is come now. They are across on the Big Island, we are just going over to see them. Mr. Campbell and me and Esther Blake and Fred and Mary came on. Well, off we goes, a pretty day, I would like for you to see it.

A spectacular drawing of a loon, Northern Diver, *in the unpublished Ballingall Diary, artist unknown.*

Well, we has been over on Big Island and saw the most of them, how changed … all can talk English and dress like the people of another country. They has a picture of the World Fair in different forms.

My dear friends, my time is too short to write much longer. We are now going to get our winter fish while we can. Men, women and children all does what they can to get something for the winter, for people that don't try to get something in the summer will not have much to carry off to their winter places. Our winter house and gardens is about seventy or eighty miles from here. We are never in want yet, although my old man and me are getting past seventy and no one but us to work for us but a poor crippled boy and a young girl, an orphan, and our daughter-in-law and her little girl, our own little Ella, our little pet. Her father has been gone for three years in the States. Well we grows our own potatoes and turnips for the winter and we gets plenty of trout for the winter, fresh trout caught thro the ice, and we gets plenty of partridges, white and spruce ones and rabbits and other provisions we got in the summer time. But we has no milk. We gets cranberries, as much as we wants for the winter. We gets a fox now and then and marten and others. Their skins is valuable. We gets seals in the spring on the ice. Oh, we never stops work unless we are eating or sleeping in the night or singing or reading prayers. On Sunday then we has a spell, on that happy day.

I remember one Christmas Day we, in my father's house, was wishing that we could see some lady to help eat our good Christmas fare. We thought that someone was coming since the dogs was barking but no one came at that time. No other house near to ours than about thirty miles distant, but we would enjoy ourselves pretty well for there was my sister Hannah to be talking and reading with me, Father and Mother and an old Englishman by the name of Robert Best, my best friends, I thought. That was all that was living together as our eldest sister was married and away. We had not many to speak to.

Hannah and me, we would go and slide on the Mountaineers sleds, what Father would buy from them, and we were thought a good deal of by the Mountaineers. They would bring some pretty snowshoes to us two sisters, and some pretty deer skin shoes to wear in or out, they all painted so pretty. It was and is our custom to give anyone, dark or white, something to eat while they are in our house, and bedding, so the Indians was always kind to us. Poor despised Indians, the traders selling them rum and the foolish people buying up all they could, and getting lost, falling overboard, losing bodies and souls ... but that has all changed now.

Lydia Campbell, *Sketches of Labrador Life.*

… I do not hesitate to say, that if I were obliged to earn my living, were proficient in some useful art, and knew what I know now, I should not hesitate for a moment between the wide, free life of Canada and my probable lot in over-crowded England!

ELLA SYKES, PREFACE TO
A Home-Help in Canada.

Bibliography

We are fortunate to have our past chronicled by such excellent references as the *Dictionary of Canadian Biography*, *The Canadian Encyclopedia*, *The Oxford Companion to Canadian History and Literature*, and above all, the magnificent red and gold volumes of the Champlain Society.

Both the *DCB* and *The Canadian Encyclopedia* are now available online and there are many sites devoted to women writers, such as *A Celebration of Women Writers*, created and edited by Mary Mark Ockerbloom: *digital.library.upenn.edu/women*.

New editions continue to appear, including Barbara Williams' *A Gentlewoman in Upper Canada: The Journals, Letters, and Art of Anne Langton* (Toronto: University of Toronto Press, 2008), and *The Woman Who Mapped Labrador: The Life and Expedition Diary of Mina Hubbard* (Montreal & Kingston: McGill-Queen's University Press, 2005), introduced and edited by Roberta Buchanan and Bryan Greene, with an illuminating biography of Mina Hubbard's life after Labrador by Anne Hart.

What follows are the editions from which the various excerpts included in this volume have been drawn.

Aberdeen, Lady. *The Canadian Journal of Lady Aberdeen (1893–1898)* edited by John Saywell. Toronto: The Champlain Society, 1960. 53, 60–62, 69–70, 85, 313–14, 332, 378–79. Courtesy of the Champlain Society.

Allison, Susan. *A Pioneer Gentlewoman in British Columbia.* Edited by Margaret A. Ormsby. Vancouver: University of British Columbia Press, 1976. 69–72.

Beavan, Mrs. F. *Sketches and Tales Illustrative of Life in the Backwoods of New Brunswick.* St. Stephen, NB: Print'N Press Publications, 1980. 10–17. First published 1845 by G. Routledge.

Bompas, Selina. *A Heroine of the North: Memoirs of Charlotte Selina Bompas (1830–1917).* Compiled by S.A. Archer. London: Macmillan, 1929. 131–47.

Campbell, Lydia. *Sketches of Labrador Life.* St. John's, NL: Killick Press, 2000. 30–31, 49–52. First published 1894 by St. John's *Evening Herald.* Courtesy of Killick Press.

Carr, Emily. *The Book of Small.* Toronto: Oxford University Press, 1942. 75–88, 90–93.

Caswell, Maryanne. *Pioneer Girl.* Preface by Grace Lane. Toronto: McGraw-Hill, 1964.

Dufferin, Lady. *My Canadian Journal, 1872-1878.* Edited and annotated by Gladys Chantler Walker. Toronto: Longmans Canada, 1969. 254–259.

Ewing, Juliana Horatia. *Canada Home: Fredericton Letters, 1867–1869.* Edited by Margaret Howard Blom and Thomas E. Blom. Vancouver: University of British Columbia Press, 1983. 164–66, 188–90.

Far, Sui Sin. *Mrs. Spring Fragrance*. Edited by Amy Ling and Annette White-Parks. Urbana & Chicago: University of Illinois Press, 1995. 220–24. First published 1912 by A.C. McClurg.

Fisher, Mary. "The Grandmother's Tale" in Peter Fisher, *The First History of New Brunswick*. With notes by W.O. Raymond. Woodstock, NB: Non-Entity Press, 1980. 126–27, 128–30. First published anonymously in 1825.

Hargrave, Letitia. *Letters of Letitia Hargrave*. Edited by Margaret Arnott MacLeod. Toronto: Champlain Society, 1947. 136–37. Courtesy of the Champlain Society.

Hopkins, Monica. *Letters from a Lady Rancher*. With introduction by Sheilagh S. Jameson. Calgary: Glenbow Foundation, 1981. 40–45, 122–27. Courtesy of Glenbow Foundation.

Hubbard, Mina. *A Woman's Way Through Unknown Labrador*. New York: McClure Company, 1908. 126–37.

De l'Incarnation, Marie. *Word from New France: The Selected Letters of Marie de l' Incarnation*. Translated and edited by Joyce Marshall. Toronto: Oxford University Press, 1967. 197–202.

Jameson, Anna. *Winter Studies and Summer Rambles in Canada*. With introduction by Clara Thomas. Toronto: McClelland & Stewart.1965, 154–65. First published 1838 by Saunders and Otley.

Langton, Anne. *A Gentlewoman in Upper Canada: The Journals of Anne Langton*. Edited by H.H. Langton. Toronto: Clarke, Irwin & Company Limited, 1950. 113–28.

McClung, Nellie. *Clearing in the West: My Own Story*. Toronto: Thomas Allen, 1935. 54–66.

Michener, Margaret Dickie in *No Place Like Home*. Edited by Margaret Conrad, Toni Laidlaw, and Donna Smyth. Halifax: Formac Publishing Company Limited, 1988, 102–13.

Morin, Marie. *Histoire simple et véritable: les annales de l'Hotel-Dieu de Montréal 1659–1725*. Edited by Ghislaine Legendre. Montréal: Les Presses de l'Université de Montréal, 1979. 134–37. Translated by Barbara Robertson.

Murphy, Emily F. *Janey Canuck in the West*. London: Cassel, 1910. *http:// digital.libraryupenn.edu/women/murphy/west/west.html*. 172–82.

Riedesel, Friederike Charlotte Luise, Freifrau von. *Baroness von Riedesel and the American Revolution; Journal and Correspondence of a Tour of Duty 1776–1783*. Translated by Marvin L. Brown and Marta Huth. Chapel Hill: University of North Carolina Press, 1965. 115–17, 120–25.

De Sainte-Croix, Cécile. *Marie de l'Incarnation: Ecrits spirituels et historiques*. Edited by Dom Albert Jamet. Paris, 1929–39 (Letter LIX, vol. 3) Translated by Barbara Robertson.

Salverson, Laura Goodman. *Confessions of an Immigrant's Daughter*. With introduction by K.P. Stich. Toronto: University of Toronto Press, 1981. 121–28. First published 1939 by Faber and Faber. Courtesy of Julie Salverson.

Shadd, Mary A. *A plea for emigration: or, notes of Canada West, in its moral, social, and political aspect … for the information of colored emigrants*. Edited, annotated, and with an introduction by Richard Almonte. Toronto: Mercury Press, 1998. 43–49. First published 1852.

Sykes, Ella C. *A Home-Help in Canada*. London: Smith, Elder & Co., 1912. 108–29.

Traill, Catharine Parr. *I Bless You in My Heart: Selected Correspondence.*
Edited by Carl Ballstadt, Elizabeth Hopkins, and Michael A. Peterman.
Toronto: University of Toronto Press, 1996. 236–38. Courtesy of the
editors.

(Warren), Mary Schäffer. *Old Indian Trails of the Canadian Rockies.*
Edited and annotated by E.J. Hart. Banff: Whyte Museum, 1980.
20–27. First published 1911 by G.P. Putnam's Sons.

Queen's University Archives, David James Ballingall fonds, Locator #2403, A.ARCH 2403-B12.

Sleigh Scene, by James Edward Alexander.

About the Editors

MARY ALICE DOWNIE has written and edited twenty-eight books for children and adults. Her many books include *And Some Brought Flowers*, with Mary Hamilton, and *The Well-Filled Cupboard*, with Barbara Robertson. She lives in Kingston, Ontario.

BARBARA ROBERTSON, now deceased, earned degrees in history from the University of Toronto and Queen's University. She was also the author of *Wilfrid Laurier* and co-editor of *Ottawa at War*.

ELIZABETH JANE ERRINGTON is currently dean of arts at the Royal Military College and also teaches at Queen's University. Her research interests centre on life in nineteenth-century Upper Canada. She lives in Kingston, Ontario.

Of Related Interest

Much to Be Done
Private Life in Ontario from Victorian Diaries
by Frances Hoffman and Ryan Taylor
978-1-55002-772-3
$21.99 £11.99

Victorian Ontario included people from all walks
of life from homeless beggars to wealthy gentry.
In *Much to Be Done*, we glimpse how life was lived
in nineteenth-century Ontario, not only in the grand mansions but also
in the farmhouses and streets where our ancestors lived. Diaries, with
some contributions from letters, newspapers, and reminiscences, assist
in promoting a historical understanding that links people of today with
the Ontario of the past.

Pearls & Pebbles
by Catharine Parr Traill
978-1-89621-959-2
$21.95 £14.99

How fitting to close out the twentieth century
with a brand-new edition of *Pearls & Pebbles* by
the noted chronicler of pioneer life, Catharine
Parr Traill. Published in 1894, Pearls & Pebbles
is an unusual book with a lasting charm in which the author's broad
focus ranges from the Canadian natural environment to early settlement
of Upper Canada. Through Traill's eyes, we see the life of the pioneer
woman, the disappearance of the forest, and the corresponding changes
in the life of the Native Canadians who have inhabited that forest.

Available at your favourite bookseller.

DUNDURN PRESS
www.dundurn.com

What did you think of this book?
Visit www.dundurn.com
for reviews, videos, updates, and more!